LUCA DAL MONTE

# THE GENTLEMAN

## Gianluca Vialli and How He Changed English Football Forever

B L O O M S B U R Y   S P O R T
LONDON • OXFORD • NEW YORK • NEW DELHI • SYDNEY

BLOOMSBURY SPORT
Bloomsbury Publishing Plc
50 Bedford Square, London, WC1B 3DP, UK
Bloomsbury Publishing Ireland Limited,
29 Earlsfort Terrace, Dublin 2, D02 AY28, Ireland

BLOOMSBURY, BLOOMSBURY SPORT and the Diana logo
are trademarks of Bloomsbury Publishing Plc

First published in Great Britain 2026



A catalogue record for this book is available from the British Library

Library of Congress Cataloguing-in-Publication data has been applied for

ISBN: HB: 978-1-3994-3182-8; eBook: 978-1-3994-3184-2

2 4 6 8 10 9 7 5 3 1

Typeset in Bembo Std by Lumina Datamatics Ltd
Printed and bound in Great Britain by Clays Ltd, Elcograf S.p.A.

FSC www.fsc.org MIX Paper | Supporting responsible forestry FSC® C018072

*For Olivia and Sofia,*
*and for Lodovica and Nicolò*

# CONTENTS

Coors

# AUTHOR NOTE

Gianluca Vialli and I knew each other since nursery school. I was four when he arrived; he was three. As was customary in those days at our school in Cremona's Quartiere Po, each of the 'older' children was paired with a younger one, and I was joined with Gianluca. Our friendship started then. The nursery was divided into classes, each identified by a colour. Ours was blue. Little did he know . . .

We played together – football, yes, but not only football – through nursery, primary and middle school. On the eve of the 1990 World Cup, when Gianluca was Italy's golden boy, I remember my mother saying, out of the blue, that whenever he came round to play at our house when we were in school together, she would fix him bread with butter and sugar.

When it came to football, we played at the Cristo Re parish ground, where his talent stood out more clearly with each passing day, without that ever turning into arrogance on his part. I played on the same team as him, and I played against him. The last time I shared the football pitch with him was in May 1982. By then Gianluca was already a regular in the first team of US Cremonese, the cherished club of our town, yet now and then he still came back to the parish ground. Perhaps the club knew, perhaps they didn't. In any case, to avoid any risk of injury, on those occasions he played as a goalkeeper. That last night we played until dusk set in.

When Gianluca made his debut with the Italian national team in autumn 1985, I was abroad for my university studies, so I sent him a note to congratulate him. That Christmas, back in Cremona for the holidays, we happened to end up in the same restaurant. When he saw me come in, he stood up from his table and came over to thank me for the note – apologising, on top of that, for not having replied yet. And, of course, he was the one making his debut with the national team, not me.

In the year of the Scudetto with Sampdoria, we settled into a routine. A group of four of us from home would call Gianluca by noon on Wednesday to tell him how many of us would be coming to Genoa the following Sunday. Then, on match day, we would turn up at the stadium and find passes waiting for us – either for the press tribune or pitch side, where, cameras in hand, we would pretend to be photographers.

We all grew up, and Gianluca went first to Turin, then to London. But he never lost touch with any of us. A phone call, a chat, a sandwich at Ugo Grill when he was back in Cremona, or *penne alla Vialli* at his beloved Osteria San Lorenzo when we visited him in London. And whenever we did meet – Cremona, London, it hardly mattered – it was straight back to the Cristo Re days of our youth. We never talked about the Champions League or World Cups. All we ever talked about was Father Angelo and the gang at Cristo Re, about matches played on that unforgiving pitch, about friends – and friends we had lost.

VIALLI
9

# PART ONE

# LONDON

## 1. CHELSEA, 1996

'English football has always been my obsession.'

GIANLUCA VIALLI

Change was never something Gianluca Vialli feared. He had always known how to leave – gracefully, on his terms. So when the moment came to part ways with Italy, he did it with his head held high and his mind already fixed on what lay ahead.

The contract was generous. Three seasons, a strong foreign currency, a fresh challenge in a new country. London would be home now – more precisely, the blue section of it: Chelsea FC. A smart address in Belgravia was waiting. A Jaguar, too, gleaming like a promise. Glasgow Rangers had made a richer offer, but money had never been the whole story. 'English football,' he would say, 'has always been my obsession.'

'The Bosman rule – which banned restrictions on EU players moving within clubs – made your life as a professional footballer so much easier,' he would recall years later. 'No transaction involved, your current club didn't even have to speak to anyone, it was just you and the club you wanted to join. It was a major opportunity for a guy like me who wanted to play away from Italy.'

Not without a touch of humour, Gianluca Vialli described himself as 'an emigrant with a Vuitton suitcase'. The phrase stuck. It captured the man – elegant, grounded, aware of the page he was turning. Albion welcomed him with open arms. 'His arrival was the start of something thrilling for English football,' they say now. And they were right. Vialli wasn't just another foreign signing. He was substance and spectacle. His football, like his manner, was perfectly tuned for England's tempo: fast, physical, full of fire.

Chelsea, at that point, were dreaming big. The chairman, Ken Bates – part jolly pirate, part property mogul – and vice-chairman Matthew Harding didn't always see eye-to-eye, but they sang from the same hymn sheet on one thing: make Chelsea a club that wins – and wins big. No more mid-table meandering. They had Europe in their sights, and they were going all-in. That's why they'd brought in Ruud Gullit first – a midfield general with AC Milan pedigree – and now Vialli. 'Luca had just won the Champions League and was a charismatic player, a leader of men,' they recall at Chelsea today.

Dutch star Ruud Gullit had already sprinkled a bit of stardust over Stamford Bridge, and his name alone had made England take notice. But Vialli was the cherry on top. Better still, he came on a free after parting ways with Juventus, meaning Chelsea landed a world-class striker for peanuts – 'cost relatively little but brought immense value in terms of skill, leadership, quality and personality.'

The adventure kicks off properly on 17 June, 1996. Looking the part, as ever, Gianluca Vialli steps into the spotlight at Stamford Bridge, razor-sharp in both suit and scalp. Two seasons under Marcello Lippi at Juventus have polished his style to a high gloss, and now, holding up the Blues' No. 9 shirt, he's the picture of suave ambition.

The press room is rammed. More Italian journalists than English ones, all jostling for a quote. But Vialli sets the tone before the first flashbulb goes off: 'Gentlemen, we talk Chelsea. No Juve, no Italian national team, not a word.' Clear as a referee's whistle. This wasn't just a move abroad, it was a line drawn in the sand.

In those same days, Arrigo Sacchi's Italy are knocking about England for Euro '96. Vialli, very conspicuously, is not part of the squad – left out after a long-running bust-up with the high priest of pressing himself. In 48 hours, Italy are due to face Germany in a must-win match. Vialli's response? Shrug and switch allegiances. Five days before the Chelsea press conference, he'd already made waves by saying that, just as he backed Brazil at USA '94, now his money was on England. Cue the *Daily Sport* going full back-page barmy, plastering the country with headlines that left English fans grinning and the Azzurri camp reaching for the smelling salts.

Oddly enough, no one does push Vialli on Juve. He left Turin with the handshakes and hugs of a gentleman's exit. But the situation with Sacchi is still raw. A few days earlier, Gianluca couldn't help but fan the flames when poked by a snide question from one of his countrymen, responding: 'Since he arrived [as manager of the Italian national team] the atmosphere has changed – it has become oppressive, obsessive.' A swing of the boot, well placed. But today, Vialli's not biting; no more angry words on the national team or its manager. Two days later, Italy will limp to a goalless draw against Germany and pack their bags early. One can't help but wonder, if Vialli had been leading the line, would the story have ended differently?

But Gianluca isn't dwelling on what's happening in Italy. He's got his eyes firmly on this new chapter in London. And he's got a plan. 'I want to entertain and enjoy myself,' he says. 'We can win, but in the way they like it here – not necessarily by finishing first, but by getting the very best out of ourselves.' Classic Vialli: results with a touch of romance. A nod to the formula that brought glory at Sampdoria.

He's nearly 32, but there's no urgency in him. London's energy and the thrill of English football have given him a second wind. He's sharp. Serene. Ready.

'He was a beautiful soul, an Italian man with great charm, but a quiet kind of charm. He knew he was a great footballer, of course, but he never made you feel it. And more than anything, he was curious about the world around him.' That's how they still speak of him in England – the man who rocked up in the summer of '96, suitcase in hand and eyes full of wonder.

The English press are quick off the mark. First question: why Chelsea? Vialli doesn't miss a beat. London, he says – always London. 'Living in London was always my dream', a line he repeats so often it could've been printed on the back of Chelsea's season ticket. But it wasn't just the pull of Hyde Park's views and a decent espresso in Knightsbridge. From a footballing angle, it was about playing under a mate – Ruud Gullit. A friend, a fellow player, and now the Chelsea coach. That connection, Gianluca insists, made all the difference. Later, that line might carry a hint of irony, considering what's to come, but the respect between them, at least in those early days, is genuine.

Gullit, who'd gone to great lengths to get Vialli into a Chelsea shirt, makes his case plain: 'When I got here, Hoddle told me I was needed to shake things up. Now we play an interesting game. People like it. But we were missing an experienced man, someone who could teach attacking movement. With Gianluca, we'll get to goal in a way that's different from the traditional style. I don't care how many goals he scores. I just hope he helps the team grow.'

Not your typical English managerial quote, but then again, Gullit wasn't your typical English manager.

As pre-season loomed, Vialli began to ease into London life while the Italian press clocked his every move like a hawk in a trench coat. Giovanna, Vialli's childhood sweetheart from Cremona, was spotted in town 'house-hunting and preparing for the move'. Meanwhile, Vialli took up residence in one of those plush hotels overlooking Hyde Park – just until the furniture arrived. He was relaxed, upbeat, relieved. 'After 15 years of stress and too much attention,' he told the crowd at his unveiling press conference, 'I can finally have a normal life. In London, no one bothers you on the street.' Journalist Amy Raphael would later remember, 'He was happy to be just another person, not recognised, not stopped in the street. Except by Italian fans, of course!'

It's true – Londoners don't usually collar players for a signature while they're queuing for a flat white. Different culture. Bit more reserve. But let's not kid ourselves, the English tabloids play a far nastier game than anything in Serie A. With a vast network of tipsters – hotel porters, cabbies, waiters in the West End – they've got eyes everywhere. One minute you're leaving a quiet dinner, next you're flashbulbed like a Bond villain outside a top London restaurant. That's life in English football. No mob on the pavement, but the long lens never sleeps.

Gianluca Vialli's first week in London wasn't exactly quiet. In fact, it played out like a tabloid hat-trick – three headline-grabbing moments, each more farcical than the last. First up: a paparazzi ambush outside a Chelsea restaurant. Vialli's just finished dinner with the sons of Juventus president Giampiero Boniperti, a friendly bite with old ties. But the press reads it as a coded message: Vialli might be in blue now, but his heart's still trimmed in black and white. After all, he had just lifted the Champions League trophy with Juve. The cameras click like mad.

Next, the unveiling press conference. The room's buzzing, Gianluca's beaming and suddenly, in she struts.

A model kitted out in hot pants and a stare that says 'accidental photobomb' louder than any flash. She's not lost. She's been planted, courtesy of a cheeky lensman. The mission? Snag a saucy shot to stir up scandal. Stamford Bridge's press room has never felt so close to a tabloid sting. And then, the pièce de resistance – a pure work of fiction. Word gets out that Gianluca's had dinner in a Chelsea eatery, San Lorenzo. Same day, earlier on, Princess Diana had lunch there. That's it. That's the whole story. And somehow, that wafer-thin coincidence is spun into a full-blown romance, complete with front-page headlines.

But Gianluca, ever the pro, learns fast. Soon enough, he'll master the art of ignoring the snappers. Not dodging them – there's no need for disguises or back-door escapes. Just that calm, knowing shrug. Let them shoot. He's got bigger things on his plate.

From the off, he throws himself into the job. He knows what's at stake. It's not just about taking a payday abroad, this is a real project, a real chance. And he's under the microscope. Chelsea fans are watching. The London press is watching. The football world is watching. Back in Italy, they're watching, too. Some cheer him on, seeing the move as gutsy, romantic even – a player choosing joy and freedom over comfort and convention. Others are sharpening knives, waiting for him to trip, to fall flat on his well-tailored face.

## 2. CREMONA, 1964–1980

'Cremona helped make me the man I am.'

GIANLUCA VIALLI

From the moment his polished Italian loafers hit English soil, Gianluca Vialli fell for London. It was love at first sight, and the affair never ended. But if the British capital became his adopted home, he never once turned his back on his roots. Not when he first arrived in the mid-nineties, and not in the 30 years that followed.

Through it all, his love for Cremona – his hometown tucked away in the flat, steamy-in-summer, foggy-in-autumn Po Valley – remained unwavering. A part of him never left. And unlike the countless footballers with rags-to-riches backstories, Vialli's upbringing didn't come with grit and struggle. He was no scrapper from the margins. 'I had a good childhood,' Gianluca never tired of saying. 'I grew up in the Quartiere Po neighbourhood in Cremona. I played football in the courtyard.'

Someone once put it perfectly: 'Even after years in London, Vialli carried a deep, almost instinctive bond with his homeland and his people. It was the kind of gratitude you find in those who leave, see the world, and never forget where they came from.' And when the fame, accolades and silverware piled up, Vialli didn't reinvent himself. He just said it straight: 'I'm proud to be called a provincial. I wouldn't have wanted to be born in a bigger city. Cremona fits me – my personality, the things I love. They say it takes a village to raise a child. Besides my family, besides my parents, I must thank Cremona. It helped make me the man I am.'

For Gianluca, Cremona wasn't just a place, it was *the* place – a world unto itself. A place where the memories were warm and uncomplicated. Where the Cristo Re parish meant football and friendship, not fame. Where his mates didn't care that he'd become a star striker – maybe because they always knew he would. 'Luca was always three, four steps ahead of everyone else,' they say now. 'Even back on the parish pitch, he was something else. You knew he would make it big.'

Growing up in Cremona in the 1970s meant many things. For Gianluca Vialli, it meant harmony. While much of Italy was wracked by fear and fury – left-wing Red Brigades, neo-fascist Ordine Nuovo, bombs, kidnappings, political killings and pitched battles on university steps – Cremona felt a world apart. The chaos played out on the nightly news, with headlines sounding like dispatches from a distant front. But if you were raised in the Quartiere Po district, like he was, the storm never quite reached your door. There were no bombings in Cremona. No mass strikes shutting down factories. No students occupying schools and quoting Marx between history lessons. For Gianluca, the unrest belonged to somewhere else. Cremona was quiet, Quartiere Po even quieter. Leafy. Safe.

The neighbourhood itself had sprung into life in the early 1900s, its sycamore-lined avenue stretching towards the Po River like a promenade in a postcard. By the time young Gianluca and his siblings were chasing footballs and dreams, the area still went by its old name: Villaggio Po. A village within the city. Tucked away. Its own little world outside the city walls, erected in medieval times and torn down at the turn of the century.

The Vialli family's first home sat at the corner of Via Adda and Via Mincio, just across from the new church, built in 1958 – six years before Gianluca was born. But once Gianluca, the fifth child, arrived, space got tight and noise levels went up. So they moved, this time to a new flat at the far end of Viale Po, just a stone's throw from the Baldesio rowing club, where Gianluca's parents were members.

The family were tightly knit, still are. Their roots led northward to the Alpine village of Cles in Trentino. During the war, Gianluca's grandfather, Giovanni Vialli, had been a key figure in the anti-Fascist Partito d'Azione. After the 1943 armistice, his office in the city centre became a hidden headquarters for Il Comitato di Liberazione Nazionale, the Italian Resistance working against Mussolini's fascists.

Gianluca's father was a solid, dependable, building contractor. His mother, Maria Teresa, came from the nearby village of Casalmorano, part of that same stretch of the Cremona countryside that also produced one of Italy's finest left-backs, Antonio Cabrini. In her school years, his mother had been a competitive track and field athlete. Gianluca often spoke of his upbringing not with pride, but with grounded gratitude: 'My parents helped me keep my feet on the ground.' And that, perhaps, was the foundation of everything.

Football wasn't exactly the lifeblood of the Vialli household – five kids, four boys: Mila, the eldest and the only girl, then Nino (born Giovanni, after his grandfather), Marco, Maffo and Gianluca. Not then, anyway. 'There wasn't much passion for the game at home,' Gianluca would later say. 'My father is a Juventus fan, but not a die-hard. There were five of us siblings, and only one really cared about football. But for me, it was a lightning strike. I remember my first boots, my first ball.'

Gianluca grew up in the afterglow of Inter Milan's glory years of the mid-1960s and in the long shadow of that legendary 4–3 epic match between Italy and West Germany at the 1970 World Cup in Mexico. Football wasn't just a game – it was a national fever. 'Football was everywhere. The whole country could feel it,' he would remember.

On 1 October, 1970, just months after that historic night at the Azteca, Gianluca started elementary school. But school was always a warm-up to the main event. 'I had worked out a system,' he remembered. 'In the morning, I paid close attention in class, so, right after lunch, at home I could finish my homework fast. After that, it was only football. All day long. Until late in the evening, when my brother and I played in our room with a paper ball. Endless, wild matches in a tiny space. And while we played, we did the commentary ourselves.'

The brother in question is Maffo – the one who shared Gianluca's obsession for football. Just two years older, just as gifted. The two formed a tight unit, the heart of every courtyard classic. And what a courtyard it was. Tucked between four apartment blocks, lined with garages that doubled as goalposts, a scattering of trees and just enough green to dream on, but the pitch was cobbled stone. Not exactly Wembley turf, but perfect for toughening up a young striker's touch.

Afternoons blurred into marathons of four-a-side matches, with Maffo always by his side. And on Saturdays, the talk turned to English football – the real deal. The matches beamed in from across the Channel lit their imaginations. The kits, for one – those bold horizontal stripes, worn by teams such as Queens Park Rangers – you'd never find on an Italian pitch. The drama. The freedom. The style. It all felt like another world.

'We were all really good,' a 17-year-old Vialli once said of his courtyard pals in an early interview. And you'd believe him. Those courtyard kickabouts weren't just fun, they were the foundations of his career. 'I was born into football in that courtyard,' he'd say years later. 'A huge courtyard, a bunch of friends. Everyone was crazy about the game. We started playing at four, five years old. The matches went on forever, right until it got dark. That was where I knew – this was my passion.' Gianluca Vialli always knew his love for the game had started not in some academy with perfect pitches and pristine kits, but in a dusty courtyard behind the flats on Via Toti. That's where he became the kind of striker who could bend a match to his will.

The layout of that courtyard played no small part. 'I was always a forward, but because the field was so wide, I had to cover the entire attacking front,' Gianluca explained in his first book. 'I'd drift wide to receive the ball, sending countless crosses into the box. Exactly the kind of striker I would become – one who liked to roam across the attack.' Fabrizio Frittoli, his best mate and long-time partner-in-crime on that makeshift pitch, agrees. 'Makes sense, makes sense . . .' he nods.

Those garage doors weren't just storage, they were goals. 'We pounded the wooden garage doors with our shots,' Gianluca recalled. 'They were our goals, of course. Sometimes, people watched us from the balconies overlooking the courtyard. That was our crowd. And when we had a crowd, we played even harder, shouting, running, pulling off fancy touches, calling out the plays like we were in a World Cup Final.'

Speaking of World Cups, Argentina '78 left a lasting mark. Maybe it was Mario Kempes, maybe it was the magic in those sky-blue and white stripes that rang freedom in an oppressed nation. Frittoli remembers it vividly: 'During the '78 World Cup, whenever Argentina played, we'd rush outside right after the game, fired up from watching them on TV.' It should therefore come as no surprise then that when the boys finally entered a parish tournament, they turned up in full Argentina kits – ready to play, and ready to dream.

The courtyard had its own rhythm, its own rules. 'We could play from four in the afternoon until dinner time,' Frittoli recalls. 'In the summer, we'd get out there again from 8.30 to 9.30 in the evening.' Neighbours did their best to put a lid on the ambition of the local prodigies. They failed, of course. At best, they managed a few passive-aggressive acts of resistance. 'Sometimes the ball would fly off, stain someone's laundry, or land on a balcony and never come back,' Gianluca would remember. 'So we'd all pitch in and buy a new one.'

And when school was out, the Vialli clan moved operations 10 miles down the road to the small countryside village of Grumello Cremonese. Their grandfather had purchased a villa there – Villa Affaitati, known locally as *Il Castello* (the castle) – surrounded by open fields and boundless sky. 'My brother and I spent hours practising bicycle kicks, flying backheels and wild headers,' Gianluca recalled. 'The ground was so soft you couldn't get hurt, even if you landed on your head – which happened a lot. It might sound simple, but it wasn't a coincidence that acrobatics became one of my trademarks.' Those overhead kicks – the kind that echoed Pelé's picture-perfect finish in *Escape to Victory* – weren't born under floodlights, they were born under blue skies and summer heat, rehearsed over and over on forgiving grass until they became second nature.

As the years passed, new players entered the scene. Schoolmates joined the courtyard crowd, and soon it was Courtyard vs. Rest of the World. 'Sometimes, we'd play against teams from the San Pietro parish,' Frittoli says. He, too, played up front – more of a winger than a true No. 9. But there was one match that stuck. 'Once, at San Pietro, I played as a goalkeeper and let in thirteen. Luca lost his mind that day while I kept conceding one goal after another. He was furious,' Frittoli laughs. 'Luca was a good guy. Honest. He never faked anything. If he had something to say, he'd say it to your face. He wasn't afraid to, not even as a kid.'

And then came the first real step up – the Cristo Re parish tournament. An older lad from the courtyard, Fausto Melgari, made it happen. 'Fausto was the first to get me and Luca Vialli into the Cristo Re tournament,' Frittoli recalls. 'We were too young, officially out of age range, but Fausto convinced Don Angelo, the parish priest, to make an exception. Thanks to Fausto, we got the chance to play against the older lads. I remember it well – it was our first real tournament. I played at the back wearing a No. 5 jersey. Luca, of course, was up front.' Fausto remembers it just as clearly: 'The "kids" were really good. We thought we'd do well with them in the team. Instead, we got buried in goals every game. But those two – those two were the real deal.'

---

That's, then, how it began: with garage doors, paper balls, Argentine stripes and the unshakeable belief that football was everything.

And then, of course, there was Don Angelo.

For Gianluca Vialli and his brothers, for Fabrizio Frittoli and the rest of the courtyard crew, and for hundreds of kids born between the late 1950s and mid '60s, Don Angelo Scaglioni wasn't just a priest, he was a presence. A mentor. A whirlwind in a cassock. Less a distant holy figure, more of a one-man youth system with a theology degree and a strict moral compass. He cared deeply, but he didn't miss a trick. And he had the sort of photographic memory that made trying to slip back in after a red-card-worthy afternoon an exercise in futility. Step out of line and you were gone for the day. Best keep your head down and hope tomorrow brought forgiveness.

Don Angelo was just 25 when he arrived at Cristo Re, buzzing with ideas and with not much patience for outdated rules. First order of business? Tear down the iron gate separating the boys' and girls' sections of the oratory. The girls' side was little more than an afterthought. Meanwhile, the boys had a footballing paradise – two pitches (the *Campone* and the *Campetto*), a pair of basketball courts, and a volleyball court thrown in for good measure. Don Angelo didn't see fairness in the divide, he saw an opportunity to build a proper community. And build it he did.

Over the next 14 years, Don Angelo broke more rules than he followed, but always in the name of something better. Under his guidance, Cristo Re became the heart of the neighbourhood, and a source of mild envy throughout Cremona. 'The first years of my ministry at Cristo Re,' Don Angelo would later recall, 'were a whirlwind. The number of boys and young people kept rising at an incredible pace. The oratory became an essential gathering place for nearly every kid in the neighbourhood.' Come Sunday at 10 a.m., Mass was standing room only. 'They were everywhere, sitting on the floor, under the altar . . . lively celebrations, maybe not always perfect from a liturgical point of view, but deeply felt by the kids and their families alike.'

But it was outside the chapel, on the pitches, where Don Angelo's kingdom truly came alive. Under his steady watch, a thousand boys found their identity – and their team. Football at Cristo Re wasn't just a pastime, it was gospel. And one thing was sacred above all else: everyone played. It didn't matter how good you were, or what your parents did, or if you'd ever touched a real leather ball before. The most well-off families took turns buying the balls, and every day Don Angelo would line up a few of them at the edge of the Campone before unlocking the gates, the signal that another day of joy – and tackles – was about to begin. And in 1970s Italy, where not every child had the luxury of their own boots, let alone a ball, that mattered.

Coming from well-off families, Gianluca and Frittoli had a leg up on most of their peers – they had their own footballs. But even that didn't always guarantee an easy afternoon at the Campone. Sometimes, showing up with your own ball was asking for trouble. 'If you brought your own ball and the older kids saw it sitting there unused, they'd take it. And getting it back at the end of the day wasn't that easy,' one of the Cristo Re veterans still remembers. So, one afternoon, with no ball in hand and a pitch full of older lads circling like hawks, the two friends hatched a plan. To a pair of primary schoolers, it must've seemed nothing short of genius.

'That day, we decided to climb over the back fence to get to the ball first,' Frittoli says. 'We were small, and we knew the older boys would outrun us. So, we climbed over. But we had barely taken a dozen steps when Don Angelo spotted us – and that was it. Out! Both of us sent home until the next day.' That was the rule. Fence-climbers were shown the door – no excuses, no loopholes, no second chances. Don Angelo didn't do favourites.

But there was another moment between Gianluca and Don Angelo. A different kind of moment. The kind you carry with you long after your boots have been hung up. 'It was probably the only "life lesson" that was ever explicitly taught to me on a football pitch,' Gianluca would say, many years later.

He was 10. Playing on the Campone. A defender passed the ball back – routine stuff – but the goalkeeper slipped. The ball trickled over the line. Own goal. Cruel luck. A few kids laughed. Some groaned. Don Angelo, ever the impartial referee, pointed to the centre circle. Goal given. But young Gianluca wasn't having it. Not because it was against the rules, but because it wasn't right. Not in the spirit of things. A goal like that felt like a hollow win. So, on the next play, Gianluca did something rather unusual and unexpected. He tracked back into his own penalty area, waited for his moment, then blatantly handled the ball. A handball so obvious that it couldn't go unnoticed. Penalty for the other team. Balance restored. Job done. Or so Gianluca thought. The trouble was, Don Angelo had a different idea entirely.

'He ran straight at me,' Gianluca would recall. 'Grabbed the ball and started lecturing me. I can still see him, wagging his finger right in my face. "No! You don't do that! I know why you did it. You thought the last goal wasn't fair, so you tried to even the score. But you think that's sportsmanship? That's not sportsmanship. Sportsmanship means accepting what happens on the field – whether it goes your way or not."'

It wasn't the telling-off that stung – it was the clarity of it. A moment that cut through childhood pride and stuck fast, long after boots and kits were traded for suits and dugouts. 'It wasn't the deepest message, but it stayed with me all these years,' Gianluca would later reflect. 'Don Angelo taught me that in life, when things happen beyond your control, you must accept them and move forward.'

And he did. From missed penalties to lost finals, from bruising defeats to moments of personal triumph, Vialli carried that lesson with him. Even – especially – when, years later, he came up against the one opponent no one ever wants to face. The one who doesn't play by rules or reason. The most unwelcome opponent of all.

Every spring, Cristo Re staged its own football tournaments. Small-sided games, hard tackles, bragging rights on the line. The kids had their own categories, but everyone knew which event really mattered: the adults' tournament – the only one open to players from all over town and not just from the neighbourhood.

In spring 1980, Gianluca is 15. Having already signed youth terms with US Cremonese, he won't give up this tournament. After all, he's the defending champion now, ever since the courtyard team from Via Toti lifted the trophy last year. Gianluca signs up the gang, with his brother Maffo as captain, under a team name of The Warriors, in English. He pays the 3,000-lire individual fee, and on 30 April, he plays his first match. Picked up a booking, too. Problem is, the word spreads fast: Gianluca Vialli is playing in the Cristo Re tournament. By evening US Cremonese know. And when they know, they step in, ordering him to quit.

At this point Gianluca offers to referee a few matches – anything to stay close to the football at his parish ground. But one afternoon, after a disputed call, the crowds turn on him, shouting and swearing. He stood there, 15 years old, taking it all in. That was more than enough. Refereeing wasn't for him. For the rest of the tournament, he watched his brother and his friends play from the touchline.

## 3. CHELSEA, 1996

> 'No regrets about leaving Italy. English football has always been my dream.'
>
> GIANLUCA VIALLI

The next chapter in Gianluca Vialli's English footballing life kicks off at high noon, Wednesday, 10 July, 1996, as Chelsea FC report for duty at Stamford Bridge to begin pre-season training for the 1996–97 campaign. The Blues are gathering, hopes high, shirts freshly pressed. The first man to speak is the new boss, Ruud Gullit – still something of a curiosity in English dugouts, full of continental ideas and cool swagger. But by half past twelve, the spotlight shifts. The real headline steps up: Gianluca Vialli.

'I'm really excited about this new adventure,' he begins, cool as you like. 'I'm convinced that with Ruud, we'll do great things. He's a smart man, and he'll bring the best of what he learned in Italy to this team. As for the rest . . . I'll take care of it,' he adds, with that cheeky grin of his – the kind that says, I probably shouldn't have said that, but I'm glad I did.

Gianluca looks like a man at ease. Tanned from two weeks seaside in Ischia and Sardinia, a rare Mediterranean glow in a very English press room. He's clearly in good spirits – up for it, in every sense. His English is still rough around the edges, but he's diving in, headfirst. No translator. No excuses. 'I bought a couple of popular newspapers,' he jokes, 'and found some fantastic interviews. Too bad they were all made up! There I was, giving opinions on my teammates . . . Well, maybe I'll have to get used to this, too,' he says, flashing again that wide, boyish grin. It gets a laugh. But not from everyone.

Turns out one of those imaginary interviews ruffled a few feathers – namely Dennis Wise's. Wise is no shrinking violet. He's been at Chelsea since 1990, captain since '93. The sort of player who tackles hard, talks loudly and is fully committed. He's also the sort of lad who doesn't forget a slight. On or off the record. Gullit, so the whispers go, is considering a change of captaincy: Gianluca in, Wise out. And Wise? He's not having it. 'I don't like it,' he told *The Sun* just days ahead of the press conference. Given Wise's tenacious track record on the pitch, it's fair to say this little spat wouldn't be over soon.

Wise might have been rattled, but he was very much the exception. The rest of the Chelsea squad took a more pragmatic view of Gianluca's arrival. They saw what it meant. A step up. A signal of intent. Vialli wasn't just another flashy signing, he was the kind of player who could take them somewhere. Somewhere real. The Premier League. Europe. Silverware.

Meanwhile, out in the club shop, the No. 9 shirts are flying off the racks. Fans have barely seen him kick a ball but they already want a piece of him. And as the cameras click, Gianluca smiles, waves to the crowd, and heads off to join his new teammates for the grind of pre-season. It is going to be his sixteenth season as a pro – his first outside Italy. 'No regrets about leaving Italy,' he says. 'English football has always been my dream.' It had been, for years. What nobody in London suspected – not the fans, not the media, not even most of the staff at Chelsea – was that this move wasn't some last-minute opportunity. Chelsea had really always meant something special to Gianluca.

Back in that cramped bedroom on Via Toti – where he and brother Maffo turned scraps of paper into footballs and lined up Subbuteo players for epic battles – Gianluca treasured a Chelsea team scarf. A friend had brought it back from London, and it became a prized possession. Scarves like that were gold dust in Cremona. And then, years later, another friend returned from England with a Chelsea jacket. The colours weren't a million miles off Sampdoria's, so he started wearing it to training with his Italian club. Quietly. Proudly. It was never just a fashion statement, it was something deeper. And now here he was, about to walk out for Chelsea. A boyhood fantasy turned fact. His debut had to wait – he would miss some pre-season friendlies with a calf strain – but he recovered in time for Chelsea's league match on 18 August, away at Southampton.

All eyes were on him. It had been a busy summer for Serie A exports. Fabrizio Ravanelli, his old teammate at Juventus, had gone north to Middlesbrough. Roberto Di Matteo, another Italian international, had joined Chelsea, too. But even with a few Azzurri now scattered across the English topflight, fans and pundits knew there was only one Gianluca Vialli.

His first official appearance comes at The Dell – and it starts with a whimper. A goalless draw. In the first half, Gianluca looks like a man dropped into someone else's dream. Not lost exactly, but surprised. Bemused, even. Chelsea doesn't play like a team. Not in the way Gianluca understood teamplay from his days in Italy. Up front, he is stranded. Balls are pinged in his direction, but rarely to him. Gone are the one-touch combinations with Mancini.

The delicate timing of Baggio. The clever link-up with Ravanelli or Del Piero. Here, it is different – full throttle, blood and thunder, but no real pattern.

It is only now, perhaps, that Gullit's words from July begin to sink in. Chelsea needed players like him not just to score goals, but to shape the very way the team played. Less hustle, more head. Less direct, more deliberate. Less English, more European. Vialli, to his credit, doesn't sulk. He adapts. Quickly. In the second half, he drops deep, almost into midfield. If no one is going to bring him the ball, he'd go find it himself. He begins linking play, moving the ball with purpose, pulling defenders around. And when it comes back to him, he is ready. Now he is in the game. Now he looks like Gianluca Vialli. The message is clear: if Chelsea are to rise, they'd have to change – not just the players, but the football itself.

But another issue becomes clear under the Southampton lights, one that has nothing to do with tactics or tempo. Some of Gianluca's new teammates don't seem too eager to give him the ball. Maybe it's resentment, maybe just the usual teething problems. After all, the media frenzy has been all about him since he stepped off the plane. The headlines. The interviews (real and imaginary). The shirts flying off the shelves. In any dressing room, that kind of attention comes at a price. And yet, Vialli doesn't flinch. Just over 10 minutes into the second half, he starts to carve open the game with moments of sheer class.

In the 56th minute he fires a rocket from the right, forcing the keeper into a scrambling save. A minute later, he's in again, bearing down on goal, only for the keeper to throw himself at his feet and deny him. At Sampdoria or Juventus he might have squared both chances. But today? Who would he pass the ball to? Who can he trust to finish the job better than he can – especially from a tight angle, with defenders closing and the keeper flying out?

Then, the moment. The moment that makes you gasp and look at the stranger next to you and say, 'That was worth the ticket.' Twenty minutes from full-time, Gianluca takes flight. An overhead kick, pure Vialli. Left foot. Clean connection. The ball arcs high, slow-motion perfection. The keeper's beaten. But the post – the damned post – says no. It rattles. So close to a debut wondergoal, the kind to make the back pages. But even without the net ripple, the message is sent: Gianluca Vialli has landed.

Chelsea are no lost cause, either. There's plenty to work with. Dan Petrescu and Michael Duberry offer width and energy from the back. Dennis Wise – still wearing the armband, still playing like he's got something to prove – runs himself into the turf, fiery as ever. Frank Leboeuf, the French import with a cultured left foot and calm presence, already looks like a man who'll steady the ship. And Roberto Di Matteo, who must've had a few of his own second thoughts during the chaos of the first half, shows signs that he can bring real shape and vision to a midfield crying out for both. Up front, Gianluca has Mark Hughes beside him – a proper striker's striker. Old school, elbows and elegance. A player once admired by none other than Gianni Agnelli himself, the owner of Juventus and troubled automotive giant Fiat. And then there's Gullit; 34, still nursing an injury, but with footballing wisdom in every dreadlock. When he returns, he'll have his say.

The breakthrough comes in Chelsea's third match of the season. Coventry City. Home. Gianluca's first goal in English football. It's classic Vialli – tenacity, timing and thunder. Fifteen minutes from time, he picks his spot and rifles a right-footed strike from outside the box. The move was quick, sharp, improvised in a flash. Gianluca peeled away from his marker, met the cross with the inside of his boot, and guided it past the keeper with the composure of a man who'd scored in European finals. No fuss. No flourish. Just pure, fierce precision. The moment the net bulges, the release is electric. He races away, arms wide, then collapses on the pitch as his teammates flood around him.

Three minutes later, he almost doubles the tally – left-footed this time, just wide. But by now it doesn't matter. The crowd are already singing his name, over and over, and this time it's not just polite applause. It's affection. Fast and real. Three matches in and Gianluca Vialli is a fan favourite at Stamford Bridge. The kind of favourite that sticks. The kind whose name would linger in chants for decades. Chelsea win. They climb to second in the table with seven points. Vialli has opened his account. The new signings are bedding in. And Gullit is nearly fit. The wheels are turning, and the dream is beginning to take shape.

# PART TWO

# GREAT EXPECTATIONS

## 1. CHELSEA, 1996

'I'm here to win. Not just matches, but respect.'

GIANLUCA VIALLI

Ruud Gullit's Chelsea hadn't exactly set the Premier League alight the previous season, they finished a forgettable eleventh, but there had been a spark in the FA Cup, a run to the semi-finals that hinted at promise. And now, with Glenn Hoddle off to take the England job, Ruud – still lacing up his boots when the occasion called – had stepped up as manager.

For Gianluca Vialli, that mattered. The Dutchman, with his elegant touch and Serie A pedigree, was one of the main reasons Vialli had chosen Chelsea. Gullit had played for AC Milan and then Sampdoria – the club that had shaped Gianluca, and that he, in turn, had led to the summit of European football. They spoke the same football language. Understood the game the same way.

It was Gianluca's turn to become the face of hope. The fans had placed their faith in Gullit the season before; now they turned their eyes to Vialli. Not just as a striker, but as a catalyst – someone who could lift the team from mid-table mediocrity to something much more ambitious. Of course, this wasn't the Chelsea of the future. There was no Roman Abramovich yet. No bottomless war chest. No Champions League regularity.

In the summer of 1996, Chelsea was still a club with a romantic soul and a modest honours list. A league title from 1955 won with poise, then followed by decades of inconsistency. A League Cup in 1965, a bright moment in a shifting era. The FA Cup in 1970, won after a famously bruising replay against Leeds, still spoken of in pubs and matchday programmes like folklore. And the Cup Winners' Cup in '71 – their lone European jewel – secured in Athens after a replay, back when European nights felt like glamorous excursions into the unknown.

These were fine moments. Glorious. But they stood apart, like well-framed photographs in a hallway that never quite led anywhere. For every high, there had been a tumble – financial troubles, relegation, the bleak days of the Second Division. Stamford Bridge had nearly been lost to developers. The club had survived, yes. But survival and success weren't the same. Respectable, certainly, but hardly the stuff of dynasties.

Yet something was shifting. There was a hum in the air around Stamford Bridge – low, uncertain, but building. It wasn't just about the results, which remained a work in progress, it was about the feeling. The sense that Chelsea, long seen as stylish but brittle, might be on the cusp of something sturdier. That perhaps – with the right players, the right character – they could stop being a team of perennial outsiders and start writing a different story.

And Vialli had arrived not just with reputation, but with presence. Even in his first few games, there was a weight to him. A way that he held himself. A way in which the ball seemed to trust him, just as much as the fans wanted to. He hadn't started every match, and there were whispers about fitness, but some fans were still pinching themselves. This was a man who had lifted the Champions League just weeks earlier, now walking the King's Road in tailored coats and speaking about tactics in English. 'Vialli at Chelsea – imagine that,' one supporter was quoted as saying in the *Evening Standard*. 'We're used to signing hopefuls, not heroes.'

And he had already scored. His first goal had come against Coventry on 24 August – a low, instinctive finish at the near post, the kind of goal that strikers score when they've done it a hundred times before. It wasn't a wonder goal, but it was a pure one. A striker's goal. Stamford Bridge had roared – not just for the goal, but for the promise in it. For the idea that this wasn't just another foreign signing trying his luck in England. This was Gianluca Vialli. And he knew exactly what he was doing.

'I'm here to win,' Vialli had said in one of his first interviews. 'Not just matches, but respect.' And that line – earnest, slightly foreign in phrasing – had landed well. Chelsea supporters, so often promised revolutions only to be handed rebuilds, were inclined to believe him. He looked the part. And more importantly, he had lived it.

In training, Gianluca was all intensity. In interviews, disarming and articulate. He wore his elegance lightly, but it was there – in the cut of his coat, the flick of a pass, the way he spoke about the game as if it were both a craft and a calling. 'He's a gentleman,' Gullit said. 'But also, a killer. That's rare.' And off the pitch, Gianluca was quietly beginning to do what few foreign players managed in those days, he was settling. Finding his rhythm. Reading the city. Watching and listening, as he always had, before stepping forward.

In London, the Chelsea fans knew what Gianluca had done with Sampdoria. How he'd helped turn a modest club into a side that took on giants – and beat them. Serie

A, Coppa Italia, even a European trophy. He'd filled their cabinet. And now, around Stamford Bridge, hope was quietly rising – maybe, just maybe, he could do it again. This time, in blue.

## 2. SAMPDORIA, 1984

> 'It was clear – he had something special. He was a player with real quality, and he was going to go far.'
>
> IVANO BORDON

Gianluca Vialli learned he was going to Sampdoria from the man who ran his first professional club like a family estate – Domenico Luzzara, US Cremonese's big-hearted, romantic president.

An entrepreneur who had once cared little for football, Luzzara fell in love with the game after the tragic death of his only son, a devoted supporter of the team. He became president to honour his memory and led the club with the tenderness of a father and the loyalty of a lifelong fan. He treated players and managers not as employees, but as kin. It was Luzzara himself who told Gianluca the news – direct, heartfelt, like a father sending a son out into the world.

But the real twist was that Gianluca had already been a Sampdoria player for a year. 'It was the end of the 1983–84 season, and only then did I find out that Samp had purchased me a year earlier,' Gianluca later recalled. 'President Luzzara gave me the news over the phone and asked me to come see him immediately. When I arrived, to my surprise, Sampdoria president Paolo Mantovani was there, too.'

It had all been handled quietly, behind the scenes, the way Italian football worked in those days. Everyone, of course, had expected Vialli to join Juventus. The Bianconeri-famed president, the great former forward Giampiero Boniperti, had come calling first. And in those years, when Juve showed interest, it was usually game over. No one said 'no' to *La Vecchia Signora*. Most clubs didn't even try to compete. Gianluca, for his part, was open to the idea. Juve were the kings of Italian football. The destination. And when he realised the interest was real, he welcomed it.

But then Boniperti hesitated. 'A lot of scouts had come to see him,' Luzzara revealed years later, 'but they told Giampiero that Gianluca wasn't Juventus material. And so he told me, "'Go ahead, give him to Mantovani."' Sampdoria didn't blink. They came in with two billion lire (around £600,000–£800,000) and got their man.

Years later, family friend Antonio Cabrini would reveal to me that Gianni Agnelli had personally tried to bring Gianluca to Juventus. The meeting was arranged quietly, in Cabrini's Turin apartment. Gianluca arrived with his father. Gianfranco Vialli wasn't his son's agent – Gianluca would go through most of his career without one – he was simply the parent. A man outside the game, but with the wisdom to guide his young son. His advice was invariably clean, without any personal interest. When father and son arrived from Cremona, Agnelli was already waiting. Cabrini left them alone. Agnelli made his pitch. Gianluca declined. Juventus would have to wait.

For Vialli, still just a teenager with a dazzling future, going to Sampdoria turned out to be exactly the right move. Big talents with big expectations and big price tags often make the wrong jump – too soon, too fast – and disappear just as quickly. 'I don't think he was ready for Juve yet,' says Marco Nicoletti, his friend and strike partner from the Cremonese promotion season. 'So, his decision was well thought out and, ultimately, the right one.' Plenty agreed. 'Looking back, Gianluca made the right call going to Sampdoria rather than Juve,' say the journalists who'd followed his story from the start. 'At Samp, he immediately got something he wouldn't have had at a big club – attention.'

Ironically, Gianluca Vialli's first league match in a Sampdoria shirt came against none other than Cremonese. The club that raised him. The club he'd just left. It was the sort of fixture that writes its own subtext. Manager Eugenio Bersellini gave him the No. 11 shirt and sent him out under the Marassi floodlights. On the surface, Gianluca looked composed. Business-like. Maybe it was a blessing the match wasn't held at the Zini back in Cremona, where the emotions might have spilled over. He ran hard, full of youthful urgency. Took his chances. Made things happen. But the match-winner against a gritty Cremonese side didn't come from the new boy, it came from Graeme Souness – the no-nonsense Scotsman and one of Sampdoria's two international stars, alongside England's Trevor Francis.

The real heartbeat of that side, though, was Alessandro Scanziani, captain and midfield general, who'd been with Sampdoria since 1981. The man calling the shots from the touchline was Bersellini, newly returned to Genoa and bringing with him the hard edge of a winner. Just a few years earlier, he'd led Inter Milan to a Scudetto and two Coppa Italia trophies. He knew how to build teams. He knew how to win. And winning – proper winning – was exactly what Sampdoria were after.

Since Paolo Mantovani had taken over the club in 1979, back when they were still languishing in the Serie B second division, the plan had been simple: build. First, promotion to Serie A. Then, silverware. Something real. Something new. Something Sampdoria had never tasted before. At the time, the club's trophy cabinet was more a wish than reality – practically bare, even compared to Chelsea's modest haul in 1996. To be fair, Sampdoria were a relatively young outfit. Born in 1946 from the merger of Sampierdarenese and Andrea Doria, they were known more for their striking kit – blue with a crisp white, red and black band across the chest – than for anything they'd won. Their best Serie A finish was fourth, back in 1960–61. And they'd only been promoted to the topflight twice since – once in 1966–67, and again in 1981–82. It was thin stuff, especially in a city where neighbours Genoa CFC boasted nine league titles and the weight of history.

But Paolo Mantovani wanted to write a new story. And to do that, he needed players. Not just good ones – the right ones. 'We were lucky because we had a president who didn't worry too much about the cost of players,' captain Scanziani recalls. 'He bought the ones who, in his view and in the view of the managing director Paolo Borea, could make a real contribution to building the team. One of those players was Luca.'

Gianluca Vialli – not just another signing but a signal – arrived at Sampdoria full of good intentions and a quiet determination to prove himself. He didn't come in swinging any ego around, quite the opposite. He kept his head down, listened, and learned. 'Luca was a humble young lad, very humble. He was well-mannered. You could tell he came from a good family,' recalls Ivano Bordon, the seasoned goalkeeper in that side. 'Being the youngest, he followed the older players, the ones who had been at Sampdoria for a long time. He immediately became well-liked as a teammate. And even then, it was clear – he had something special. He was a player with real quality, and he was going to go far.'

In Genoa, Gianluca found an anchor of sorts – a fellow Lombard. Narciso Pezzotti, from Offanengo, a tiny village on the outskirts of Crema, just a short drive from Cremona, had joined the staff as Bersellini's assistant. The two would share the next eight years at Sampdoria and reunite at

Juventus. 'He arrived as a young and ambitious forward from Cremonese, fresh off their promotion to Serie A. I came as Bersellini's assistant coach,' Pezzotti recalls. 'Gianluca was a 20-year-old with a thick mop of curly hair – respectful, cheerful and a prankster off the pitch, but creative and fearless on it. Even though he didn't start as a regular, he quickly carved out an important role within the squad, making a key contribution.'

That first season, his role was still being worked out. He wasn't handed the keys to the attack straight away – he had to earn them. 'When Bersellini arrived as coach,' remembers Scanziani, 'the three forwards were Mancini, Vialli and Francis. Francis was a phenomenon – not just because of his technical ability, but also because, being a bit older, he had much more experience. For the two younger ones, who were strong both physically and technically, it was a matter of waiting for their turn.' Gianluca had to wait. But not for long.

'Bersellini wanted to get to know him first, to understand how best to use him,' says Bordon. 'But I think he realised very quickly that Gianluca needed to play – often, if not always. His physical qualities made a difference. He gave everything for the full 90 minutes, ran tirelessly, never held back . . . and then, of course, there was his technique.' That was the beginning. Not just of a player finding his feet, but of something much bigger – a bond with a club, a city and a generation of fans who would one day call him their own.

Despite their friendship, in Bersellini's Sampdoria system Gianluca Vialli and Roberto Mancini found themselves vying for the same space in the spotlight. There were no harsh words, no training ground bust-ups, but make no mistake, the competition was real. For Gianluca, this was his first big stage. He was hungry to play, but he handled the situation with a calm maturity beyond his years. 'At the start, I was the regular alongside Francis, and Mancini was the backup,' Gianluca recalled that first winter in Genoa. 'Then Roberto won his spot back, and it was my turn to suffer on the bench. I'd come on late in games. It was tough to make an impact. But now my moment has come again, and I don't intend to get off this rollercoaster.'

That moment came on Matchday 12 – Sunday, 16 December, 1984. Sampdoria were hosting Avellino at the Stadio Luigi Ferraris. The match was headed towards a stalemate, a cold Ligurian afternoon destined to drift into memory without a spark. But then, in minute 73, Mancini, drifting wide, twisted through two defenders with that signature swerve of his and hit the byline. Then came the cross – left-footed, whipped and wicked. Vialli, loitering at the far post in that classic striker's pose, timed his run. He rose, met it clean. A header angled back across goal, past the keeper and into the net. His first goal for Sampdoria. His first in Serie A. And the start of something big.

He was wearing No. 15 that day, having come on in the 49th minute for Evaristo Beccalossi. After scoring, he sprinted straight for the stands, towards the Blucerchiati faithful who were already on their feet. But with one hand, he searched for Mancini. Found him. And pointed. The pass had been perfect – so perfect it hardly needed more than a touch. Whatever the competition between them, the respect was already there. The bond was and would always be real. To the end.

After the match, Gianluca could have basked in the moment. Could have spoken about the goal, the emotion, the relief. But when he faced the RAI TV microphone, he didn't talk about himself. He talked about the team. About the final 20 minutes. About how Sampdoria had pushed and pushed, and how that collective effort had made the difference. Serie A had welcomed him. And Gianluca, with that quick wit and easy eloquence, returned the favour. 'A likable guy, quick-witted, well-read and mature in his judgment,' the journalists wrote.

But it wasn't just his football that left a mark.

'He was a great person, even before he was a great player – right from that first season,' remembers his first captain. 'Whenever I misplaced a pass – too long, too wide – he would stretch out in a slide, pretending he had only just missed it by a few centimetres, even when it was clear that I had messed up the pass. Then he would turn around and apologise to me. He did it so that the fans wouldn't whistle at me.' That was Gianluca. Already a class act. Already a teammate who players would follow anywhere.

Sampdoria maintained their place among Italy's elite throughout the 1984–85 season, finishing fourth in the table – matching their best-ever finish from 1960–61, a time when half this squad hadn't even been born. But as spring rolled around along the Ligurian coast, there was a nagging sense among fans that something more had been within reach. 'We could be fighting for the Scudetto right now if Bersellini had put Gianluca Vialli in the team at least a month and a half ago,' came the murmurs from the bars and balconies along the Riviera.

The league campaign might have been locked, but there was still the Coppa Italia to play for. And on the eve of the semi-final's first leg, Bersellini stuck to his plan. Vialli, once again, was left on the bench. But in the return leg, he changed his mind, and Vialli didn't just repay the trust, he repaid it with interest.

Starting from the off, Gianluca scored, fought and led the team to a commanding 3–1 victory over Fiorentina, sending Sampdoria to the final against AC Milan. When he and Trevor Francis were subbed off with 20 minutes still on the clock, the result secure, the Marassi crowd stood to salute them. It was more than applause, it was the sound of belief catching fire. 'After the win over Fiorentina, there was great enthusiasm because we had realised – first us, then the fans – that we were a great team, playing to win as much as possible,' says Scanziani.

And just like that, the celebration could begin.

On 3 July, 1985, under the warm Genoa sky, Sampdoria lifted their first trophy. They'd gone unbeaten in the Coppa Italia. Three days earlier, in the first leg at San Siro, a goal from Graeme Souness had handed them the advantage. And now, in the second leg, they did it – 2–1 over AC Milan. Mancini scored from the spot. Vialli, of course, got the other. Francis was injured, so the two youngsters who'd spent the season fighting for the same role started side by side – and they delivered. A glimpse of the future, ready to take shape.

'Before the second leg, I can't say that we were sure of victory, but we had already shown at San Siro that we were the better side,' recalls captain Scanziani who, that evening, lifted at Marassi the first trophy in Sampdoria's history. 'We had outstanding defenders, strong midfielders and even stronger forwards. There was a huge sense of optimism. Something new to Sampdoria. I remember that, before the match, President Mantovani gathered all the fan club's representatives and asked them not to flood into the pitch in case of victory. In return, he gave them his word that the team would do a lap of honour with the cup.'

Sampdoria stitched the victors' tricolour cockade onto their shirts. The first stone in making history had been laid. Mantovani beamed. His vision of football – not just as a sport, but as an antidote to the gloom of daily life – was beginning to take shape. Gianluca shone. 'In the second leg of the final, Luca Vialli had been the best player on the pitch. He ran, fought, set up his teammates, took his chances and scored the most beautiful goal of the match,' the press reported the next day.

Italy fell in love. Vialli's talent had never been in question, but now, with each match, each impossible goal, he was no longer just a great young player. He had quickly become something more. A national figure. A footballer who belonged to everyone. 'He has a culture beyond that of his peers,' journalists wrote. He handled interviews with poise. Never a word out of place. No scandal. No spin. Just sense.

Even as his fame grew, Gianluca remained, somehow, ordinary. Not because he lacked brilliance, but because he chose to stay grounded. 'He's traditional,' the press discovered and revealed, 'and deeply loyal to his girlfriend Giovanna, 18, the girl-next-door, whom he met in Cremona when they were both teenagers.'

But he also stood out – effortlessly, even stylishly. 'Off the pitch, he is a character – and he wants to be one. His immense popularity isn't just about his incredible skill and competitive fire. It's about the way he has shaken up a sport that doesn't like to change.' Gianluca Vialli was the first Italian footballer to wear an earring. The only other player in the league bold enough to do the same was Maradona. In 1980s Italy, an earring on a man was enough to spark headlines. But with Vialli, no one blinked. It didn't feel like a challenge to the establishment – because it wasn't.

## 3. CHELSEA, 1997

'Cheer up, LUCA – We love you xx.'

DENNIS WISE

Gianluca Vialli settled quickly at Chelsea – on the pitch and off it. He wasn't there to float above the squad on reputation alone. Quite the opposite. When he realised some of his new teammates were a little overawed by his name, his medals, his history, he made a deliberate effort to meet them eye-to-eye. 'I have not come to England to be the big star,' he said that summer. 'In Italy things were there for me when I wanted. I was waited on. But here when I want something I am careful to ask for it with manners.'

'When he arrived, Gianluca gave himself completely to Chelsea, and we gave ourselves completely to him,' they still say today around Stamford Bridge. 'Gianluca did everything to fit in, to be like the others, to become – as he used to say – the perfect English gentleman.' And it worked.

'Such modesty comes as a shock. The severe haircut and ferocious grimace that sears his face when he plays give the impression of a short-tempered bighead peering imperiously down from the top of his wallet at the common life scurrying below,' the press reported. 'Nothing like it. Vialli turns out to be a most gracious of men, thinner and younger than he looks on the field, with piercing blue eyes and a devilish sense of humour.'

On the pitch, Vialli started like a man with something to prove. There was no easing in, no polite adjustment period. He came with pedigree, but in England, pedigree meant nothing without proof. So, he gave them proof – week by week, goal by goal.

He scored in the derby against Arsenal, a match that always carried extra weight. It wasn't just a goal – it was a message. Chelsea hadn't beaten Arsenal in a league match for nearly a decade. Vialli helped end that run with a poacher's instinct and a finish that skipped off the wet turf like it had somewhere urgent to be. The fans in blue roared louder than they had in years. The supporters finally had what they had long been craving – a forward with teeth.

Next came Nottingham Forest. Then Leicester, where he scored again – quick movement, clinical touch, the kind of goal that looked easy only because he made it so. There was one more in a frustrating home loss to Wimbledon, where Chelsea's fluid build-up met the brutal resistance of the Dons' old-school defending. Vialli still found the net. Even when they lost, he gave them something to cheer about.

But the real headline came at Old Trafford. It was early November, and Manchester United were as imperious as ever. Chelsea were not expected to win. But they did – and it was Vialli who delivered the moment. A clever dart inside the box, a touch to settle, and then a low shot through Peter Schmeichel's legs that silenced the Stretford End. The away end exploded. That was the goal of a man who's been there. Who's done it. And who's not afraid to do it here.

By then, it was clear – he wasn't just scoring, he was lifting the side. Raising their level. You could see it in the confidence with which they played, in the body language of players who had spent too many seasons playing for scraps. Chelsea were climbing the table. Not fast, not flash – but steadily, with purpose. And at the centre of it all was Gianluca Vialli, sleeves rolled, jaw set, goals flowing. It was early yet, but you could feel it. Something had begun.

But just as everything seemed to be falling into place, something cracked. The relationship with Ruud Gullit – so full of promise – began to unravel.

It hadn't been part of the plan, of course. Vialli had chosen Chelsea, in no small part, because of Ruud. They shared a footballing past – Serie A alumni, both veterans of Sampdoria and international stars for their respective countries. They spoke the same tactical language, respected the same values: intelligence, movement, flair with discipline. But somewhere between the handshakes and the team sheets, the connection began to fray. Quietly at first: a substitution too early, a start denied. Then a pattern. Finally, silence.

There were no dramatic confrontations, no tabloid-ready outbursts – not in so many words. But Gianluca, proud and still adjusting to English football, began to feel sidelined. 'When I play, I score,' he told the press, without bitterness, but with purpose. Gullit, for his part, never explained much. His selections seemed to drift from merit to message. And the message, increasingly, was that Vialli's role would not be guaranteed – not by reputation, not by history, not even by goals. A growing distance. A clash of personalities. Maybe a power struggle. Maybe something subtler – tactical tensions, differing visions of how to rebuild the club's identity. The irony, of course, was that this was why Gullit had brought Vialli to Chelsea in the first place.

By the autumn, things had shifted significantly.

'His ego was as big as Amsterdam, and he didn't even try to disguise it. Ruud had to be the top man in any way,' said English midfielder Rob Lee, who would later experience a similar rift under Gullit at Newcastle FC. 'Ruud loved conflict; he enjoyed being at loggerheads with certain players . . . At the start I thought Ruud liked me, we seemed to get on, but he didn't like being disagreed with and . . . by the end, he didn't speak to me at all. He didn't want me anywhere near the training ground.'

By the time Gianfranco Zola arrived from Parma – Chelsea's third Italian signing in as many months – Vialli had been relegated to the bench. When he played, he still made an impact. Between November and December, Vialli scored against Newcastle and Everton. In January, he put two past Liverpool in the fourth round of the FA Cup – an old-school striker's performance. But his appearances were limited, his rhythm broken. In the league, he went three long months without a goal. And while Gianluca sat, Zola soared.

Zola was magic – floating past defenders, scoring spectacular goals, lighting up the Premier League with a grin and a backheel. By season's end, he'd be crowned Chelsea's best player. And for Vialli, it only deepened the shadows.

Still, the fans never wavered. Every time Gianluca stepped onto the pitch, they sang for him – 'That's Amore', Dean Martin's old hit, turned into a love song for their Italian No. 9. It started as a bit of terrace fun, a nod to his charm and continental flair, but soon it became a chant of defiance. A way of saying: he's one of us. We believe in him. Even when he sat on the bench, the song would ring out – louder, almost pointed. Fans didn't understand why Gullit had started to sideline Vialli. To them, it didn't make sense. Vialli had delivered goals, big moments, a touch of class. He had become more than just a marquee name – he was a presence, a player who made the crowd sit up and the team play better.

But between player and manager, the break was final.

'You see? I put Luca in, and we got beaten. Maybe it's a coincidence, but we always lose with him,' Gullit said after a 3–1 league defeat against Coventry City. No tact. No grace. Just a line that cut deep and told the whole story. The comment wasn't just undiplomatic, it was cruel and fictitious. Public, casual and devastating. Vialli didn't respond in kind. That wasn't his way. But something shifted that day; the hurt was obvious, even if he didn't say so. Whatever trust had once existed between them was gone.

The team stood behind Gianluca. That much was clear. In football, loyalty is rarely loud, but it finds its ways to speak. And at Chelsea, that message began to show, quietly but unmistakably, through the cracks in the dressing-room silence. Even Dennis Wise – the captain and heartbeat of the squad – made his loyalties known. Wise had once bristled at Vialli's arrival, suspicious of the fanfare and foreign pedigree. But now, he saw the bigger picture. He saw what Vialli meant to the players, to the fans, to the very idea of Chelsea daring to be more.

So, when Wise scored against Derby County at Stamford Bridge in January 1997, he didn't just celebrate – he made a statement. He lifted his shirt to reveal a plain white vest underneath. Nothing flashy. Just a message, handwritten in thick black marker: Cheer up, LUCA – We love you xx. It was raw, simple, and unmistakably human. The crowd saw it. The cameras caught it. The Bridge erupted. 'Vialli frustrated but not forgotten,' the press would comment the next day.

Gullit saw it, too.

He didn't say a word. Didn't gesture. Just stood there on the touchline, stoney-faced, letting it all play out. But when it came time to make a substitution, when the crowd and half the bench expected to see Vialli's number go up, Gullit turned, looked past his veteran striker, and called for a youngster – Paul Hughes, barely into his twenties, raw, wide-eyed, making his first-team debut. A gesture that said everything. The message had been received. And rejected.

If Vialli's league minutes were drying up, his FA Cup appearances were rarer still. One start. Four cameos. That was all. For a man of his pedigree, his pride, it felt like slow erasure. And even when the big day came – the final at Wembley, the kind of occasion every footballer dreams of – Gianluca was left on the margins.

This was supposed to be the storybook moment. A kind of redemption. Five years earlier, he had stood on the same turf in a Sampdoria shirt, heartbroken under the twin towers after losing the Champions League final to Barcelona in extra time. That match had never left him. He carried it, quietly, in the spaces between words. And now he was back in 1997 – with Chelsea, in a different shirt, chasing a different trophy. The opponent was Middlesbrough. But his name wasn't on the team sheet.

Ruud Gullit sent him on with one minute left to play. Sixty seconds. The score was already 2–0 after goals from

Roberto Di Matteo and Eddie Newton. The match was done. And everyone knew it. Gianluca entered the pitch not like a champion seizing his chance, but like an extra in a play he should have been starring in. He replaced Gianfranco Zola. And Zola, ever graceful, ever aware, didn't jog off with a high-five. He stopped, turned, and bowed – deeply, deliberately – to the man taking his place. It was a gesture that carried weight. Respect, solidarity, maybe even apology.

The fans understood it, too. They'd waited the whole afternoon for a glimpse of their No. 9. And when Gianluca finally stepped onto that famed turf, they rose as one. VIALLI! VIALLI! VIALLI! VIALLI! The chant echoed around Wembley, not just for the player, but for the man and what he represented – for style, for dignity, for being denied. A roar of defiance from the stands. And it cut deeper than any whistle.

Playing in an FA Cup final at Wembley had been one of Gianluca's boyhood dreams. Back in Cremona, they'd simply called it La Coppa d'Inghilterra – spoken with reverence, as if it were a faraway myth. No one cared that it wasn't the league. In England, this cup mattered. It was theatre. Glory. History. The kind of match that made legends out of men. They all dreamed of playing in it. So had the young Gianluca.

But one minute? One minute isn't playing. It's a footnote. A formality. A line in a match report that says you were there but doesn't tell the truth. And for a man like Gianluca Vialli – a champion of Europe, a captain of Juventus, a scorer of great goals – it could have been the final straw. A reason to pack up, go back to Italy, find somewhere he'd be treated with the respect he'd earned. But Gianluca typically didn't walk away. He never had. Not when it was difficult. Not when it hurt. Gianluca Vialli didn't leave things unfinished.

'I'm not going back to Italy. Next season, I'll still be playing in England – I still have a lot to prove here,' he said. These should have been glorious days, filled with confetti and champagne. Instead, they felt like a cruel joke. A great player, side-lined. A dream, soured. 'In my own country, I did what I had to do. In London, on the other hand, I've done far too little. I won't deny it – of all the Italians who came to the Premier League, I'm the one who's done the worst.'

He said it calmly, without bitterness, and with far more grace than anyone had shown him that season. He didn't name names. Didn't point fingers. He left out the truth that everyone else could see, who's really to blame for how it had all unfolded so far. Back in Italy, the rumour mill turned. Atalanta had made overtures. Gianluca's old US Cremonese coach, Emiliano Mondonico, was coaching there now, and he'd welcome Vialli with open arms. But Gianluca wasn't entertaining the idea of going back. Certainly not like this.

Despite his limited minutes – and the fraying relationship with his manager – he was still Chelsea's top scorer in the league, with nine goals. Years later, he would admit, 'I was thinking of maybe leaving.' On his shortlist were Celtic, Rangers and, most notably, Crystal Palace – where Attilio Lombardo, his old teammate from Sampdoria and Juventus, was about to land. Palace would have meant a fresh start, but more importantly, it would have meant staying in London. And Gianluca loved London.

Most didn't know the half of it. Late at night, Vialli would often hop on a red double-decker – the iconic London bus – just to drift through the city, watching it roll past, soaking it in like a boy seeing it for the first time. 'He came with an open heart and filled it with London,' recalls Rick Glanvill, Chelsea's official historian. 'He fell in love with London and with Chelsea, and we opened our hearts to him and filled our hearts with him as well.'

'Here, I feel a real sense of freedom,' Gianluca once said of his adopted home. 'I do what I want without the fear of being watched, not like in Italy. People respect privacy. At the supermarket, the cinema, the museum – no one bothers me. In London,' he added, 'there are five or six places where we're always welcome. It's not like in Italy, where footballers get the red-carpet treatment in every restaurant and club. More than once here, as I wasn't recognised, they wouldn't even let me into a nightclub.'

He stayed. At Chelsea. Not because there was peace with Gullit – there wasn't. If anything, part of his decision to remain may have been rooted in stubborn pride. Not to give Ruud the satisfaction of watching him walk away. Gullit had made his position plain enough: I don't want any player to leave, every player here is welcome to stay. But if the player himself said he wants to leave, then it is difficult.

Everyone knew who he meant. It was an invitation, barely veiled. But Vialli declined it.

UMBRO

# PART THREE

# FAULT LINES

## 1. CHELSEA, 1998

> 'For Chelsea fans watching back home or huddled in the away section, something became clear: the story wasn't over. Not even close.'

Ruud Gullit left Gianluca Vialli on the bench for the curtain-raiser to the 1997–98 season: the Charity Shield, the 75th edition of English football's traditional clash between the league champions and the FA Cup holders. A statement game. A chance to set the tone. Wembley again. The big stage. But not, it seemed, for Gianluca.

Chelsea faced Manchester United – a heavyweight fixture made for players like him. Yet he sat and watched, waiting, while the minutes ticked by. Gullit finally turned to him, with the game level at 1–1, in the 77th minute. Vialli came on for Mark Hughes. Thirteen minutes to make a difference. Not much, but something. He ran, chased, carved out a half-chance. He knew the drill. He'd been here before.

Then came penalties. No extra time. Straight to the shootout. Vialli, ice-cool by nature and habit, was down to take the fifth spot-kick – possibly the decider. A moment of pressure. A moment he was built for. But it never came. Two Chelsea players missed before it got to him. United, ruthless and precise, scored all of theirs. The match was lost and Gianluca's penalty, like so many opportunities during his time under Gullit, was denied him. The season had barely begun, the kit was still crisp, the story still unwritten. But the message was all too familiar.

Gullit's big idea for the new campaign was 'rotation' – a nice word when it means options, a less-nice one when you're the one left out. With Chelsea now juggling four competitions, including the Cup Winners' Cup earned by that FA Cup triumph, squad depth was crucial. But after watching the first trophy of the season slip away from the bench, Gianluca was put back into the starting eleven for Chelsea's second league match: away at newly promoted Barnsley. And in Yorkshire, on a pitch still dizzy from its own fairytale, Vialli did what strikers do when they know they've got something to prove. He scored. Four times.

It was Barnsley's second Premier League home game – just two months after the club's historic rise to the topflight. The ground was a sea of red and white scarves, grown men wiping tears from their cheeks. But on this afternoon, sentiment met steel. Vialli unleashed all his frustration on the pitch, and Barnsley took the full brunt of it.

The first goal came with his right foot – hard, low, drilled from the edge of the area. A turn so fast it barely registered, only the finish told you what had happened. The second was sheer persistence: a scuffle with the keeper, one touch with the foot, one with the head, and somehow the ball ended up over the line. The third was all about speed. A clever ball into the box, Gianluca ghosted in, unmarked, beat the keeper to it, finished clean. And the fourth – three metres out, left foot, instinctive smash. Job done.

It was the only four-goal match of his entire career. And he did it without a flicker of celebration. After the third, Gullit rose from the bench and applauded. A smile flickered across his face – one that may have carried the faintest trace of discomfort. Gianluca didn't grin. He didn't raise his arms. No fist pumps, no badge kissing, no messages. Just a nod to Zola, who'd set up the first, and quiet embraces with teammates. Businesslike. Efficient. Professional. Each goal felt like a step towards the next. That's all.

After the match, Gullit offered praise, but with an edge. 'He looked fitter and sharper,' he said, then added with a hint of theatre, 'and he's given up smoking.' The implication was clear: if Gianluca had been benched last season, maybe it hadn't been a manager's whim after all. Vialli responded in kind, without bitterness, just with that unmistakable glint in his eye. He admitted he'd trained hard over the summer. Hit the gym. Rode his bike. 'But mostly,' he added, deadpan, 'I made love as much as possible.' A line delivered with the kind of humour English fans were growing to love. But also, possibly, a subtle jab at his manager. A playful nod to Dutch football's progressive view of players, wives and . . . extracurricular preparation – something Johan Cruyff's '74 Holland side had famously normalised. It was quintessential Vialli, direct, elegant and a little mischievous. A man still scoring goals, still winning hearts – and still writing his own story.

Chelsea were growing, they were no longer just a club of potential, but one cautiously building towards something more. Over the summer, they'd moved with intent in the transfer market. Norwegian striker Tore André Flo had arrived, tall and angular, with a knack for the unexpected. Gustavo Poyet, a Uruguayan with an eye for goals and a head for battle, brought bite and late runs from midfield. Celestine Babayaro, all energy and promise, came in to strengthen the flanks. And Ed de Goey, the towering Dutchman, added both reach and reliability between the posts.

It wasn't always tidy. Ruud Gullit's Chelsea still played like a side in mid-construction – flashes of brilliance, moments of confusion. The Dutchman's ideas were ambitious, fluid – sometimes too fluid. He wanted style and structure, but they didn't always arrive together. Even so, there was movement. Shape. Something resembling a proper team was beginning to emerge. And within that group, Gianluca Vialli was still very much a presence. He trained hard, spoke softly but carried influence. Players respected him. Some admired him outright. He'd been a star before many of them had turned professional. He might not start every match, but his shadow still stretched across the dressing room.

The season had begun and Gianluca was ready – sharp, focused, aware that chances might be limited but determined to make each one count. While league minutes remained unpredictable, the Cup Winners' Cup offered a different stage. A chance to lead from the front, to play with freedom, to remind people why he had come to England.

He started the opening match away against Slovan Bratislava and helped Chelsea to a confident 2–0 victory. It wasn't just the result that mattered, it was the way he played. Intelligent movement, deft touches, that unteachable awareness of space and rhythm. After the match, he spoke not of his own performance but of something deeper. 'On Thursday, I played up front with Zola; but from the bench, Flo and Hughes were my biggest supporters. That shows we're a team.' It was classic Vialli – elegant, modest and quietly powerful.

He scored in the return leg at Stamford Bridge. Back then, the European cups were knockout ties from day one – no second chances, no group stage to paper over a poor night. Every goal mattered. Every moment was a test of nerve. But the night that etched him into Chelsea legend – the night fans still talk about – came in Norway.

On 23 October, 1997, second round, first leg. The opponent: Tromsø. A name that sounds like a whisper. A place almost at the top of the world (it is located in the Arctic Circle). Tromsø sits so far north that, until 1963, they weren't even allowed to play in Norway's top league, they had their own, separate, polar circle championship. And when Chelsea landed, they understood why. The field was frozen solid. The wind screamed down from the Arctic. A snowstorm swept across the sky. The sort of weather that would stop traffic in London and make headlines in Milan. In Tromsø? It was just Thursday.

Tromsø were no European giants. In the second leg, back at the Bridge, they'd be taken apart. But tonight? On a pitch glazed with ice, they had the upper hand. Chelsea players slipped and struggled. Staying upright was an achievement. Playing football? Almost reckless. And somewhere in the middle of that frozen chaos was Gianluca Vialli.

He played like he was back at Cristo Re, on the parish pitch that turned to mud in autumn, to concrete in summer, and to something quite like this in winter – except that in Cremona, it never got this cold, of course. A field that taught toughness and touch in equal measure. 'Of all the images that define Vialli as a Chelsea player,' wrote the English press, 'none is more unforgettable than his slalom run on a snow-covered pitch, just steps from the Arctic Circle in Tromsø, weaving through the ice to score a magnificent goal – while many, including his own manager, who had injured his ankle kicking a rock he mistook for a snowball, could barely stand on their feet.'

That night Gianluca Vialli rose to the occasion. Scored twice, led the line with elegance and fire, fought through the cold and the chaos like a man who refused to be reduced by conditions or circumstance. The goals were sharp, instinctive – vintage Vialli. But it wasn't just the finishing. It was the performance. The movement, the timing, the authority. He played like a captain without the armband. That night, in the far north of Europe, he wasn't a sidelined veteran. He was the man. And for Chelsea fans watching back home or huddled in the away section, something became clear: the story wasn't over. Not even close.

That performance in Norway should have settled the questions. Two goals in Arctic conditions. A complete display of leadership, poise and finishing. It was the kind of night that should silence debate, secure a place, end the whispers. But somehow, it didn't.

That autumn Vialli was playing more than he had the previous season, there was no doubt about that. He was fitter, sharper, more integrated. But not regular. Once again, not untouchable. The starts came, but so did the omissions. The rhythm of being a first-choice striker never quite materialised. The shirt never felt entirely his. Or rather, not his alone.

'I was playing more, but I was frustrated with the rotation system, which didn't really make sense,' he said later, reflecting on the first half of that second campaign. Rotation sounded modern, sophisticated, necessary for a club chasing on multiple fronts. But to a man who had built his career on rhythm, timing, confidence – on knowing when he'd play and who he'd play with – it was maddening. One week he was the match-winner; the next, back on the bench.

Vialli's relationship with Gullit remained polite but distant, icy in that peculiar way that footballing relationships can become – all handshakes and eye contact, but no warmth. The camaraderie they once shared, rooted in Serie A memories, international stardom and mutual respect, had quietly dissolved into something cooler, more transactional.

'Last year, we had some misunderstandings. But on a personal level, there was never a problem,' Gianluca offered in the autumn of 1997, still the gentleman. Still measured. Still protecting the dignity of the role, and the man above him. It was a generous comment, all things considered. A player of lesser character might have said more. Much more. But Gianluca had always played the long game – on and off the pitch.

Yet something was shifting beneath the surface. The air around the club felt taut, heavier than before. Gullit, for all his charisma, was becoming harder to read. His decisions more erratic. Players sensed it. So did staff. And Vialli, who had lived through title races in Italy and Champions League finals in Europe, knew what tension looked like when it was starting to turn into fracture.

The balance was tipping. The lines of loyalty and leadership were beginning to blur. And things were about to take a sharp turn.

## 2. JUVENTUS, 1992

> 'Never had an ex-player been welcomed back with such warmth and kindness.'

Having lifted the Scudetto with Sampdoria in 1991 and lost the European Cup final to Barcelona the following spring under the towers of the old Imperial Stadium at Wembley, Gianluca Vialli made the biggest move of his career. In the summer of 1992, he left Sampdoria and joined Juventus – the club that had first come for him a decade earlier.

Back home in Via Toti, his childhood mates were quick to pounce. Now all in their thirties and still clinging to their football loyalties like heirlooms, they teased him mercilessly.

His move to Juve was, they said, a betrayal. A broken oath, forged on afternoons spent whacking a ball off the garage door in Cremona, dreaming of glory – but never in black and white stripes. Most of them, Gianluca included, were Inter Milan fans. All of them, once upon a time, believed they too might become footballers. And they'd made a pact: none of them, ever, would play for Juventus.

But this was real life, and Gianluca had a different kind of responsibility now. 'I want to be a leader for a team built to win,' he said upon his arrival in Turin. 'Motivation, enthusiasm, responsibility – it's a weight I can handle with my experience, and it's the kind of things that extends a career.' He was still young. At the height of his powers. And he knew it. 'I just turned 28. I'm at the peak of my physical and mental abilities, and I have no intention of letting down those who believe in me. As a man, I'll adapt to this new environment. As a professional, it's clear – I came to Turin to chase even greater victories.'

The fans welcomed him warmly. And he gave it back, placing his faith in their belief. 'I'm starting from zero, but I'll overcome any difficulty quickly because I know I have everyone's help.' Giovanni Trapattoni – the legendary manager brought back to Juve for a second spell – had pushed hard for the transfer. He admired Gianluca's drive, his intelligence, his work ethic. 'He works with almost too much generosity,' Trapattoni said after an early intrasquad match, in which Gianluca's side won 4–2 and he scored twice. When the club's owner, Gianni Agnelli, called to check on the new arrivals, Trapattoni didn't hesitate: 'We all know Vialli. There's a lot of responsibility on him, and that will push him to do well – to leave his mark on the season.'

But football isn't always scripted, and despite early goals, Juventus didn't click. Not with Vialli at the tip of the attack. As autumn settled in, questions began to swirl – not just outside but inside Trapattoni's own head. Doubts crept in. Adjustments followed. Between October and November, the manager began to reshuffle. He moved Roberto Baggio up front, closer to Vialli. Behind them, Andreas Möller – the gifted but enigmatic new German playmaker – was tasked with pulling the strings. Pierluigi Casiraghi and Fabrizio Ravanelli watched from the bench. David Platt watched from the stands.

The results were patchy. So was the mood. Vialli stopped scoring, and in Italy, that's all that counts for a striker. 'The critics are ready to stress every mistake I make,' Gianluca admitted on the first Sunday of November. His last goal had been a stunner – a free-kick at the San Paolo in Naples on 5 October. Since then: silence. 'Today, no one forgives anything. You'd have to be perfect all the time. But I make sacrifices for the team,' he said, 'and I do it willingly.' It was true. He was running. Battling. Working between the lines. But the goals weren't coming, and the press were circling.

Trapattoni stepped in. 'Gianluca knows his role is important, just like Schillaci's was last year,' he said, trying to steady the ship. 'Players like him, unlike Möller and Baggio, rarely have the space or strength to shake off defenders and go for goal. They need the team to create for them. I won't lose sleep if Vialli isn't scoring. What matters to me is that we keep creating chances. I'd be worried if we didn't – or if Vialli weren't giving his all. But he always does.' It was a fair defence. And a necessary one. But the weight of the Juventus black-and-white shirt is heavy. Especially when the goals stop coming.

As always in his career, Vialli gave everything. But the comparison to Salvatore Schillaci – made by Trapattoni, certainly with the best intentions – must have echoed through Gianluca's nights. Everyone knew how that story ended: Schillaci, once the golden boy of the Italia '90 World Cup, was fading from the spotlight and leaving

Juventus with more regret than legacy. And yet, there was something else. Something more radical. Trapattoni had started to imagine something apparently unthinkable. He was beginning to see Gianluca Vialli not as a striker, but as a midfielder.

It was a tactical idea and, in part, a return to something older, buried beneath 10 years of goals, trophies and reputation. Back in his early days at Cremonese, Gianluca had never been the out-and-out No. 9. Managers Guido Vincenzi and Emiliano Mondonico had often deployed him wide, as a winger, a runner. He was versatile. But that was before Sampdoria, before the transformation, before Vialli became the Italian centre-forward of his generation. At Sampdoria, he had become a symbol. A force. With Mancini and the gang, he had powered his team to a Scudetto, three Coppa Italia wins, a Supercoppa and a Cup Winners' Cup. He wasn't just a forward. He was *the* forward. And now Trapattoni wanted him to play deeper.

On 3 January, 1993, as the league resumed after the break and the internationals returned, Vialli started behind Baggio and Casiraghi – a deep-lying playmaker in a Juventus shirt. 'It was an idea I had been toying with for a while,' Trapattoni admitted. 'It's an option I might use in special cases – when I need to add another forward without weakening the attack. Vialli knows how to press, he's intelligent, he plays first-time passes. He's a natural midfielder. He just needs to adapt to the role.' The manager assured everyone that Vialli was on board: 'Gianluca agrees. We have an open dialogue. It's a solution to keep in mind.' But Gianluca said nothing. No statements. No interviews. No clarifications. Just silence.

'Gianluca Vialli elegantly sidesteps all questions about his potential transformation into a midfielder,' the press were quick to note. Some called it 'diplomatic', others 'strategic'. Gianluca had his reasons. He was caught between two visions. Trapattoni, who saw him now as a playmaker, offered examples to sweeten the move – Giampiero Boniperti, Valentino Mazzola, Roberto Bettega, Alfredo Di Stéfano, even Johan Cruyff himself. All men who reinvented themselves for the sake of the game and their careers. And then there was Arrigo Sacchi, the new Italian national team coach, with whom Gianluca had clashed before. But Sacchi, whatever else, had always seen Vialli for what he was: a striker. A finisher. A man for the box.

The debut of this new experiment – Vialli the playmaker – was inconclusive. Juventus drew at home against Parma. Both he and Baggio scored. But Trapattoni didn't get what he was after: control, flow, a win. 'The experiment didn't go perfectly,' he said afterwards. 'But I'll keep going. Vialli didn't do bad, but the team lacked fluidity. He's not yet natural in the role. He relies too much on power. If he struggled against Parma, if he doesn't feel comfortable going on, we'll talk about it. But in my mind, the experiment should continue.' Still, Vialli said nothing.

In the midst of this tactical storm, Gianluca returned to Genoa – his first time at Marassi in a Juventus shirt. It could've been cold. It could've been hostile. But it wasn't. 'Never had an ex-player been welcomed back with such warmth and kindness,' the papers wrote the next day. Sampdoria hadn't forgotten their golden boy. Two banners told the whole story. THE JERSEY IS BLACK AND WHITE / BUT THE HEART IS BLUCERCHIATO, said one. HIS SOUL IS OURS / HIS BODY IS YOURS, said the other. And then, from the South Stand, three enormous banners unfurled. At their centre, a giant white heart. Four words, in English, for all the world to read: WE LOVE LUCA VIALLI.

When the teams are announced, the Juventus players are greeted by a chorus of whistles, as the worst habits of our football demand. Then comes number 9. The stadium announcer pauses, stretches out Gianluca's name, and waits. The whole stadium answers with an ovation Marassi had rarely heard before – and never for a man in the shirt of the opposition.

As the sides emerge, Gianluca hangs back a few steps from his new teammates. Almost as if he didn't want to hurt the people who once adored him by appearing to belong elsewhere. Perhaps he is even quietly grateful that Juventus has chosen the yellow kit instead of the famous – or infamous – black and white.

By the time he reaches the centre circle, the whole ground is on its feet. Scarves whirl. Hands sting from the applause – just like the old days. Thirty thousand voices chant his name. Gianluca, who had walked out with his eyes lowered so as not to meet the gaze of faces he had known for years, finally gives in. He stops, alone in the middle of the pitch, and blows kisses in every direction. Now the crowd is in tears. His former teammates come to greet him. Mancini pulls him into a long, warm, meaningful embrace.

Gianluca had a mind of his own that day at Marassi. It was meant to be a return – the kind that reminds a player of who he is, of where he came from. And perhaps that's exactly what happened. Because during the match, he began to drift. Ignoring Trapattoni's instructions, he slipped out of midfield, pulled wide, pushed forward, went where instinct took him. The manager barked at him from the touchline, voice rising over the roar, calling him back to position. But for that one afternoon, Vialli was playing his own football.

After that match, though, something gave way. Gianluca gave in. He took on the role he didn't want – the midfielder's burden, deeper on the pitch, further from goal. And anyone watching could tell that it didn't suit him. It wore on him. He played, but he didn't look like himself.

And as the weeks dragged on, the questions weren't just about where he played. They were bigger than that – existential, even. Did he still belong in this Juventus? Was there room for a striker who no longer struck? 'Why spend a fortune on a recycled Vialli, a Vialli who is no longer Vialli?' jabbed one headline, mercilessly. Worse still, while he was being pulled away from goal in Turin, he was being pulled out entirely with the Azzurri. Sacchi made it plain: there would be no call-ups. Not now, not for the foreseeable future.

The goals dried up. Nostalgia crept in. He missed Genoa. Missed Sampdoria. Missed the looseness, the laughter, the sense of belonging. Then came the week of Napoli away. Worn down and off form, Gianluca did something few professionals ever do, he walked into Trapattoni's office and told the manager to leave him out. He needed rest. He needed air. The Coppa Italia semi-final against Torino was just around the corner, and he wanted to be ready for it. The league was lost, but a cup could still save something. Trapattoni agreed. But fortune was not on Juventus' side that year. The two-legged semi-final against the cross town rivals was settled in Torino's favour by the rule then in force, whereby away goals (1–1 at Torino's grounds; 2–2 at Juventus') counted for double.

By then, Vialli hadn't spoken to the press in months. No interviews. No statements. Just silence. But the frustration had never been more visible. It clung to him. And then, at the end of May, after Juventus lifted the UEFA Cup against Borussia Dortmund – in a two-legged final in which the Bianconeri scored a total of six goals – Gianluca, despite starting both matches, was left without one of his own and finally broke his silence. And when he spoke, as always, he didn't waste words.

Out of nowhere, he dropped a bombshell on the evening news. Not in a press conference. Not filtered through a journalist's pen. His voice, his message. 'I'd love to return to Sampdoria. Their style of play suits me,' he said, firm and clear. He'd learned the power of speaking directly. The few times he chose to speak now, it was always on television – unfiltered, undistorted. 'My first season at Juventus hasn't satisfied me, but it's up to the two clubs to reach an agreement. I'll say it again: I'd gladly go back to Sampdoria.' And then he laid it bare. 'I haven't spoken until now,' he said, 'because I had nothing special to say. And the important things – well, those, I wasn't allowed to say.'

A return to Genoa was, of course, never likely. Too many moving parts. Too much politics. And besides, Gianluca Vialli wasn't one to walk away because the road got steep. But that outburst – measured, but unmistakable – said it all. It was the voice of a man tired of pretending. Of smiling through a role that didn't fit. Of sacrificing his footballing self for a system that didn't seem to want him, only what he represented. He had played 32 times in the league, but only scored six goals. He was there. But rarely decisive. Rarely himself. And it showed.

He was tired. Not of the game, but of what the game had become for him. Tired of sacrificing himself for a role that didn't suit him. Tired of reading the papers and seeing one new striker after another being paraded at Juventus, while he, once the most feared predator in the box, was being reshaped into a playmaker. A forward who no longer played forward. A star who'd been asked to step aside. It wasn't just tactical. He could feel it. This was about status. About value. About trust. He had been moved deeper by Trapattoni, handed a new script – but it wasn't a starring role. And Gianluca Vialli had never been a supporting actor.

But even after his public statement – his plea for a return to Sampdoria, his subtle admission that this Juventus wasn't working – his teammates didn't turn on him. They knew. They knew what he meant to the side – not just as a footballer, but as a figure. A leader. A presence in the dressing room. A man who gave everything. Andreas Möller, the elegant and often enigmatic German whose role had become entangled with Vialli's, didn't hesitate: 'If Vialli wants to play up front, he's welcome to. I'm happy to drop deeper to make room for him. What matters is that all three of us – Baggio, Vialli, and me – can play together.' That was the tone around the club. There was no mutiny. Just understanding.

In the end, Trapattoni's old-school wisdom and Gianluca's own sense of duty prevailed. They didn't trade shots, they traded perspective. Trapattoni, always ready with a wry line and a sharp memory, smiled as he addressed the moment: 'These were the same things Boniek and Platini used to say – confessions from champions who always demanded more from themselves.' The names weren't chosen at random. Zbigniew Boniek and Michel Platini weren't just world-class players, they were icons who had shaped the club's golden years under Trapattoni 10 years earlier. Mentioning Vialli alongside them wasn't just flattering, it was Juve's coded way of saying: we get it. You're one of us. And more importantly, it was a signal that they were still willing to build together.

Always pragmatic, Gianluca knew when to speak and when to settle the air. 'I'm sorry if the fans misunderstood me – or maybe I didn't explain myself well,' he said. 'I only meant that I wasn't happy with how I'd been used at Juventus, and that, in terms of style, I preferred Sampdoria's way of playing. Genoa has been good to me, but that's in the past.'

He didn't storm out. He didn't retreat. He stayed. And in doing so, he helped write one of Juventus' finest chapters.

The following season would not necessarily prove happier than his first in Turin. A foot injury kept him out for long stretches. An unwelcome exile from the pitch where he longed for continuity. But the year after that, helped in part by the departure of Trapattoni and the arrival of a new manager in Marcello Lippi, Gianluca finally found his footing. Turin would never replace Genoa. Juve would never be to him what Samp had been. Yet, by 1995 he would win a second personal Scudetto. And the year after that he would lift the Champions League trophy.

## 3. CHELSEA, 1998

> 'I have a lot to learn, of course. But I hope I can repay the trust the club has placed in me.'
>
> GIANLUCA VIALLI

With his contract set to expire on 30 June, 1998, Ruud Gullit spent months negotiating a renewal with Chelsea's owners. He was fresh off a FA Cup triumph – the club's first piece of silverware in 26 years – and felt he had leverage. He wanted a new package. More than that, he wanted control over his future.

The club had ideas of their own. They wanted Gullit to retire as a player and focus solely on management. He, however, was reluctant to hang up his boots. And just to be clear, he let them know he had options. Feyenoord and PSV were keen to bring him back home. Rangers, north of the border, were circling, too.

Eventually, the endless back-and-forth wore Chelsea thin. 'We told him we couldn't accept his financial demands and that he would have to give up playing,' said vice-chairman Colin Hutchinson. 'We were prepared to make him the highest-paid manager in England. But in the end, we realised he wouldn't accept, so we called it off. This situation was only hurting Chelsea.' And just like that, Gullit was gone. No testimonial. No warm goodbye. Just a ruthless, clean break. For a club that had won so little before him, there was no room left for gratitude. Not now. Not here. Not in football.

If the sacking stunned the football world – including Gullit himself, who would later admit, 'I found out through the television' – what happened next left jaws on the floor. Because his replacement wasn't a household name in the dugout. It wasn't a seasoned manager. It was one of Ruud's own players. 'It's a joke. It has to be a joke,' said Roberto Di Matteo when he first heard who the new Chelsea manager was.

Gianluca Vialli!

Like the rest of the squad, Di Matteo had no idea what was happening behind closed doors. None of them did. Except for one. This wasn't just a dismissal, for Gullit, it was humiliation. The man he had pushed to the fringes, left on the bench, sidelined, questioned, was now taking his seat in the manager's office.

The irony was staggering. But it hadn't come out of nowhere.

Some time earlier, Chelsea had quietly approached Vialli. They knew his frustrations; not just with Gullit's tactics, but with his style of leadership – leaving players guessing, locking up decisions like state secrets. The club had asked Gianluca, discreetly, whether he'd be interested in stepping up at the end of the season.

At the time, Gullit still had a contract, and Vialli respected that. Still, he was intrigued. Management could be a new chapter. He was turning 34 in the summer, and while he'd often said his dream role was something closer to Giampiero Boniperti's – a player turned executive, guiding from the top floor – this, too, was a path. A challenge. A way forward. But he hadn't expected it so soon.

As Gullit's negotiations dragged on, Vialli's willingness became Chelsea's safety net. Then it became their solution. On Monday, 9 February, Gianluca met directly with the club's vice-chairman. Two nights later, the offer came in: player-manager until the end of his contract, then two more years as manager alone. Gianluca didn't blink. 'I made the decision in five minutes,' he later said. And that was that. Chelsea didn't wait. They cut ties with Ruud on the spot.

'We felt Vialli was the best replacement,' said Colin Hutchinson, stepping out to explain what, to many, still felt like a surreal twist in Chelsea's story. 'Last season, he earned universal respect for the dignity with which he handled being benched and his difficult relationship with Gullit. After the FA Cup final, he was deeply downcast. I spoke to him for a long time,' Hutchinson recalled. 'And I realised that beyond being a great player, he was intelligent and mature, someone who truly understood the game.'

And Hutchinson didn't stop there. He'd done his homework.

'Later, I went to Turin and spoke with Lippi and some Juventus executives. They all agreed – Gianluca had the makings of a manager.' So, while it felt sudden – one shock after another, Gullit out, Vialli in – this wasn't an impulse. The foundation had been laid well in advance, quietly, carefully.

But even with the groundwork in place, no one looked more stunned than Gianluca himself. 'I'm still a little confused but I'm very happy and I hope I can be the right person for the right job,' he admitted, still catching his breath after the announcement. And then came the emotion. 'This is the most unbelievable thing that's happened in my career. I have a lot of great memories, but this is something different even from the feeling of scoring a goal.' His voice trembled with the weight of the moment. 'If you consider that I've been in football for 17 years, you'll understand that's no small thing.'

It wasn't.

Overwhelmed by the chance not just to play, but to lead, for Vialli, this wasn't simply a new chapter, it was the beginning of a brand-new story.

Colin Hutchinson wasn't the only one who turned to Marcello Lippi. When the time came to decide, Gianluca Vialli picked up the phone and called his old manager – the man who had guided him through Juventus, who had seen his strength, his struggle, his transformation. Vialli wanted advice – not permission, just clarity.

'I rang a few friends, Lippi among them, and asked for advice,' he admitted when the news became official. 'They encouraged me. They told me not to be afraid, that I had everything it took to succeed at the highest level.' And yet, as always, Gianluca never lied to himself. 'I know full well there'll be pressure, new responsibilities. I must be honest – I'm a beginner at this. I'll need everyone's help, their support.'

He knew what he was stepping into. The spotlight. The scrutiny. The burden. Years later, with hindsight and the calm that comes from experience, he'd say the same thing – word for word: 'It's true, I was an experienced player. I had worked under some of the best managers in the game. I wanted to be a manager, and as a player, I studied tactics, training, the physical side of football. But in many ways, I was still just a novice.'

But in this moment, Vialli admitted, 'I have a lot to learn, of course. But I hope I can repay the trust the club has placed in me.'

And repay it he would.

# PART FOUR

# IN CHARGE

## 1. CHELSEA, 1998

> 'I was one of the lads, and I still am, but some things will have to change.'
>
> GIANLUCA VIALLI

Looking back with perspective – past the stormy 1996–97 season, past the silent benching, past the strained relationship with Gullit and the refusal to become a 'Vialli case' – the English press would one day write: 'The drama was intense, but Vialli's decision to stay had paid off, and over the coming two years, he established himself not as a bit-part player but as a pivotal figure in the club's recent history.'

The signs of that pivot were there from day one.

His first training session as manager was behind closed doors. It had to be; the attention was feverish. The press wanted every detail. The fans were watching. Two global stars had traded places – one out, one up. No one in or around the club could think about anything else. The Italian media showed up in numbers rarely seen in London outside of a Champions League final. The cramped press room at Stamford Bridge was bursting to the seams. Health and safety officers would've had a field day.

Five days remained until his first test: the second leg of the League Cup semi-final against Arsenal. The first leg, lost 2–1 at Highbury, had left Chelsea chasing the tie. The return leg would be Gianluca's debut. His trial by fire. A baptism under the floodlights. 'I know that for the players it will be a bit difficult to go through this unusual situation, but I hope they can go through it with maturity, which is the most important thing,' Vialli said on the eve of the match. 'I was one of the lads, and I still am, but some things will have to change and what I want to do is improve the relationship between the manager and the players, which is the key to any successful team.'

And there it was: the first real mission statement of Gianluca Vialli, manager; not tactics, not formations, not possession stats but relationships. Because in the end, the man who once learned the values of sport on a parish pitch in Cremona had never forgotten that you never win alone.

Wisely, Gianluca Vialli made one of his most important decisions before the first whistle. He asked Graham Rix to stay on as assistant. Rix brought something that even Gullit never quite possessed: experience. More than once during Ruud's time in charge, Rix had been the steady hand, the voice of reason in the tactical fog. 'After I had got over the shock,' Rix recalled, 'I went down to see Luca in the dressing room. I was pleased when he said he wanted me to stay on. I wished him all the best and his first words to me were, "Graham, I need your help." It was amazing. I had waited 18 months for Ruud to say that to me.'

Gianluca was still a player; he still shared the dressing room, still jogged through training drills, still joined the banter. But after the sessions – once the boots were off, the massage done, the autographs signed – he would now head upstairs to face the press, sharp suit replacing sweat top. 'Impeccable in his London look, with his shaved head and neatly trimmed goatee,' the journalists noted, watching as Vialli navigated his first big pre-match press conference on the eve of the League Cup return leg against Arsenal.

Gianluca admitted he hadn't decided whether he'd play. It was the kind of match made for him – big stage, big opponent, backs to the wall. A battle. But this time, the decision had to go beyond instinct. It wasn't just about him anymore. He spoke carefully. No grand declarations. Less laughter now, the Italian press observed. He was already speaking and thinking like a manager. And, of course, the inevitable question came: which of his old managers would he try to emulate?

Too sharp to walk into that trap, he answered with poise. 'Lippi was a great example for me. But I also learned a lot from Boskov, from Vicini, from Sacchi.' The signs, however, were clear. It was Lippi's Juventus that would be his compass. 'I hope to give Chelsea the same spirit, the same mentality as Juve, which for me remains the model to follow,' he said. 'I want to structure the club like the Bianconeri – meticulous planning in both fitness and tactics, perfection in the details.' It wasn't just about proving something to Ruud. It was about answering another voice from his past. Because maybe, just maybe, this was also about settling a quiet old score with Arrigo Sacchi.

And finally, the moment of truth came.

Wednesday, 18 February. Stamford Bridge. Arsenal in the neighbourhood. Gianluca Vialli makes the call. He puts himself in the starting XI. Leads the line as centre-forward, flanked by Zola and Hughes. No more 5-3-2. Gullit's system is gone. Vialli brings in the Lippi model: a fluid, aggressive 4-3-3. High tempo. Clear roles. Controlled ambition. He knows it by heart. Knows what it brought Juventus. Knows what it can give to Chelsea.

When Gianluca Vialli was named manager, not everyone was convinced. To some, it felt like a mismatch. Here was the son of an Italian construction magnate, raised in a Renaissance manor with dozens of rooms and a private tennis court, a childhood wrapped in comfort, far from the noise of the terraces, and now he was taking charge of a club rooted in working-class grit. Chelsea, for all its new ambitions, still bears the scars and soul of the King's Road – the chants, the cigarette smoke, the muddy fight of midweek fixtures. Now they were being led by a man who sips his espresso with style and quotes Dante before kick-off. But despite the reservations of some sections of the press, Chelsea fans had no doubts, and they were on his side from the very first match.

The reception is spine-tingling. As the teams walk out onto the pitch, the big screen at Stamford Bridge lights up with a single word – LUCA – painted in the green, white and red of the Italian flag. The roar that follows is pure emotion, a tidalwave from the stands. The Chelsea faithful, who had taken him into their hearts from the very first moment, now sing his name as if to will this new era into existence. Even those who still carry affection for Gullit feel it: this isn't betrayal. This is transition. The page has turned. The club has moved on. This is Vialli's Chelsea now.

Before stepping out under the lights, Gianluca did what only he could think to do. Champagne – not for victory, but for new beginnings. He brought two bottles into the dressing room. Glasses for everyone. And, one by one, he filled them himself. A toast, before battle. Not after. Not for what they'd done, but for what they were about to try. A quiet, unconventional touch. A signal. 'An early sign of what was to come in terms of managerial style,' the English press would write later. Because if Vialli was going to lead, he would do it his way – elegant, human, defiant, surprising.

And the team responded. They weren't just sharper than they had been under Gullit, they were committed. United. This wasn't yet a side sculpted in Gianluca's image. It couldn't be; that would take time. But tonight, they played for him. Because he had earned it and they wanted him to succeed. And, of course, he gave it all. Like in the old days. Like he had at Samp, at Juve, on frozen pitches in Tromsø and giant nights in Turin.

During the match, he's all in. Player and coach, mind and body. Every sprint forward is matched by a glance to the dugout. He jogs to the touchline to confer with Rix. Fine-tunes instructions. Adjusts details. This isn't about ego. It never was. It's about doing what's needed. It's about knowing what's required. It's about leading. He covered the front line. He dropped back when needed. He chased, tackled, pressed. Inspired. He took knocks – this was England, after all – but each time he hit the turf, he got back up. Even when limping, he got up. Because that's what you do here. That's what he does. And on the touchlines, in the stands, in the press box, everyone saw it: Gianluca Vialli was alive again.

'He looks ten years younger,' wrote the Italian journalists who had tracked him since the early days at Sampdoria. 'If Lippi were here, he might just feel a twinge of regret,' they added. And somewhere, perhaps, he did. Because this wasn't just a man surviving the pressure of his new role, this was a man thriving in it.

Chelsea led 1–0 at half-time. Hughes had put them in front just 10 minutes in. The aggregate score now level. The Bridge, alive and rumbling. But three minutes into the second half, the tide turns properly: Patrick Vieira is sent off. Arsenal are down to 10 men. Three minutes after that, a flash of magic from Di Matteo, the kind that lifts an entire stadium onto its feet. Stamford Bridge doesn't simply celebrate, it believes. And then, as if riding a wave, another three minutes later, Romanian Dan Petrescu lashes it home to make 3–0 on the night. The final beckons.

Vialli plays on until the final 10 minutes. Then comes the moment only a manager can make. He pulls himself off and on comes Eddie Newton. A midfielder for a striker. A calm, calculated shift. Game management, they'd call it now. But on the night, it was a signal: we've done enough, now let's see it through. As Gianluca jogs off, the whole of Stamford Bridge rises in unison. A standing ovation – not for the goals, not just for the win, but for the man himself. The one who had been cast aside, then called up. Who had stepped into fire and walked out roaring. The man who, tonight, proved he belonged.

'Chelsea fans saw a clear display of Vialli's tactical and motivational abilities tonight,' the press wrote the next morning. 'It was fantastic,' Gianluca said afterwards. 'We changed a few things in the way we played, but in the end, it was heart that won us the match. I'm proud to be the manager of these lads.'

And after the storm came calm.

That evening, Gianluca made his way to Osteria San Lorenzo. Italian in name, refined in spirit, it was a favourite of the London elite, yes, but for Gianluca, it was something else entirely. A haven. A second home. The owners knew him well. Knew what he liked. They'd even named a dish after him: Penne alla Vialli. Not for show, but because it fitted.

'Now I just hope I can sleep,' he confessed. 'These last few days, I've barely closed my eyes, always thinking about what I had to do. The tension –' he admitted without hesitation, 'felt just like the night before the Champions League final in Rome.'

Because for all the noise, the tactics, the touchline decisions – for all the champagne, the press conferences, the chants echoing across Stamford Bridge – Gianluca Vialli was still the same man who had walked into finals with butterflies in his chest and a duty on his shoulders. Still the man who carried the pressure with grace, even when it kept him awake at night. A champion who understood that leadership doesn't mean being fearless. It means being brave anyway.

## 2. JUVENTUS, 1996

> 'I knew that was going to be my final game with Juventus, I knew I was going to come to Chelsea and so, probably, last chance for me to play in the Champions' League final.'
>
> GIANLUCA VIALLI

With a second Scudetto now in the bag, Gianluca Vialli had only one thing on his mind – the Champions League. The one that got away. The one he should have lifted at Wembley three years ago, wrapped in the colours of Sampdoria, alongside Mancini and the brothers-in-arms who took a provincial club to the gates of European glory.

This time, he meant to finish the job.

With Roberto Baggio gone, the captain's armband was his. At Juventus, he had long been a leader in the shadows, a voice in the dressing room, a presence in training, a standard to match. Last season, in Marcello Lippi's debut campaign, he had become one on the pitch. Now it was official. Not just a nod to talent, but to will. To character. To the kind of leadership you don't inherit – you earn. Not even at Sampdoria had they handed him the armband. But now, in Turin, it was his. And with it came the weight of Europe.

The Champions League, in only its third season under the new name and format, was merciless from the start.

There was no gentle welcome back. After nine years away from the continent's top table, Juventus were drawn into a brutal group: Glasgow Rangers, Steaua Bucharest and, most daunting of all, Borussia Dortmund. And to crank the tension higher, the first match was away in Germany, without their main strikers. Both Ravanelli and Vialli were suspended. The frontline was toothless on paper. But Lippi didn't back down. 'If anyone thinks we've already reached the summit [with the Scudetto],' he warned, 'they're making a big mistake.'

He was right. Even without their attacking pair, Juve stormed to a 3–1 win in Dortmund. Goals from Michele Padovano, Antonio Conte and a brilliant Alessandro Del Piero gave them the start they needed. Two weeks later, for the home debut against Steaua Bucharest, Vialli was back. He didn't score, but he made sure others did. Del Piero, Angelo Di Livio, Fabrizio Ravanelli – all on the scoresheet. Four minutes into the second half, it was Vialli who slid in the assist for Ravanelli to open the floodgates. A simple finish made easy by his vision and timing. After that, he hunted. Stalked the box like the old days, sniffing for a goal to mark his return. It didn't come, but the message was clear: Juventus were here, and so was he. The Champions League was calling, and this time, Gianluca Vialli intended to answer.

Juventus marched on. In mid-October, they demolished Rangers 4–1 at the Delle Alpi. Two weeks later, they went to Glasgow and did it again – another four-goal masterclass. By the time Borussia Dortmund snatched a narrow win in Turin on 22 November, it barely mattered. Juventus were already through.

Marcello Lippi knew exactly what he had in Gianluca Vialli. First, he had convinced him to stay – after the chaos of that first year under Trapattoni, after the injuries and doubts of the second, after the frustration that had nearly driven him out the door. Then, he had motivated him. Finally, he had waited. And now, as Juventus swept through Europe, so much of it flowed from Gianluca. 'He has always had the heart of a leader,' Lippi said. His teammates didn't hesitate either. 'His presence on the pitch changes everything,' Ravanelli believed. 'And more than that, Gianluca always finds the goal when it matters.'

On 6 March, Juventus travelled to Madrid for the first leg of the quarter-finals. Vialli didn't. The previous weekend, away at Padua, he'd taken a brutal knock and left the pitch with a deep gash in his foot. Eleven stitches. No chance of playing. Juve lost 1–0 at the Bernabéu. Not fatal – it kept Juventus alive – but it was not ideal, either, and now everything hinged on the return leg at the Delle Alpi and return of Vialli.

The press circled. The pressure mounted, 'The guns are aimed at him. The spotlight won't blind him. He has no excuses, and he doesn't want any.' Gianluca understood. He always had. On the eve of the match, he cut through the noise with his usual no-nonsense approach: 'If we go through, they'll put us on a pedestal. If we don't, they'll beat me with a stick.'

And then he did what he always did: he showed up. Juventus beat Real Madrid 2–0.

Vialli didn't score. He didn't need to. He led. He pressed. He bled for the cause. At full-time, the Delle Alpi erupted. All eyes on the captain. 'Some thought Gianluca wasn't fit enough, that he'd struggle tonight,' said Lippi. 'But I knew he'd give everything. And he did. You all saw how exhausted he was at the end. He never pulled out of a tackle. He led by example.'

Juventus marched into the semi-finals. Waiting for them was Nantes, who had just dumped out Spartak Moscow. On the other side of the bracket, Ajax – the defending champions – prepared to face Panathinaikos.

But in Turin, all eyes were already on a dream. A rematch. A reckoning. Ajax in the final, 1973 avenged. Vialli triumphant. And for Juve fans, hearts now bracing for goodbye, that dream meant everything. Because they knew what Gianluca had given. And they knew, deep down, that the final in Rome might just be Gianluca Vialli's last match in black and white.

In the first leg of the semi-finals in Turin, Gianluca finally broke his European goal drought. His first strike of the Champions League campaign, it should've felt cathartic. A moment to savour. Instead, he barely celebrated. 'It had to happen sooner or later,' he shrugged afterwards. 'It was bound to come. Just a poacher's goal.'

It mattered – of course it did – but it wasn't his kind of goal. Not one to replay in your head. Not one you write home about. And he knew it. Earlier, though, he had tried something different. Something pure. Something Vialli. A bicycle kick – instinctive, acrobatic, audacious. The kind of moment few would attempt in a European semi-final. And it nearly came off. Only a top-drawer save from French keeper Dominique Casagrande kept it out. That – that was the goal he wanted. The crowd knew it. They roared not just for the goal, but for the intent, the art, the heart.

'Stay with us!' they chanted, over and over. Gianluca felt the love. He always had. But tonight, it cut deeper. He turned to both ends of the stadium, arms wide, saluting them all. 'Tonight, more than ever, I felt the fans behind me,' he admitted, voice thick. 'These things get to you. Respect and love from the supporters – they mean everything.' But he was captain now. Not just in name, but in posture, in poise. On the pitch. In the dressing room. In the press room. And captains don't get carried away. 'I'm happy with 2–0. It's a good result, but it's not enough to make us feel safe. We can't let ourselves think we've already qualified.'

They didn't. In France, Juve held their nerve. Despite a 3–2 defeat in the second leg, they booked their place in the final.

But the atmosphere in Nantes was poisonous. Nantes manager Jean-Claude Suaudeau had been lighting fires since the final whistle in Turin. He'd blamed Vialli for the red card given to defender Carotti. Said Gianluca had gone down too easily. Stirred the pot with every interview. And when Juve arrived in France, Suaudeau poured on more fuel. He called Vialli a 'provocateur, a bully, a cry-baby who runs to the referee for protection.'

Gianluca didn't rise to it. No fireworks. No fury. Just steel. 'No need for me to be my own lawyer,' he said, calm and composed. 'The Nantes manager started setting the stage for the second leg the moment they lost in Turin. A questionable tactic, but one that suited him. I'm not offended. Everyone picks their own way to get what they want. When you're struggling, you'll try anything. Even if it means using someone else as a pawn.'

That was Gianluca. Elegant when praised, gracious when attacked. No outbursts. No nonsense. Only focus. Because just over the horizon, something bigger waited. Rome. The cup final. One more night. One last chance.

---

Just like four years earlier, the Champions League final at Rome's Stadio Olimpico would be Gianluca Vialli's last match for the club he played for. Back then, it was Sampdoria. Now, it was Juventus.

The decision had been made. He was going to London. He was going to Chelsea. And that made the stakes heavier than ever. 'For me, that match was quite similar to the match I played with Sampdoria at Wembley four years earlier with Barcelona in the final of the Champions'

Cup,' he would recall years later, 'because I knew that was going to be my final game with Juventus, I knew I was going to come to Chelsea and so, probably, last chance for me to play in the Champions' League final . . . again, final game with my club. I was desperate to win. By far the most complicated game, for me, mentally, to prepare for . . .'

Juventus were ready. He was ready.

'Physically, we were the best team in Italy, maybe even in Europe,' he would recall. 'Peruzzi was the kind of guy you'd go to war with – an absolute rock. Up front, we played in a way that was rare – three top-class strikers: me, Del Piero and Ravanelli. And all three of us worked for the team. We scored, but we were also the first line of defence when we lost the ball. And then there was Lippi. To me and the rest of the squad, he was like a footballing Messiah. The cherry on top. The absolute leader of a group full of leaders.'

That night in Rome, the Olimpico was a sea of black and white. Scarves waving. Flags fluttering. Hope burning. Juventus struck first – Ravanelli sneaking one in. The place erupted. But then came Jari Litmanen. Ajax found the equaliser: 1–1 at full-time; 1–1 after extra time. It would come down to penalties. And then, for the first time in a long, long while, Vialli hesitated. 'I was nervous when we got to the penalty shoot-out,' he later admitted. 'I had taken two penalties in the last six years in Rome, in that very stadium. One was at the World Cup, against the United States – I hit the post. Two years later, I took one against AC Roma, broke my foot, and was out for 120 days. So, I didn't have good feelings about it.'

Lippi came over and looked him in the eye. 'Luca, do you want to take one?' Vialli didn't lie. 'I said, "I'm here if you need me. But if you've already got five who want to take one, I'll sit this out."' Lippi nodded. 'Alright, let me see. You might be sixth, if it comes to that.'

It didn't.

From the spot: Ciro Ferrara. Gianluca Pessotto. Michele Padovano. Vladimir Jugović. All perfect. No need for a fifth. No need for a sixth. No need for Vialli. Juventus won 4–2 on penalties. And finally – finally – Gianluca Vialli lifted the Champions League trophy. The one he had turned down when Sacchi's Milan came calling. The one that slipped through his fingers at Wembley four years earlier. Now, at last – it was his.

'A goal would have been the cherry on top,' he said after the match. 'But I wanted the whole cake.' And this – this was the cake. The victory. The vindication. The final word in a story of pain and persistence. 'It was amazing. It was basically the defining moment of my career,' Gianluca would later reflect. 'When you're 20, you're just happy. You don't realise what you have done. But at 31, with the pressure on your shoulders, time running away and so many sacrifices, then I got really emotional. I nearly fainted on the pitch.'

Coca-Cola

# PART FIVE

# FORTUNE FAVOURS THE BRAVE

## 1. CHELSEA, 1997

> 'We stayed patient, we believed. We deserved to go through.'
>
> GIANLUCA VIALLI

It was a dream start, but football has a way of reminding you just how quickly dreams can turn. After the jubilation came the sting.

Three straight defeats follow Gianluca's electric beginning: first, away at Leicester – a scrappy, stumbling performance that feels more like a hangover than a match. Then a sobering night at Stamford Bridge against Manchester United, who are starting to look inevitable again. And finally, Aston Villa – compact, clinical and ruthless – come to west London and take all three points. It's a hard run. A spell that strips away the euphoria and lays bare the job ahead.

Vialli responds not with excuses, but with goals. A brace in a 6–2 demolition of Crystal Palace stops the bleeding. It's a statement not just from a manager, but from a player who can still lead by example – and still score. But even that can't resurrect the title chase. By now, it's no longer

Chelsea's race to run. The Red Devils and the Gunners have already broken free – a two-horse sprint towards May, all but settled before the dugout at Stamford Bridge even changed hands.

Still, Vialli's Chelsea are alive on two other fronts. The league might be slipping away, but silverware is still in reach. And one of those paths leads to a final before March is out. The League Cup: England's youngest domestic prize, the least glamorous, the least romanticised. No sepia-toned memories. No fanfare. But it's the first trophy of the season. And it counts.

Wembley, 29 March. Chelsea vs Middlesbrough. Gianluca Festa and Gascoigne in red. A clash of styles, of personalities, of footballing moods. And on this day, Gianluca steps back. Leaves himself out entirely. No tracksuit, no boots, no shirt hidden under a blazer for a late cameo. He takes his seat in the dugout dressed to the nines – charcoal-grey tailoring, sharp lines, calm posture, eyes locked on the pitch. Manager first, player second. He makes his decision not on sentiment, but on structure. On what the team needs, not what the crowd might want. It's a quiet declaration that this is his team now. That his ambition has shifted – not away from the pitch, but above it. And that perhaps – just perhaps – the man who once lifted trophies in a game shirt will soon be lifting them in a suit.

It's a bruising affair. Tight. Nerve-jangling. Both defences drilled to the inch. No room to breathe, let alone break lines. The forwards scrap, chase shadows, lash shots from distance. Possession is messy, progress even messier. Still, Chelsea start to edge it. The rhythm shifts. The pitch tilts in their favour. But the scoreboard doesn't budge. Ninety minutes. No goals. Extra time.

Then, finally, the door cracks open. Frank Sinclair strikes in the 95th – a shot low and true, threaded through a crowd and past the keeper. Relief, not celebration. There's still work to do. Middlesbrough press on. Gamble. But the next blow is fatal. Di Matteo, calm and clinical, buries the dagger in the 107th. The final whistle sounds. Chelsea lift the cup. Forty-five days after taking Gullit's seat in the dugout, Gianluca Vialli is a trophy-winning manager.

Praise rains down. For the win. For the setup. For the decision. The next morning, the papers line up in agreement: 'Vialli's selflessness primes Chelsea's deserved victory. The victory justified Gianluca Vialli's brave and selfless decision to leave himself out. His compensation was a trophy.' A cup in the cabinet. And a new era, perhaps, just beginning.

And there, in football's grand temple – Wembley – where six years earlier he had come so close in a Sampdoria shirt, Gianluca Vialli, now impeccably dressed, beaming, steps forward. He takes the trophy from the hands of the Home Secretary, Jack Straw. No shorts. No boots. Just a grin, a suit and the steely satisfaction of having made the right call.

His first trophy as a manager.

But there's no time to dwell. No time to savour it, not properly, because Thursday brings another battle. A European night. Away to Vicenza, Italy. The first leg of the Cup Winners' Cup semi-final.

---

Under manager Francesco Guidolin, Lanerossi Vicenza FC are living the finest season in their history – greater even, by most accounts, than the Paolo Rossi-led fairytale two decades earlier. Guidolin has taken the Biancorossi from Serie B to the topflight. He's given them silverware – Coppa Italia champions – and now, improbably, a place in a European semi-final. They don't have pedigree, but this season they don't need it. Guidolin's men are drilled, disciplined, dangerous. A unit built on belief and intelligent football.

The first leg is in Italy.

And Chelsea? They flatter to deceive. Or perhaps more accurately, Vicenza play exactly the way their manager wants them to play – compact, clever, unyielding. They soak up pressure, strike on the break and never lose their shape. Chelsea look like the bigger side, but not the better one. The Blues escape with a 1–0 defeat, spared a harsher punishment only by their goalkeeper, who pulls off two extraordinary saves to keep the matter alive. 'We're still in it thanks to De Goey,' Gianluca Vialli admits post-match. 'We made mistakes, and we paid for them. But I won't criticise my players – we gave everything. If we want to go through, though, we'll need to be perfect.'

Gianluca plays in Vicenza. Comes close to scoring. Leads the line with purpose, but the goal doesn't come. And he starts again in the return leg at the Bridge. It's pouring. The rain lashes down, the pitch slick and greasy, every touch a risk, every tackle a slide. Conditions like these level everything – form, reputation, expectation. And after half an hour, disaster. Vicenza strike first: 1–0 on the night; 2–0 on aggregate. And worse – an away goal. Under the rules of the day, it cuts twice. Chelsea now need three.

The Blues bite back. Gus Poyet levels just before the break with a clever finish – controlled chaos in the box, a lifeline. Stamford Bridge breathes again. Then, just after the restart, Zola pounces: 2–1. Chelsea now within touching distance. But not enough. They still need a third, because Vicenza's away goal stands like a locked gate. It counts double. The maths is cruel, and the clock is ticking.

And then – minute 71 – Gianluca makes the move. Jody Morris off. Hughes on. A striker for a midfielder. It's bold. A gamble. But the right one. Five minutes later, it pays off. The substitute scores. A classic finish, all power and instinct, straight from the soul of an old-school centre-forward. It's 3–1. Chelsea are through.

Gianluca Vialli tastes the full thrill of changing a game not with his boots – but with his brain. That's what great managers do. They read. They risk. They get it right. And tonight, that call – his call – sends Chelsea into the Cup Winners' Cup final. At full-time, the young manager is jubilant. 'Even after going behind,' he says, 'we kept playing well. We stayed patient, we believed. We deserved to go through.'

They did. And so did he.

## 2. SAMPDORIA, 1990

> 'Last year, just getting to the final felt like a victory. This time, only winning will do.'
>
> GIANLUCA VIALLI

In May 1990, 12 months after falling 2–0 to Barcelona in the first European Cup final of its history, Sampdoria found themselves in another Cup Winners' Cup final. This time in Gothenburg, Sweden. The opponent was Anderlecht.

The word on the street was this Belgian side might even be stronger than the Barcelona that had shattered their dreams in Bern the year before. The Blucerchiati needed more than a good performance, they needed to exorcise the ghosts of the previous final. 'There's a heavy air in the dressing room,' Gianluca Vialli admitted before kick-off. 'We're focused, but mostly afraid. Afraid of another Bern.'

Roberto Mancini, ever the voice of mischief and mischief-managed, tried to lighten the mood. 'Last year we were knackered, half the team held together with tape. Now we're fresh, fit. No excuses.' And Gianluca – this time – was fit, hungry and ready. The past was still fresh, but the body, finally, was not broken. 'A year ago, I was playing on one leg after a brutal season. I'd peaked too soon. Now, I've had my rest. We're ready. Last year, just getting to the final felt like a victory. This time, only winning will do.'

They stepped onto the pitch aggressive, determined, hungry. Anderlecht bunkered down. Held their shape. Survived. In the first half, Gianluca came within a whisker, a left-footed strike flashing just past the post. Pietro Vierchowod rose like a mast from a Mancini corner, only for the ball to be blocked by dumb luck on the line. Mancini, floating like only he could, dinked the keeper – denied again by a last-ditch clearance. The ball, it seemed, was being difficult. Maybe Boškov was right: 'Ball goes in when God wants.'

Second half. Same story. Sampdoria swarmed. Anderlecht held. The Belgian keeper flattened Fausto Pari. Attilio Lombardo flew down the wing. Giovanni Invernizzi had a go. Nothing. For Anderlecht not a single knock on Pagliuca's door. Ninety minutes. No breakthrough. Extra time. And time – at last – for Vialli to change everything.

Just before the first half of extra time ticked out, Fausto Salsano let fly from the edge of the box. The ball slammed against the post and spun into chaos. The keeper, still down from his dive, reached. Fumbled. But Vialli was already there. Already moving. He flicked the ball away with his right, settled it with his left – and bang. Into the net. Sampdoria were in front.

'Not a beautiful goal,' he'd say later. 'The keeper got hold of the ball, then lost it, and I got there first . . . an opportunist's goal, let's say. But a crucial one. It won Sampdoria our first European trophy.' It would always be, in his words, 'the most thrilling goal' of his career. Not for how it looked, but for what it meant.

Gianluca didn't stop running. He leapt the advertising boards and charged towards the stand where the Blucerchiati faithful were losing their minds. It looked like a dance – arms spread wide, bouncing, drunk on joy – until his teammates caught him and buried him beneath a heap of blue shirts and roars. A goal that defined a career.

But he wasn't done.

Three minutes into the second half of extra time, Sampdoria struck again. Lombardo and Salsano sliced through the Belgian defence with quick passes. The ball found Mancini, tight to the byline, just outside the area. Roberto looked up. Picked his moment. Curled the cross. And then Vialli rose. Timing. Power. Poetry. Goal. 2–0. Another sprint. Another smile. Arms wide, raised to the sky. A leap. And then the crush of teammates – again.

Now there was only the waiting. And the whistle. When it came, the Anderlecht players queued for his match shirt. Defeated, yes – but with reverence. Vialli had earned that tonight. Sampdoria had won the Cup Winners' Cup. 'This was the win we were missing,' Gianluca said afterwards. 'It fills a gap, erases that label of an immature team, or worse, a great unfinished work. Maybe if we had believed in ourselves a bit more, it would have come sooner.'

He was happy for himself – scoring twice in a European final wasn't something you did every day. But he was even happier for others. For his teammates. For the fans. And for the man who stood behind it all, the volcanic football maestro Vujadin Boškov. And for the Sampdoria president, of course. The man who had believed in him when others had not. 'I'm happy for Mantovani too,' he said. 'He's demonstrated that in Italy, you can win and still be a gentleman.'

That night, Gianluca Vialli didn't just win a European trophy. He became something more than a footballer. He became the face of a club's transformation. The proof that dreams, when met with sweat, stubbornness, and the right amount of poetry, can become real.

## 3. CHELSEA, 1998

'This is no longer just Vialli the player or Vialli the icon. This is Vialli the manager.'

The European Cup Winners' Cup final is set for Wednesday, 13 May, 1998 – exactly three months to the day since Gianluca Vialli took Ruud Gullit's place in the Chelsea dugout. Three months in which he's lifted a trophy, reached a European final and shown – despite inevitable bumps in the road – that he has what it takes. Not just to win, but to manage.

First, by repeatedly benching himself, he's proved that the team matters more than his own ego. Second, though he hasn't reinvented Chelsea's style, he's given them something else: sheer determination. The kind that once made him such a force on the pitch. Now it's contagious. And third – perhaps most important of all – he's shown humility. He listens. Especially to Graham Rix, his assistant. A man who knows the game like few others. With Rix at his side, Vialli has shown a beginner's mind, without surrendering authority.

But none of this has been as easy as Gianluca makes it look. Not as effortless as the smile, the warmth, the good humour suggest. Especially not on the personal side. Managing players who, until yesterday, were teammates – that demands a kind of emotional amputation. And not everyone can make the cut clean. 'At Chelsea, his teammates adored him. Then, suddenly, the moment he became manager, Luca – so to speak – became the enemy,' an insider recalls.

No one felt the shift more than Roberto Di Matteo. Once thick as thieves off the pitch, now there's a gap between them. One that Di Matteo can't pretend isn't there. 'I've just lost a friend,' he says. 'Our relationship has changed. We never go out now because he is the manager.

I would like him to be the way he was before. It's sad for me because I miss him as a friend, and I can't have him back as a friend as long as he is a manager.'

Gianluca knows. Of course he knows. He doesn't pretend otherwise. The job demands it. Still, he wonders aloud about what friendship really means. 'It must be possible to be angry sometimes with your friends,' he says. Perhaps, he suggests, managers should speak of bond rather than friendship – but even that, he knows, changes the meaning. The truth is: everything has changed.

But the squad accepts the change. More than that – they respond. 'I'm now playing more in the way that I did in Italy,' says Zola. 'I've been asked to do more work when the ball is with the opponents. I accept that.'

Under Vialli, Chelsea become runners. Press conferences. Compact. Disciplined. Gullit had wanted artistry, control, possession. The beauty of the ball. Vialli wants work. And the players feel the shift. 'There's more discipline now in the way we play,' they say. Captain Wise backs him. 'You have to respect the decisions a man with his experience makes.' And yet, even he leaves a door ajar. A quiet doubt. 'It's hard to say whether he has the ruthlessness necessary,' Wise concedes. 'He's not been in the job long enough yet. But not a lot has gone wrong, except dropping form in the League a bit.'

It's true. The League slipped away during the transition. But trophies are still in sight. And the next one – a big one – awaits in Sweden.

---

When Gianluca Vialli's Chelsea and Joachim Löw's Stuttgart – coached by the man who would one day lead Germany to World Cup glory – meet in Stockholm on the second Wednesday of May, 1998, there's no clear favourite.

These are the two best teams in the competition, that much is certain. The Blues have taken the long road. Slovan Bratislava in the first round, Tromsø up near the Arctic Circle in the second, then Real Betis and finally, Vicenza in that dramatic semi-final at Stamford Bridge. Stuttgart's path has been less turbulent. IBV from Iceland, Germinal Ekeren of Belgium, Slavia Prague. Lighter fare. But then again, this is the Cup Winners' Cup in the 1990s; a tournament built for variety, one team per country, full of curious detours and unfamiliar names. For most of Europe's giants – especially outside England – the domestic cup is, sadly, no one's priority.

But tonight, it all matters. On the eve of the final, Gianluca Vialli wrestles with the big question. 'I could play. I want to play. That's my first instinct. But I need to work out if it's better for me to stay on the bench,' he says, carefully. Perhaps cryptically. Is it genuine doubt or a touch of gamesmanship? Keep Löw guessing. Because even now, at 33, Vialli remains a lethal threat. Nineteen goals across all competitions this season. Six in Europe. A hat-trick against Tromsø.

Then he decides to play. Centre-forward. Leading the line alongside Tore André Flo. Zola, not yet fully match-fit, is held in reserve. Vialli dials things back. Out goes the expressive 4-3-3, and in comes a solid 4-4-2. Pragmatic. Grounded. Built to match Stuttgart's discipline. But also, to leave room for a spark, if one is needed. As always, Gianluca leads with more than just tactics. 'Let's turn a great season into an extraordinary one,' he tells his players in the dressing room.

The match is tight. A proper final. No space, no rhythm, no margin for error. Vialli himself has a crack at goal but can't find the net. The clock ticks. The game inches towards extra time, where the Golden Goal rule hovers like a guillotine – one shot, one swing, and it's over.

With 20 minutes left, Gianluca makes his call: Flo off, Zola on. And then – magic. Gianfranco Zola, still feeling his way back from injury, touches the ball for the second time. One flick. One finish. One goal. Minute 71. Chelsea 1–0.

Löw's men are stunned. Zola's strike proves enough. Chelsea lift the cup. And as for Gianluca, he lifts his second trophy of the season as manager. He gambled. He played. He led. And once again, as for Gothenburg in 1990, Rome in 1996, he stood at the centre of something unforgettable.

Zola is the man of the hour. Of course he is. The one who settled it all with a stroke of genius and a second touch. But on this night in Stockholm – just three months since stepping into management – Gianluca Vialli's stature as a coach grows tenfold. His decision to abandon the 4-3-3 in favour of a tight, matter-of-fact 4-4-2 is hailed in the morning papers as a 'tactical masterclass'. Stuttgart had no room to breathe, no rhythm to find. Everything they'd prepared for was undone by a system they never saw coming.

But Gianluca, typically, is quick to redirect the spotlight. 'It was my assistant, Graham Rix,' he says. 'He had a feeling. And he was right.' That's Vialli through and through. Honest. Generous. Always ready to praise the team around him. But the truth is plain for all to see. This was his night. His win. And his arrival. The Cup Winners' Cup triumph silences any doubters still clinging to the old clichés about star players-turned-managers. About rookies with clipboards and romantic notions. About charisma without cunning.

'Lucky Luca' they call him now – not in jest, not in the cheap tabloid sense, but in the way Napoleon meant it. A man blessed by fortune. A man who wins. The English press doesn't hold back. 'Vialli has won more trophies in half a season than most managers do in a lifetime,' one media outlet proclaims, only half exaggerating. And it's true. The League Cup. The Cup Winners' Cup. Two pieces of silverware in less than three months.

But Gianluca isn't necessarily satisfied. 'We're delighted we won,' he says, steady in the post-match press room, champagne somewhere just off camera. 'But we don't want to stop here. The next step is the Premier League.'

He says it plainly. No bold promises. No grand statements. Just the tone of a man who means what he says. Because this is no longer just Vialli the player or Vialli the icon. This is Vialli the manager.

10

# PART SIX

# COOL HAND LUCA

## 1. CHELSEA, 1998

'With Luca, Chelsea are now a real team. They look formidable to me . . . I think this is just the beginning.'

PETER BONETTI

In the 93 years since its founding in 1905, Chelsea Football Club had managed to win the English league title exactly once. That solitary triumph came in the 1954–55 season – back when ration books had only just vanished from British kitchens and Winston Churchill was preparing to leave 10 Downing Street for the second and final time. It was a different England, black-and-white in more ways than one. Since then, the United Kingdom had cycled through 10 prime ministers – not quite Italy's revolving door, but a reminder all the same: time had moved on. Football had, too. Chelsea hadn't.

Before Gianluca Vialli arrived in west London, Chelsea – technically rooted in the borough of Hammersmith and Fulham, despite borrowing its name from the rather posher neighbouring district – had enjoyed only two true golden spells. The first came in that storied '54–55 season: a league title and the Charity Shield to go with it. The second bloomed briefly between 1969 and 1971, when a swaggering, stylish generation – Peter Bonetti, Peter Osgood, Charlie Cooke, John Hollins – lifted the FA Cup and then conquered Europe with a celebrated Cup Winners' Cup victory over Real Madrid in a replayed final.

The first encounter ended level, so the teams met again 48 hours later. By then, most of the crowd from the original match had already flown home – back to their jobs in London and Madrid. Since that night, the team that had lived longest in the collective memory of Chelsea fans had been the Lions of Athens. The team that, for one glorious moment, had stood atop Europe.

And it was one of that side's great figures – goalkeeper Peter Bonetti – who gave Gianluca Vialli his seal of approval following the Blues' Cup Winners' Cup victory over Stuttgart, 28 years later. 'With Luca, Chelsea are now a real team,' Bonetti told reporters. 'They look formidable to me. They've got so much talent, and I expect them to win – and win a lot. I think this is just the beginning. They won the FA Cup last season, finished fourth in the league this year. That shows consistency. Now, I feel they can become the number one team in England.'

Coming from Bonetti, it wasn't just praise – it was passing the torch. Because in England, no matter how brightly you shine in Europe, you're only truly measured – at least back then – by what you win at home. By what you do in the rough-and-tumble of the FA's competitions. And now, for the first time in decades, Chelsea looked ready to rise. Ready to make that leap. The era of the Lions of Athens had lasted long enough. Now, it was time for Vialli's Chelsea.

Bonetti's reference to consistency is no accident. He knows what it means to touch greatness – and then watch it unravel. His – the side that lit up the early 1970s with style, swagger and silverware – had seemed destined for a dynasty. They had the talent, the trophies, the terrace love. But they couldn't hold it together. The unity fractured. Egos clashed. Injuries mounted. Success bred tension rather than stability. Within four years, the same squad that had beaten Real Madrid was fighting to survive – and losing. By 1975, Chelsea were relegated. Not gently, not by inches, but with a thud. A team that had danced on Europe's biggest stage had collapsed under its own weight. That memory never left Bonetti.

And now, decades later, as the Blues begin to climb again, what the glorious Chelsea goalkeeper sees is something steadier. Something earned. Concentration and intensity had always been Gianluca Vialli's strengths as a player, and now he's drilling them into his team. And the results are there for all to see: two trophies in 90 days. Then, to start the new season, a third – 1998 UEFA Super Cup – this time against no less than Real Madrid, fresh off winning the Champions League. No chaos. No collapse. Just purpose and progress. The kind of foundation Bonetti's generation never quite had.

The match was played in Monte Carlo on the evening of 28 August. Gianluca opted to take on only the role of manager. It made sense. Chelsea had just signed Pierluigi Casiraghi from Lazio – a prolific striker whose game bore more than a passing resemblance to Vialli's. Casiraghi was there to take over when Gianluca finally stepped off the pitch for good. The young manager paired him with Gianfranco Zola. At the back, Chelsea unveiled their two marquee summer signings: Albert Ferrer, the silky Spanish full-back, and Marcel Desailly, fresh from lifting the World Cup with France.

Once again, it was a super-sub who broke the deadlock. In the 63rd minute, Vialli made his move – off came Di Matteo, on came Gustavo Poyet. Twenty minutes later, the Uruguayan pounced on a Zola assist and rifled a low strike from the edge of the box: 1–0. Game over. It was far from a memorable match – early-season finals rarely are – but

Chelsea had their fourth trophy in just over a year. For Vialli the manager, it was number three in little over six months.

But as he had said from day one – and as everyone around the club openly admitted – the real target this year was the Premier League.

They started poorly.

A 2–1 defeat away to Coventry City on opening day. But after that, Chelsea became formidable. A 1–1 draw at home to Ruud Gullit's Newcastle United kicked off a run of 21 league matches unbeaten – 11 wins, 10 draws – that propelled them into the title race alongside Manchester United and Arsenal. It was a run built on belief, balance and the quiet authority of a manager who had once shared the dressing room and now commanded it. Vialli rotated wisely, kept egos in check, and never allowed the pressure to show. He let the football speak.

There were moments of style – a 4–2 win away at Leicester, a commanding 2–0 victory over Tottenham. There were gutsy draws, too – at the Bridge against Arsenal, at Anfield and Old Trafford, where Chelsea refused to bow. In every match, the team looked composed. They weren't just competing, they were controlling games. Vialli's influence was everywhere. The squad played with purpose. Zola danced. Petrescu surged. Wise and Poyet ran the show in midfield. And though his days as a regular starter were behind him, Gianluca still found a way to lead by example, just more selectively.

He saved his legs, and his goals, for the cup competitions, giving his regular starters room to breathe and rotate. And when he did step onto the pitch, the instincts were still razor-sharp. In the League Cup third round, he scored a hat-trick against Aston Villa, sweeping Chelsea to a 4–1 victory at Stamford Bridge. And just days later he put two past Arsenal in the fourth round – a match of real intensity and meaning, and another win delivered by the player-manager himself. These weren't ceremonial cameos, they were tactical choices – and they paid off. Vialli was not only managing minutes, he was managing momentum.

The team didn't just win matches, they weathered them. They controlled tempo, absorbed pressure, and struck with precision. And with each week, the conversation shifted – from 'could they?' to 'why not them?' Vialli's Chelsea were now in the thick of a title race, but this time, the momentum felt different. The pieces were in place. The squad was deep. The identity was clear. The culture had shifted. The expectation had changed. And in the dugout, with arms folded and eyes always searching, stood the man who had made it all happen.

## 2. SAMPDORIA, 1991

> 'We knew this was the match that would decide the title. But we didn't need any special speeches. Our world was already special.'
>
> GIANLUCA VIALLI

'Without false modesty, I'd say there's a lot of me in this. A lot of my teammates, too, the president, the manager, of course. But I gave everything, no question. For seven years, I let people call me immature. I let all the talk about the Azzurri national team get tangled – for me and for Roberto – because we wore this shirt. I played for three years in a stadium that was half a ground. I could have earned more elsewhere, no doubt about it. But I did it because I always believed we could do something great. I gave everything for the cause, and I'll take my fair share of the credit – on and off the pitch.'

That was Gianluca Vialli in May 1991. No false modesty. No clichés. No empty words. Just the sound of a man who had spent seven years pushing a club and a dream up a mountain and who had finally reached the summit. Sampdoria had won the Scudetto. The first in the club's history. The so-called experts had scoffed for years – too stylish to be ruthless, too young to stay the course, too reckless to grind it out. The same refrain, over and over. 'A team for the romantics, a target for the press.' And yet, here they stood, champions of Italy.

Even Vujadin Boškov, philosopher-manager and master of deflection, had once privately worried that his Sampdoria were only '*copetera*' – a word he'd borrowed from Spanish and twisted into his colourful brand of Italian. Meaning, 'a cup team' – not one built for the league, but built for the magic of single nights, not the monotony of a season. Knockout football suited them. The Coppa Italia – won three times in the space of a few years. The Cup Winners' Cup – lost narrowly in Bern to Barcelona in 1989, then won brilliantly in Gothenburg in 1990.

But the league was different. The league demanded something else. Consistency. Ruthlessness. A bit of cruelty, even. For years, they hadn't quite had it, but now they had seen the season through. They had outlasted AC Milan. Out-played Inter Milan. Out-fought Juventus. And they had done it their way.

Vialli had never forgotten the sting of being written off. The labels. The half-truths. And above all, the scar of the Italia '90 World Cup. The summer of 1990 had promised everything. It was going to be his World Cup. His moment on the biggest stage of all. And yet, within days it had slipped away – his form vanished, his role reduced, his place in the side taken. Italy's golden boy turned scapegoat. Forgotten on the bench. Ignored by the part of the country that only remembers it loves football once every four years.

Worse still, Vialli became easy prey for the usual suspects in the press. The ones who measured football not by courage or sacrifice, but by status. Who resented the boy from Cremona with the good manners and the rich family. The ones who never forgave him for smiling while being different. Envy, after all, brings out the worst in people. But Gianluca remembered; not with bitterness, but with drive. Italia '90 didn't break him, it hardened him. Made him more. And the Scudetto that followed was not just a title, it was an answer. He had given everything. And now – finally – he had everything to show for it.

When he was finally thrown back onto the pitch in the semi-final against Argentina, the speculation began. Why had he been dropped in the first place? Why was he back now? And when Italy lost on penalties, a scapegoat was needed. Never mind that he wasn't even one of the takers. Never mind that, in the Italian mentality, a penalty shoot-out is less a test of nerve than an act of Russian roulette. His head was served up on a silver platter all the same.

Italy took the field on 9 June, the second day of the Italia 90 tournament. After weeks of doubts and just as many experiments, manager Vicini settled on what had long been regarded as his first-choice strike partnership: Vialli alongside Andrea Carnevale, the forward of Napoli.

The Azzurri have failed to convince in the last friendlies before the World Cup. The press circles restlessly. Critical of both the team and their manager. The 'Champagne and phantasy' football of the Vicini's band has faded into a pale memory,' they say. Gianluca Vialli, leader of this Italy side, steps forward to take the heat. 'We were a carefree, reckless team,' he says, recalling the team that had convinced at Euro 88. 'Things have changed. There's less appetite for joking now. We feel the weight of a responsibility that has grown heavier. The boys have stopped being boys – and that isn't entirely a good thing.'

Against Austria, Gianluca is not fully fit. Four days before the World Cup opener, he had felt a nagging pain in his left calf. An immediate scan ruled out any tear. Nothing more than fatigue. Something that should pass in time.

The Azzurri may not be playing their best football tonight, but Italy easily command the match. Yet, for all their probing, neither Vialli nor Carnevale can prise open the visiting defence. With a little over 15 minutes remaining, Vicini withdraws Carnevale and sends on Schillaci. Four minutes later, Vialli reaches the byline and whips in a cross. Schillaci meets it, rises, and heads home Italy's breakthrough.

Schillaci's wild celebration flashes around the world. Italy have their opening two points. Schillaci is the hero of the night – on, scored, job done. That the assist had come from Vialli, however, goes totally unmentioned. As if that ball had arrived on Schillaci's head by some happy accident rather than being placed there with intent and rare precision.

The second match, against the United States, is a flat affair. Italy have plainly poured most of their physical and emotional reserves into the opener. Hosting a World Cup is no walk in the park. Giuseppe Giannini breaks the deadlock as early as the 11th minute. Yet, from that moment on the Azzurri struggle to find any real bite. Just past the half-hour mark, the referee awards Italy a penalty. Gianluca steps up. The goalkeeper is sent the other way, but the ball crashes back off the post. Italy win nonetheless. Two matches, two wins.

But results aside, Gianluca is far from satisfied with what he has seen – or produced – so far. 'We run a lot but we score little,' he says, 'and we're certainly not enjoying ourselves. But this is our football. Vicini tells me to run, to move, to roam, and I do it.'

The press begin to speculate that Vialli and Schillaci will start together in the next match against Czechoslovakia, already through to the last 16 along with Italy. Instead, something shifts, and Vialli suddenly finds himself on the fringes of the plan.

For the third Group match it will be Roberto Baggio – not Vialli – who partners Schillaci. The official explanation is a strain to Gianluca's right hamstring picked up in training on Sunday morning, two days before the match against the Czechs. Then, during the match, both Schillaci and Baggio find the net – and from that moment on, Gianluca Vialli's name at Italia 90 will scarcely be heard again.

Beyond the injury – real or presumed – it's the wind that has changed. For a striker, goals are usually, and inevitably, the only real measure, and at a World Cup, the man who scores holds all the cards. Schillaci, after his two goals in the group stage, scores again against Uruguay in the round of 16, and against Ireland in the quarter-finals, riding a wave no one is inclined to interrupt. By the time Gianluca is fit again, the script has been rewritten without him. He is confined to the bench, watching events gather pace from a distance.

Before the quarter-final against Ireland, Gianluca is desperate to get back on the pitch. 'When the going gets tough, the tough get going,' he cries – a message clearly intended for Vicini. 'From now on the matches are brutal. You need men with nerve. Everyone says the only thing missing from this Italy side is Vialli – if that's true, I am ready! After all,' he mischievously adds with more bitterness than sarcasm, 'it would suit everyone if I played, since when things go wrong, it's always my fault.' Vicini does not waver. Gianluca is left on the bench for the whole 90 minutes.

Then, out of the blue, on the eve of the semi-finals against Argentina, Vicini surprisingly shuffles the deck. Baggio is given a rest. Vialli is brought back in from the cold. It's 3 July, and Gianluca has not started a match since 14 June. At first he struggles to find rhythm, the game moving faster than his touch. Then he begins to run, to roam, to stretch Argentina's defence across the width of the pitch. In the move that leads to Schillaci's goal – his fifth of the tournament – Vialli is involved twice, nudging the play forward, keeping it alive until the ball finally breaks the right way.

After Italy scores, Argentina press harder and, at the 67th minute, they equalise. At 1–1, Vicini looks for fresher legs. Gianluca, three weeks without a match, cannot have 90 minutes in him. Vicini takes Vialli off and sends on Aldo Serena. Argentina will go through on penalties. Serena will miss the last and decisive one.

With Vialli back in the side, Italy was defeated and eliminated. Never mind that Gianluca didn't take part in the penalty shoot-out. The critics descend at once. The reality is more complex than that, but this is the summer of Schillaci and of swift, merciless verdicts. Italians want a villain and the villain is Vialli.

This time Gianluca refuses to stay silent. 'I'm bitterly disappointed,' he says. 'I realised I was needed only when there was a job for a workhorse,' he accuses after the semi-final defeat. 'I was asked to sacrifice myself and I did. I accepted it even knowing it may make me look bad because in this team's system one of the strikers has to sacrifice himself for the other. The result? I lost my confidence and I lost my place. It's a shame because others were given the chance to play their own game and show the full range of what they could do.'

'I am leaving – don't come looking for me. I won't be talking about football for a while,' Gianluca says at the end of the tournament. He leaves for his summer holidays carrying a promise. 'In life you always have to look for the positive,' he says. 'This experience hasn't been for nothing. Maybe, after so much bitterness, I'll come back and win the Scudetto – and finish as the league's top scorer.'

Winning the 1990–91 league title meant many things. It was the culmination of a journey that had begun four, five, six years earlier. It was the triumph of talent and sacrifice, of a spirit forged not in training manuals but in something closer to Dumas' spirit – one for all, all for one. It was proof that belief, graft and a bit of stubborn dreaming could carry you all the way to the top. But above all – though to say that it was only this would be to miss the poetry – it was a response. A response to the frustration and bitterness that had come out of the 1990 World Cup for Gianluca Vialli and his partner in crime, Roberto Mancini.

'Same age but nothing alike. Roberto was quiet, reserved. Gianluca was loud, playful, always up to mischief. One was all flair and vision, living for the joy of setting up a teammate. The other had become powerful, relentless, ruthless in front of the goal. Yet they fit together perfectly. They respected each other, they were friends, and they were never rivals,' recalls Boškov's assistant manager, Ciso Pezzotti. 'When you've got two strikers who don't care whether the other striker is scoring three goals and you're not scoring any, it's fantastic because all we wanted was for the team to win,' Gianluca would never tire of saying.

'He was the good-looking one. I was the funny one. I did the dirty work, and he scored,' Gianluca would joke. 'We really lived in symbiosis for ten years,' echoes Roberto. 'For a while we shared an apartment, then we lived next door. In the mornings we were up and on the training ground within five minutes. We had lunch together. Spent the afternoons together. Went out in the evenings together. Ten intense years. And of course, even when our paths eventually split, he remained the kind of friend you keep for life.'

This was a team with two leaders on the pitch. Some said they picked the lineup themselves. Boškov knew it wasn't true, but he let the rumour live. 'We never actually picked the team,' Mancini would say years later. 'We thought we did, though. Boškov would ask, he'd listen . . . then he'd do exactly the opposite.' That, too, was part of the Boškov magic.

After the World Cup fiasco, Mancini plotted his revenge in silence. Gianluca, on the other hand, made himself perfectly clear. The first day back at the Bogliasco training ground, he walked into the dressing room and stuck a piece of paper to a locker door. On it, a blacklist – a list of journalists he had no intention of speaking to that season. 'You lot do as you like,' he told his teammates. 'But I'm not talking to these ones.'

It wasn't just theatre. It became part of the mission. This was a team that had spent years proving people wrong. Here was one more battle – against the doubters, the critics, the haters, those who still refused to believe. That chip-on-the-shoulder energy carried them all the way to history. The senior players – Vialli, Mancini, Vierchowod and the rest – had made a pact: nobody would leave Sampdoria until they had won the Scudetto.

And as Italian football evolved, so too did its battle lines. Arrigo Sacchi was rewriting tactics at AC Milan. Gigi Maifredi tried the same at Juventus. Boškov kept the faith. His 4-4-2 remained rigid, reliable, tested. His Sampdoria had elegance, yes – but also a libero, a stopper and the kind of structure that outlasts fashion. In an age of revolution, Boškov remained the seasoned general of a well-drilled army. And that season, they didn't blink.

Moved to the centre of the attack by Boškov when he first arrived at Sampdoria, Gianluca Vialli had left nothing to chance. 'Luca loved scoring goals,' Pezzotti recalls. 'And in his early days as a pure centre-forward – because he wasn't born – his perfectionist nature kicked in. He felt the need to rehearse, over and over, the movements and instincts of the role. Especially playing with his back to goal on the edge of the box.' So, at his own request, while the rest of the squad took their afternoon rest, Gianluca stayed behind. With Pezzotti, a goalkeeper, and a handful of willing teammates, he'd spend hours repeating the same drills. Same runs, same turns, same finishes. He didn't just want to play the role, he wanted to master it.

By the autumn of 1990, it was all coming together. 'Luca is reaching full maturity. He's completing the journey that will make him one of the strongest players in world football – for technique, pace, movement, physical strength and sheer endurance,' Pezzotti remembers. 'Vialli came back from Italia '90 in rough physical and moral shape. His knee was troubling him, but more than that, his morale was shot. Other players had stolen the spotlight, and it hurt him. He started pre-season late and struggled to find his rhythm. He missed the first few games with one issue or another. But when he got going, he was unstoppable. Goals, goals and more goals – a decisive force in Sampdoria's title charge.'

The warning shots came thick and fast that autumn. Late October: San Siro. Sampdoria took down AC Milan, with a goal from the ageless Toninho Cerezo. A couple of weeks later, the real hammer blow – Napoli at the San Paolo. They didn't just beat the reigning champions, they shredded them, 4–1, with the goal twins – Mancini and Vialli – bagging a brace apiece. With the AC Milan win, they hit the top of the table. With the Napoli demolition, they put a flag in it.

Then came the third statement win to close out 1990. Inter Milan, 3–1. Two from Vialli, one from Mancini. In two months, they'd taken out Serie A's holy trinity. As for Juventus? Struggling under Luigi Maifredi's so-called champagne football – elegant fizz, no finish.

'After a strong start, the team had a dip in form over the winter,' Pezzotti recalls. 'That's when the manager's character and the squad's strength and unity came to the fore. Someone even vowed to go blonde if we won the title.' The turning point came on 23 January, 1991 – Sampdoria v Roma, a match rescheduled from December after Marassi had been drowned in a Ligurian monsoon. Sampdoria won it. From then on, they never lost again. Barely even drew.

AC Milan fell next. A 2–0 win at Marassi, goals from Vialli and Mancini. Then came Inter Milan, again, on 5 May. The last stand. 'We had already beaten Juventus, triggering their crisis, and we had taken down AC Milan,' Gianluca would recall. 'But Inter wouldn't go away. Before kick-off, there was tension, but also belief. We knew this was the match that would decide the title. But we didn't need any special speeches. Our world was already special.'

Guiseppe Dossena struck first, but then came the moment everyone would remember. A bursting run on the counter. Zenga charging out to meet him. Vialli didn't blink. A side-step and the ball was rolling past the keeper into the empty net. Inter beaten. The Scudetto in sight.

And then came the grand finale. Sunday, 19 May. Lecce, clinging to top-flight life, standing between Sampdoria and glory. Marassi was overflowing. Packed to the rafters. Before kick-off, tears rolled freely in the stands – men, women, sons, daughters – some of them old enough to have stopped believing they'd ever see this day. In the Samp end, a colossal flag unfurled. A tricolor at the centre. Bold as fate.

The match was over before it even began. Two minutes in, Cerezo hammers home a right-footed rocket after a neat layoff from Gianluca. At 13 minutes, Mannini doubles the tally with an improbable, glorious volley from outside the box – one of those shots that, nine times out of ten, ends up in Row Z. Not this time. And then, Gianluca. A spin on a sixpence. A no-look finish, straight from his playbook. One glance, one twist, one touch. The somersault that follows says everything. Three-nil before the half-hour. The rest is procession.

In the second half nothing happens. Just 45 minutes of Marassi holding its breath, locked onto the clock, willing the seconds to pass. The longest three-quarters of an hour in the club's history. Until – finally – the triple whistle. And the eruption – on the pitch, in the stands, in every heart clad in blue, white, red and black.

The players pour forward, beginning a lap of honour trailed by a wave of photographers. They hoist a giant cardboard tricolor Scudetto and pass it among themselves like a relic, like proof. Gianluca Vialli, shirt gone, shorts gone, stripped to his underwear, sprints across the turf, hair flying, face blazing. Someone tosses him a flag. He catches it, clutches it, keeps running. Next season, for the first time ever, those colours will be stitched to the chest of a Sampdoria shirt. And it will be because of these lads. Because of this.

'A well-earned victory, in every sense,' Gianluca would always maintain. 'We were 16 men, a proper team. The title was the last step in a climb where Sampdoria had been winning something every year. But if I'm honest, we only truly believed it when the maths confirmed it. With Boškov, we took the all-important final step up. He had many qualities, but above all, he knew how to work with what a player did best. He talked to us, listened to us,' Gianluca adds. 'A footballer has to believe in his manager's ideas, and the manager, well, he needs to take on board what his players tell him.'

This afternoon, many have something to celebrate at Marassi. But no one has as much as Gianluca Vialli. 'The title of courage belongs to him. As a man, he's won the real battle,' said his old mentor, Emiliano Mondonico – beaming with pride, unable to hide it. He had coached Gianluca at Cremonese at the beginning of their individual careers, and neither had ever forgotten the bond. 'He was left on his own. People took shots at him, no one gave him a pat on the back. I always knew he'd come through. Plenty treated him like a shooting star, bright for a moment and then gone.'

But now, with a Scudetto in his hands and the flag of his club wrapped around his shoulders, Gianluca Vialli is no comet. He is the centre of a galaxy. And every light at Marassi tonight shines because of him.

## 3. CHELSEA, 1998–99

> 'Management is about improving your relationship with the players and the journalists, about learning to read a game better so that you can make changes.'
>
> GIANLUCA VIALLI

In the autumn of 1998 and the winter of 1999, Vialli's Chelsea are winning – and doing it in style.

'There are various reasons for Vialli's astonishing success over the last eleven months,' the English press wrote at the time, 'ranging from his practical maintenance of the best features of Gullit's tenure to his measured but astute use of Chelsea's wealth. Yet perhaps his greatest attribute is his capacity to combine a reassuring warmth towards his players with a more searing passion to avoid defeat.' Vialli, they say, has found the sweet spot. 'He has struck a balance between sustaining a distance from the players while maintaining the camaraderie he thrives on. The lads call him Luca – not boss or gaffer – and few perspire as hotly in training.'

The truth is that Gianluca Vialli loves English football. And he loves it for its soul. What strikes him most is the passion – not just from the players, but from the terraces, the streets, the everyday fans who live for their club. On so many levels, the game is almost pure, grounded, free from the obsession with celebrity that he often found in Italy. He loves the honesty of the play – the end-to-end action, the crunching tackles, the refusal to give up. He admires the atmosphere at stadiums like Anfield and Highbury, the floodlit drama of midweek games, the sense of history stitched into every chant and scarf.

By now, Gianluca has made up his mind – he's all in. Management is no longer a transition, it's his calling. He likes managing a football squad because it means blending leadership, empathy and modern awareness. For him, being a manager isn't about barking orders, it's about leading by example and empowering players to take ownership of their roles. He believes that true leadership is quiet, consistent and rooted in trust. Vialli places enormous value on teamwork, insisting that success comes not from individual brilliance but from collective effort and unity on and off the pitch. Mondonico at Cremonese, Boškov at Sampdoria and Lippi at Juventus have taught him precisely that.

His Chelsea reflects that belief: talent shaped into cohesion. He's also acutely aware of the changing landscape of football. Modern players, he notes, are 'like small companies', with agents, brands and entourages to consider. Managing them requires more than tactical insight; it demands emotional intelligence and diplomacy. Finally, Vialli understands the pressure that comes with elite football, both as a player and a manager. He sees mental strength as crucial – resilience in the face of scrutiny, and calm in moments of consequence. For Vialli, managing a football team is not just a technical craft but a human one. It means building a culture, protecting the group and guiding individuals through a game that can be as brutal as it is beautiful.

He sticks with Graham Rix, his trusted lieutenant, and brings in Ray Wilkins, the consummate English professional. He hands over contracts and transfers to Chelsea's chief executive Colin Hutchinson. 'The way I saw it,' he'd say later, 'I already had more than enough on my plate. I've no idea how other managers do it, but I knew I couldn't.'

But it's not just the manager who wins praise, it's the man himself. Because Gianluca always carries himself just right. Confident but modest. Stylish but grounded. No swagger, just class. 'Considering his team's meteoric rise to stardom, silverware and a stake in the title, coupled with his own reputation on the back of a magnificent playing career,

Vialli has done well to keep an amazingly modest profile in his first full season in management,' reporters observe, visibly impressed. They turn to his former teammates, who speak of him with the same easy affection as always: 'He always thinks before he speaks, always. He knows what to say and when to say it.'

Beyond the football, the wins and the tactics, it's Gianluca the man who captures the heart of England's football fans. The elegance. The charm. 'Luca brought style to the Premier League,' they still say today. He had substance. He radiated calm. He spoke with precision and led with grace. And even the famously ruthless British press were taken in.

He slipped into the role with no fuss. No grandstanding. No revolutions. No manifestos. He learned the language – not just enough to bluff his way through a post-match interview, but fluently. As if he were preparing for Oxford University, not the Premier League. He did it not for show but because he wanted to speak to the people who welcomed him. Because he respected the English game. Because he respected England.

That effort, rare among international footballers, did not go unnoticed. 'A testament to his intelligence – he taught himself English in just a few months, mostly by reading children's books,' the British press would later say, full of admiration. But Gianluca didn't stop at bedtime stories and private lessons, his English became so good, so distinct, that before long he was 'famous for his use of everyday expressions, slipping into the local lingo like a natural.'

The press are spellbound – not just by his grammar, but by his grasp of the nuances, the quirks, the bits that turn a foreigner into a local. Gianluca doesn't stop at pronunciation or sentence structure, he wants slang. Idioms. The real stuff. So, he finds the perfect teacher, Dennis Wise. His captain. His mischief-maker-in-chief. A man who never needs asking twice.

They strike a deal: Wise will teach him one new phrase a week and Gianluca must use it – live, untested – during a pre-match or post-match press conference. And he does. In his best Cockney twang, straight-faced and with full conviction, he praises an opponent with a hearty: 'Well, 'ats off to them' – sounding less like a Serie A legend and more like a flower seller in Covent Garden.

Of course, there were blunders – magnificent ones. Like the time Wise told Gianluca to use the French word he'd normally slip in in Italian – *fiches* – instead of chips. Half the press room walked away convinced that Vialli had suddenly developed an improbable passion for fishing. Or when, trying to talk about Chelsea fighting on multiple fronts, Gianluca earnestly declares: 'As long as you can, you have to keep your finger in all the pies.' But none of that matters. If anything, it adds to the legend. The charm, the effort, the openness – Gianluca doesn't deal in clichés, he gives the press something real. Something human. And for these seasoned writers, that's gold dust.

In short, the English public respect what the British press call 'his roguish charm' – that respectful yet ever-so-slightly mischievous way of carrying himself, like a man forever on the verge of breaking a rule, shattering a cliché, tearing down a footballing taboo. In Italy, that kind of thing caused him problems. Here, it makes him a star. Not just a winner on the pitch, but a one-of-a-kind character. 'Cool Hand Luca,' they write, summoning Paul Newman himself.

The fans love his humanity. His humility. 'You can hear Vialli's generosity in his answers,' writes *The Guardian* that winter. 'I don't want to sound humble,' he said one Friday, just before Chelsea extended their unbeaten league run to 21 matches, 'but I think it's down to the players. They've got hunger. They've got something to prove. Chelsea have always been known for playing good football, but not always for consistency. I have my ideas on how we should play, but it's the players who must make them work.'

And they love his honesty. His refusal to play the game the way other managers do. Again, *The Guardian* commented, 'Vialli realises that most footballers respond best to such magnanimous praise but, up close, it is clear that his ease with others is a gift rather than a trick. Whether he is laughing as Gianfranco Zola leaps to slap his hand in a high-five or cuddling the old boy who brings over the practice bibs, or simply grinning and saying to me "you must be freezing your socks off" – another fine bit of slang – Vialli transcends the gruff bluster so many managers use to convey a sense of authority.'

He's doing so well at Chelsea that even Juventus fans start dreaming of his return. At a match at Turin's Delle Alpi, they unfurl a banner for all the stadium to see: LIPPI NEL CUORE, VIALLI ALLENATORE – *Lippi in our hearts, Vialli as our manager.* Gianluca is flattered. Grateful. But he doesn't take the bait. 'I'm proud that the fans remember me with such affection and that some of them want me as their manager, but my future is at Chelsea.'

And that's the truth. Partly because Chelsea is where he's building something big. Partly because his friendship with Marcello Lippi is real. Taking over from Gullit had been a sweet bit of redemption. Taking over from Lippi would feel like betrayal. And that's never been Gianluca Vialli's way.

'As a manager,' Gianluca says, 'you have to sow a seed of imagination in your players. Of course, you give them an idea of the way you want them to play tactically but, if you insist too much, they can lose a little bit of their imagination. I don't want robots. I want players who are spontaneous.' It's pure Vialli. The essence of nearly two decades in the game, distilled into a single belief. Tactics matter, of course they do, but so does instinct. So does joy. So does trust. His Chelsea side, built on these principles, carries echoes of all the men who shaped him – Mondonico's honesty, Boskov's warmth, Lippi's steel. And yes, just as clearly, it quietly rejects something else: the rigid, mechanical vision of Arrigo Sacchi. A brilliant mind, no doubt. But one whose methods never quite matched Vialli's soul.

Gianluca Vialli's idea of football is grounded in a deep love for the game's artistry, its honesty, and its humanity. For him, football is never just about tactics or trophies – it's about people. It's about character, commitment and creating a shared purpose. Raised in Italy on the traditions of Catenaccio and tactical rigour, Vialli never rejected structure or discipline. He understood the game's strategic demands intimately. But he also believed that football was a form of expression – something that should carry emotion, invention and joy.

He loves the elegance of a well-timed pass as much as the resolve in a last-ditch tackle. He admires beauty, but not at the expense of fight. Football, in his view, is both a science and an art. It has room for logic and flair, for data and guts. That belief carried into his management style. He never saw players as chess pieces but as individuals – each with a story, a psychology, a heartbeat. He valued the locker room, the mood, the bonds. He believed trust and spirit could tilt the balance of a match just as much as a formation.

And he always carried respect – for the opponent, for the referee, for the fan in the back row who pays to believe in something. To be sure, he had his moments . . . as when, still early in his career, he clashed with the ebullient rival manager Carlo Mazzone – who claimed that he cared more about his bank account than his legacy – prompting Vialli to fire back, polished quiff and all, unwilling to play the humble apprentice. The two reconciled publicly the next time they met.

Or when Gianluca stirred the waters by stating that the match commentary on the Fininvest networks wasn't just theatrical, it was openly pro-AC Milan. And no wonder, he argued: AC Milan and the broadcasters shared the same owner, Silvio Berlusconi. Not to mention when he pushed back against the Catholic Church's condemnation of Sunday football. 'Granted, I'm a Catholic in my own way,' he said, 'meaning I believe in absolute values that exist beyond any catechism, and I try, humbly, to live by them. But the proposal leaves me very perplexed because I don't believe that a football season – however fierce – can lead to damnation.'

But overall, Gianluca Vialli carried a deep, unwavering respect for his opponents, rooted not just in sportsmanship, but in character. Whether on the pitch as a player or on the touchline as a manager, he believed that true competition demanded dignity. He once said that to beat an opponent without respecting them was to win nothing at all. His career is filled with gestures that spoke louder than words – applauding rival players, embracing defeated managers, shaking hands before and after the fiercest battles. He admired those who played with heart, who gave their all, even if they played and sometimes won against him.

Vialli will always see being an integral part of football as a privilege. We are lucky, he would say, to be part of something that brings joy to millions. He played that way – with grace, with humility, with intent. And he coached that way, too. Football, in his world, is at its best when it unites – not just players and fans, but cultures, histories and dreams.

In early 1999, Gianluca has no illusions about where he stands in the hierarchy of great managers. Not yet at their level. But working. Learning. Improving. Always. 'I hope I am a much better manager now than when I started,' he says. 'Management is about improving your relationship with the players and the journalists, about learning to read a game better so that you can make changes. I hope I keep improving as a manager for the rest of my career.'

It's a modest assessment, honest and measured. He still has half a season left as a player. Then, in May, he'll hang up his boots for good. All in. All focus on the dugout. And maybe, somewhere down the road, Juve will call again. But right now, Gianluca Vialli is exactly where he wants to be. With his team. Living his new life. In London. 'Here, I can walk down the street with my girlfriend, I can go shopping, sit in a pub or go out to dinner, and nobody asks me for an autograph. That's a dream. After fifteen years of worrying, I'm finally a free man.'

---

The 21-match unbeaten streak in the Premier League comes to an end in January 1999, with a narrow defeat away to Arsenal.

From there, Chelsea loses only once more – at home to West Ham – but it isn't enough. The title slips out of reach. If it wasn't for an extraordinary Manchester United side – one that would sweep up the League, FA Cup and Champions League – or an Arsenal team refusing to surrender their crown, this might well have been the year Chelsea ended their 40-year wait for a league title.

For Gianluca, it could have been a glorious repeat of 1990–91, the season of dreams with Sampdoria, the one that ended in Scudetto glory. Instead, 20 wins, 15 draws and just three defeats aren't enough. Vialli's Blues finish third, only four points behind United. A whisper, really, in a league where a win is worth three points. The consolation prize is a first-ever place in the Champions League. Although in football, as everyone knows, no one really cares for consolation prizes.

The dream is postponed. But Gianluca will chase it now from the dugout, and the dugout alone.

The 1998–99 season ends on a bitter note – the defence of the Cup Winners' Cup falls short in the semi-finals. Chelsea are knocked out by the surprise package, Mallorca, just shy of a historic second consecutive final. A final that would've pitted Gianluca against Lazio – coached by his lifelong friend, Roberto Mancini.

And with that, Gianluca Vialli hangs up his boots. He wants no farewell match, no testimonial. He never liked them. Too staged, too sentimental – whether the tears are real or forced. That was never his style. He prefers to go his own way. His final match comes on 16 May. Chelsea at home, against Derby County.

In the 68th minute, Gianluca scores Chelsea's second goal, finishing off a perfect counterattack. Wise breaks at pace, charging half the pitch alone. Flo meets him, takes the pass and gently whips a perfect cross into the box. Gianluca cushions it with his right, then strikes with the outside of his foot. Goal! The last one of his career. The celebration is subdued. Gianluca claps his teammates for the move, then raises both fists – just once, no flourish. A quiet moment of personal triumph. This he wanted, to go out with one last goal.

And that's it.

He played only 20 games this season but still leaves with 10 more goals to his name – including a hat-trick against Aston Villa and a brace against Arsenal in the League Cup.

Counting his debut season in 1980–81, Gianluca Vialli played 19 years as a professional – 16 in Italy, three in England. The numbers tell their own story: 25 goals for Cremonese, 141 for Sampdoria, 53 for Juventus, 40 for Chelsea. Add to that 16 for the senior Italy side, and 11 more for the Under-21s. Top scorer in Serie A the year Sampdoria won the title. Top scorer at the Under-21 Euros in '86. Top scorer in the Coppa Italia in '88–89. Top scorer in the Cup Winners' Cup in '89–90. Named in UEFA's Team of the Tournament at Euro '88. And, in 1995, World Soccer's World Player of the Year.

His team honours are just as impressive. They begin, of course, with that historic Scudetto with Sampdoria, or Sampd'Oro – Golden Samp, as they still say with pride and tears on the Liguria seaside. But at Sampdoria, he also won three Coppa Italia titles, the Italian Super Cup and the Cup Winners' Cup. At Juventus, he added another Coppa Italia, the UEFA Cup, the Serie A title – and, finally, the Champions League.

Then came Chelsea. The first trophy, the '97 FA Cup, won as a player. But it was the next ones that made history – the League Cup, the Cup Winners' Cup and the UEFA Super Cup, all lifted as both player and manager. That seamless transition from pitch to dugout, from goal scorer to decision-maker. From leader on the field to leader of men.

And though more modest achievements don't always appear on a world-class player's official honours list, they shouldn't be forgotten. What he did at Cremonese, for instance – keeping them in Serie B during his first full season, when survival looked all but impossible. Then, in 1983–84, leading them to promotion to Serie A. The beginning of everything. A quiet miracle. A promise kept.

Of his former clubs – Cremonese, Sampdoria, Juventus, Chelsea, Watford – Gianluca would one day offer a telling metaphor, comparing them to past loves – some remain dear, others are best left behind, and a few settle into something resembling mutual respect.

# PART SEVEN

# ALONE

## 1. CHELSEA, 1999–2000

> 'True greatness is not measured by the number of titles you win, but by the impact you have on the game and the people around you.'
>
> GIANLUCA VIALLI

The 1999–2000 season is Gianluca Vialli's first without stepping onto the pitch in a competitive match since 1975. A full 25 years earlier, he'd made his debut in organised football, wearing the sky-blue and white of Unione Sportiva San Bartolomeo – the small club in Grumello, the town near Cremona where he and his brothers spent most of their summers.

At Chelsea, he hands the No. 9 shirt to Chris Sutton, the club's big summer signing. But just to be safe, he quietly registers himself with the FA as a player-manager. No drama, no fuss – just a fallback option. The deal with the club is clear: two years as manager, no playing, and then they'll talk about the future. Still, when winter rolls in and Chelsea are short of strikers, the thought creeps in – one last run in the Champions League, maybe? Just once. Just to feel it again.

On Monday, 31 January, 2000, Gianluca laces up his boots. No headlines, no crowds, just a reserve fixture against Leicester. He's fit – he trains every day with the first team – and it shows. A left-footed volley, clean and sharp, cracks off the bar. But that's as close as he'll come. One match, one strike, inches from a fairytale. Then he steps away – this time for good.

The goal for the season remains the same: win the Premier League. The title that slipped away the year before still burns in the background. But there's something new this time. For the first time in their history, Chelsea are in the UEFA Champions League. The draw is unkind. AC Milan, Galatasaray and Hertha Berlin. No easy rides there. They open at home, and not just against anyone – against AC Milan, favourites to top the group and one of the best sides in Europe. It finishes 0–0, but Chelsea look the better team. The Italian press say it plainly: 'Gianluca Vialli's Chelsea should have won. They dominated physically and tactically.' A solid start. But Vialli's not the type to settle for praise in the papers.

Next comes Berlin, and a slip – defeat to Hertha. But Chelsea respond; they edge Galatasaray at the Bridge, then go to Istanbul and tear them apart – 5–0, a performance that silences the doubters. A point at San Siro keeps them on course, and they finish the job at home, beating Hertha by the same two-goal margin they suffered in Germany. When the group stage ends, Chelsea are top. Hertha, the surprise package, sneak through in second. AC Milan, shockingly, finish bottom.

But that European form comes at a price. While they shine in midweek, they stumble on weekends. Between September and December, Chelsea lose six league matches. The title race soon turns into a one-horse race – Manchester United pulling away, never looking back. Even Arsenal, who will finish second, end up nearly 20 points off the pace. And yet, history is made.

On Boxing Day, 1999, Vialli sends out a starting eleven against Southampton without a single English player – the first time that's ever happened in the topflight. The fans take it in their stride, but the establishment doesn't. The old guard, the commentators, the columnists – most of them don't appreciate it. The English invented the game, after all. And here's Chelsea, led by an Italian manager, taking the pitch without a single subject of Her Majesty. That ruffles feathers. Some critics saw it as a betrayal of tradition, a step too far in the league's growing internationalisation. But Vialli's stance is clear: quality, commitment and team spirit matter more than nationality. He didn't exclude English players by design; he simply selected the eleven he believed would best serve the club on the day. For him, football is a meritocracy, not a matter of passports.

Gianluca, as ever, stays calm. 'I don't see the fuss,' he says. 'Football is like this now. Chelsea is still an English club, with English and international players. Yesterday, the internationals played.' Simple, clear, and – at least to him – completely normal. But the debate had only just begun.

Vialli respected the English game and its identity deeply. He loved its intensity, its supporters, its rhythms. But he also believed that embracing international talent would elevate standards, broaden tactical horizons and sharpen competition. He never saw foreign players as outsiders but as contributors to a shared cause. At the same time, he valued English players who met those standards – Dennis Wise, Graeme Le Saux, Jody Morris all played central roles in his squads. In other words, Vialli's Chelsea reflected his philosophy: inclusive, ambitious, forward-looking. He saw no contradiction in loving English football while opening its doors. In his view, diversity wasn't dilution, it was strength.

For four months, Chelsea don't lose a single league match. But by then Manchester United are already gone – over the hill and out of sight. The Blues will finish fifth, 26 points adrift of Sir Alex Ferguson's side. The title race, in truth, was never a race at all.

Europe, though, is a different story.

This season's Champions League brings with it a new format. Before the knockout rounds, there's a second group stage. Chelsea are drawn with Lazio, Feyenoord and Marseille. A tricky group. Lazio are storming their way to the Serie A title, but Vialli's Chelsea go toe-to-toe with them. In the end, both clubs go through. And waiting in the quarter-finals is Barcelona – Gianluca's old personal nemesis.

The first leg is at Stamford Bridge, and Chelsea don't blink. They take their chance. A 3–1 win. Zola scores. Flo bags two. No one thinks it's over, but this Chelsea side – led by Vialli and anchored by World Cup winner Didier Deschamps – knows how to handle itself. Solid. Organised. Fully switched on. Then comes the return leg – 18 April at Camp Nou.

Vialli knows all eyes are on him. 'This is the most important match in the history of the club,' he says on the eve of the game. 'We must be fearless. We can't think: Let's defend and play on the counter. It's not an option. We want to play our own game.' Gianluca can't step onto the pitch any longer, but he gives his players what he can – his edge, his belief. 'I am used to winning games and winning things. That's my mentality.' Then he adds, quietly, 'To be in the Champions League quarter-final is part of the learning curve for a club like Chelsea. But perhaps in two years' time only the final will be good enough.'

The night had promised so much. But the chances slip, the momentum fades, and the game drifts beyond them. By the end, there's only the noise of the Camp Nou and the weight of what might have been. Chelsea go into half-time 2–0 down; the tie slipping through their fingers. But just past the hour mark, Flo strikes again. A goal that tilts the balance back Chelsea's way. And then – seven minutes from time – Barcelona score again. Level on aggregate. Extra time. No more Golden Goal rule, just 30 long minutes, played the old-fashioned way.

That's when it unravels. Rivaldo scores from the spot and Chelsea's Celestine Babayaro is sent off in the 98th minute. Kluivert adds another six minutes later. Barcelona 5, Chelsea 1 on the night. 6–4 on aggregate. The run is over. For a club in its first Champions League campaign, going out in the quarter-finals to Barcelona is more than respectable. It's a marker. A signal of intent. But not everyone sees it that way. Some in the press are quick to point fingers.

'This is when Vialli's managerial inexperience perhaps shone through. Chelsea was guilty of trying too hard to avoid penalties, and goals from Rivaldo and Patrick Kluivert saw Barcelona through to the semis,' critics would write – cold and unsparing. Some questioned the way Gianluca threw his team forward in extra time, desperate to avoid a shoot-out but leaving them far too open at the back. The criticism, for now, is drowned out by the bigger picture. Glass half full. But upstairs, in the boardroom, people take note.

Coming within seven minutes of a Champions League semi-final stings. But sandwiched between the two legs against Barcelona, Chelsea book another trip to Wembley. A win over Newcastle sends them through to the FA Cup final. Thirty years ago, lifting the FA Cup meant as much as winning the league. Those days are gone, but in England, the cup still matters. It's not just silverware. It's heritage. A fifth-place finish in the league. A Champions League quarter-final. And with Wembley ahead, Chelsea's season – and their manager's – still has a chance to end on a high.

Aston Villa await in the final. They've finished sixth, seven points behind Chelsea. But this isn't just any cup final. It's 20 May, 2000 – the 119th FA Cup final, and more importantly, the last ever played at the old Wembley before the bulldozers move in. The Twin Towers. The ghosts. The history. It all ends here. Vialli makes a call – he leaves Flo on the bench. Up front, he pairs Zola with George Weah, the Liberian legend brought in on loan from AC Milan mid-season. Another international, the critics mutter. But Gianluca's never picked teams to please columnists.

As tradition demands, the manager leads his team out. At the centre circle, the Queen's Royal Guards stand at attention in red coats and tall bearskins. The FA Cup isn't just football. It's ceremony. It's memory. *God Save the Queen* rings out. Then the Duke of Kent steps forward, flanked by both captains, moving down the line to shake hands with players, subs and staff. Gianluca is last. He looks right at home. Sharp grey suit, Chelsea badge on his lapel, blue and yellow bloom at his buttonhole. Fit as ever. Calm. Ready.

The first half is no spectacle. Scrappy, tense, cautious. Two sides more afraid of losing than eager to win. The second half brings a bit more. Weah has a few chances but can't convert. Dennis Wise has a goal ruled out. And then, finally, the breakthrough – courtesy of a goalkeeping error Aston Villa will want to forget.

With just under 20 minutes to go, Zola swings in a free-kick. The delivery is teasing, dipping towards the edge of the six-yard box. The Villa keeper comes to claim it – but spills it. The ball ricochets off a defender's chest, loose in the box. Before anyone else can react, Di Matteo, the scorer of important goals, is there. One touch. One finish. The goal that wins it. The goal that secures Chelsea's third FA Cup.

Captain Dennis Wise lifts the legendary silver trophy into the Wembley sky – the same cup that's been handed to the winners since 1911, and which must be returned to the FA by the first of March the following year. But the images that circle the globe are of Gianluca Vialli beaming, holding the cup in both hands, elegant as ever in his charcoal suit. It's his fourth trophy as Chelsea manager. A BBC commentator reminds him live on air that he's now the most successful manager in the club's history. 'Am I?' he says, almost surprised. The perfect gentleman. The master of understatement. 'True greatness,' he will one day say, 'is not measured by the number of titles you win, but by the impact you have on the game and the people around you.'

Despite the FA Cup triumph, the English press show no mercy to Chelsea's manager. 'Sir Alex Ferguson once bought himself time at Manchester United by winning an FA Cup after four trophy-free seasons, but that was 10 years ago in the age of comparative innocence that existed pre-Premiership, pre-Champions League and pre-Bosman,' thundered *The Guardian*.

For a club with Chelsea's spending power, an FA Cup is not enough. Not on its own. Not even with a European trophy – unless it's the Champions League. The dig is obvious. It points straight to the Cup Winners' Cup, the silverware Vialli's Chelsea lifted in the spring of '98. And yes, the game is shifting fast. The fame, the money, the prestige – they're all being pulled towards the Champions League. But the criticism cuts deep. That Cup Winners' Cup was only the second European trophy in Chelsea's 95-year history. That matters. It should matter.

More than the quarter-final exit to Barcelona – after all, Arsenal had gone out earlier, and even Manchester United hadn't reached the semis – it was Chelsea's failure to qualify for the next Champions League that stung the most. Fifth place. No way around it. Part of it was Leeds United and their unlikely surge. But not all of it. As *The Guardian* accused on 21 May, 2000, the rest came down to 'inexplicable lapses of concentration against lesser teams' from the Blues.

And while the football media start to press the finger towards Gianluca, behind closed doors and in the quiet corridors of the club's hierarchy, the whispers are getting louder. About the future. About whether this most successful of Chelsea managers still fits their long-term plans.

## 2. ITALY, 1991

'It's not easy being Vialli.'

GIANLUCA VIALLI

After Italia '90, Gianluca Vialli spent 10 months outside the national team setup. Manager Azeglio Vicini hadn't exactly shut the door, but with injuries creeping in and the squad evolving, Italy began to move forward without him.

Vialli returned to the starting eleven on 1 May, 1991, in the fourth match of the Euro '92 qualifying campaign. A month later, he was back again – this time in Oslo. But Italy lost 2–1 to Norway. In October, he started once more in Moscow. Yet despite two matches still to come, a goalless draw against the Soviet Union confirmed it: Italy were out. The Russians advanced. The Azzurri would stay home. That same night – 12 October – Azeglio Vicini was replaced. The new Italy manager was Arrigo Sacchi.

Sacchi kept faith in Vialli. No surprise there – he'd once tried to bring him to AC Milan to partner Marco van Basten. But come autumn, Sacchi made a move no one expected: he left Vialli out of the squad for a key World Cup qualifier in Glasgow against Scotland. And that's when the storm broke. The backlash was instant. No one bought the explanation. Against a physical, high-pressing Scotland side, Vialli's strength, pace and leadership would have been priceless. He'd worn the captain's armband in Italy's last two matches. Now he wasn't even in the squad.

'Italy without Vialli?' screamed the headlines on the eve of the match. 'The risk is real.' Officially, the issue was goals. Sacchi wanted finishers. And at Juventus, Vialli hadn't scored since 4 October. Giovanni Trapattoni no longer saw him as a classic No. 9. He was to play deeper, more withdrawn. But Gianluca, in truth, was struggling to work out exactly what Trapattoni wanted from him. 'Juventus has nothing to do with this,' Vialli said firmly. 'The national team is different. No one comes here to pay a price. No one has sins to atone for.' He tried to ease the tension. Said he'd spoken at length with Sacchi. But when pressed on the content, he stayed tight-lipped: 'The details of our conversation,' he said, 'I'll keep to myself.'

Next up was an away trip to Malta – the third match in the road to USA '94. Vialli was back in the squad, but the mood was anything but calm. At the pre-match camp in Rome, Sacchi came out swinging. At the press conference, he pushed back against the criticism – taking aim not just at the media, but at his players, too. It was classic Sacchi: a challenge disguised as confrontation. And top of the list, for sheer headline weight, was Vialli.

'When I was at AC Milan, I wanted him,' Sacchi told reporters. 'Since I've been in charge of Italy, I've been waiting for him.' It sounded like praise. It wasn't. 'Just be a centre-forward, for God's sake! That's all,' Sacchi snapped. 'I don't want him running all over the pitch, starting the move and then trying to finish it. He needs to fit into my system.'

Gianluca, speaking from that same training camp in Rome, didn't wait long to respond. 'I have no desire for revenge against the manager,' he said. 'Sacchi picks me because he knows what I can offer.' Then came the promise. 'I'll fight for my place this week. I'll throw plenty of elbows to win back my Azzurri shirt.'

Saturday, 19 December, 1992. National Stadium, Malta. The Azzurri No. 9 was Gianluca's once again. Sacchi started him up front alongside Beppe Signori. The match itself was forgettable – low on drama, light on quality. But Italy got the result, and Vialli scored the second goal of the night: a poacher's finish, darting in to meet Evani's cross from the right and tucking it away. It was his 200th career goal. His 16th for the Italian national team.

On a night when the result was about the only thing worth remembering, Vialli stood out. Beyond the goal, he nearly produced something spectacular – two bicycle kicks, one thudding against the crossbar, the other grazing past the post. But despite the effort, despite the milestone, this would be his final match for Italy. By mid-January, the writing was on the wall. Sacchi never said it outright, but the message was clear. On the afternoon of 15 January, 1993, he announced his squad for a friendly against Mexico in Florence. Vialli's name wasn't on it. For Gianluca, it was a cold slap. 'I didn't expect it,' he said, clipped and curt.

The disappointment of being dropped from the national team only deepened his growing frustration at Juventus, where Trapattoni had taken to deploying him in midfield as part of an ongoing tactical experiment. But was it really about tactics? At Juve, he was caught between roles – no longer the out-and-out centre-forward he'd been at Sampdoria, and unsure what role Trapattoni actually wanted him to play. Sacchi had claimed he wanted a striker, a classic No. 9. So why the exclusion?

The press didn't buy the official line. They pointed to Baggio, who had faced similar confusion at Juventus just a year earlier and yet kept getting picked. 'So,' the papers concluded, 'the reasons must be different.' The pundits didn't hold back. They'd seen it coming. Sacchi, they said, had simply been waiting for the right moment to drop a player he'd never truly wanted 'Too unpredictable. Too independent. Too generous in his movement. Too unwilling to follow the rigid, clockwork patterns Sacchi demanded.'

What really happened between Vialli and Sacchi has remained a matter of speculation ever since. Neither man ever felt the need to fully explain. After Gianluca's untimely passing, Sacchi softened his version of events. A sign, perhaps, that over time he'd come to respect the man, if not the player. But one thing has always been clear: the clash was personal. And it ran deep.

'When it comes to the national team and his relationship with Sacchi,' says Ciso Pezzotti, who coached Gianluca for eight years and knew him as well as anyone, 'I think it was a matter of character.' Gianluca never pretended otherwise. He didn't hide the fact that he and Sacchi saw football differently 'At first, he loved me,' Vialli said years later, one of the very few times he opened up about the rift. 'Then he realised I was someone who asked questions. Someone who wanted to understand. Someone who needed more than just an order.'

There was, by most accounts, at least one key misunderstanding. And a conversation that never happened.

'I mentioned to one of Sacchi's staff that I had doubts about some things in camp,' Vialli would later admit. 'The 8 a.m. wake-ups, the strict rules at meals and on the bus, little details . . .' The message was passed on. Sacchi, hearing about the complaints, decided to call Vialli directly. But when the call came, Gianluca didn't pick up. 'Out of pride, I didn't answer,' he would later say. 'I was in camp at Villar Perosa,' Juventus training centre. This was the pre-mobile era – no texts, no quick calls. Just landlines. And one call that never quite got through.

Some say the final straw came later – during that pre-Malta camp in Rome. A prank involving a napkin and some Parmigiano Reggiano cheese. Whether it really happened or not – and some swear it did – the truth was, by December 1992 the relationship between Sacchi and Vialli had gone well past breaking point.

'I haven't given up on the national team, and I hope Sacchi will still consider me,' Vialli said in late October 1993. It had been 10 months since he'd last worn the Azzurri shirt. And then, almost as an afterthought, he added, 'If not, I will not lose sleep over it. I've had 60 caps for Italy, I think I have done my part.' But the journalist listening to him wasn't fooled. He added a quiet note of his own, 'You could see it in his eyes – he is desperate to be back,' he wrote.

Sacchi never took the olive branch that Vialli offered – whether it came through a performance on the pitch or a carefully worded remark in the press. The manager had made up his mind long before, and nothing was going to shift it. Vialli could score a hat-trick against Lazio – three goals in a single afternoon – and it wouldn't change a thing. And in fact, it didn't.

In late April 1994, Juventus thrashed Lazio 6–1. Vialli scored in the 7th, 73rd and 83rd minutes. A complete performance. But just 15 minutes after the final whistle, Sacchi released his preliminary list of 31 players – those from whom the final 22 for USA '94 would be chosen. Gianluca's name wasn't on it.

He took it with grace. Still in his kit, not yet out of the stadium, he spoke to the waiting reporters. 'I don't think it would be fair,' he said, 'for one great performance to erase a season spent in the treatment room – or to take a spot from someone who maybe didn't score three goals today but has played well all year.' A few days earlier, he'd already hinted he knew what was coming. 'If they call me, I'll go,' he said. 'But if they want to take me to America as a tourist, they should tell me, and I'll step aside. At my age, you can't handle two months of training camp without playing.'

Gianluca Vialli wasn't the only high-profile casualty of Sacchi's Italy. Others had been left behind, too – Giuseppe Giannini, Beppe Bergomi, Riccardo Ferri, Nando De Napoli, Walter Zenga. Even Roberto Mancini, Gianluca's long-time partner at Sampdoria, lasted just a year longer. Sacchi had dangled hope in front of him, playing him in a friendly against Germany just a month before naming his final squad. But when the list came out, Mancini was missing, too.

And yet, somehow, the spotlight shone more fiercely on Vialli than on anyone else. The reaction, the scrutiny, the emotion – it all seemed sharper when it came to him. 'It's not easy being Vialli,' he once said. And he wasn't wrong.

## 3. CHELSEA, 2000

> 'A year is a long enough time to prove I'm the right man to continue the job.'
>
> GIANLUCA VIALLI

On 13 August, 2000, Gianluca Vialli's Chelsea face the champions of England – the seemingly untouchable Manchester United of Sir Alex Ferguson – in the Charity Shield, the traditional curtain-raiser that pits the league winners against the FA Cup holders and hands out the first silverware of the new season.

Gianluca has enormous respect for Sir Alex. 'I get up every time I mention Alex Ferguson's name,' he would say one day. But he's not at Wembley to pay tribute. He knows exactly what this match means. 'Beating the champions at Wembley and lifting a trophy would be the best way to start the season,' he says before kick-off. Despite being the most successful manager in Chelsea's history, Vialli senses something is shifting. The support he once felt from the club's hierarchy now feels thinner. The energy has changed.

The fans, for their part, have moved past the disappointment of last season's league finish. The FA Cup helped. It always does. But English football has changed. Ambitions have changed. At the dawn of the 21st century, history doesn't carry what it used to. You can win the last-ever FA Cup final at the old Wembley – leave your mark on a century of tradition – and still be judged a failure if your side stumbles in the league.

Gianluca isn't naïve. He's read the signs. He knows there are corners of English football – perhaps not at Chelsea, but close enough – where opinion has started to turn. The charge? That he's somehow betrayed the English game. Too many foreign signings. Too few English voices on the pitch. Even though the club's ownership – the same board that had embraced a European model to push Chelsea into the elite – still backs him, the murmurs have commenced.

'We are a European team playing in the Premier League,' said CEO Colin Hutchinson at the time, without a hint of irony. But the criticism had begun long before. It goes back to Boxing Day, to that match at Southampton, when – for the first time in English football history – an English club fielded a starting eleven with not a single English-born player. That club was Chelsea. That manager was Vialli.

'I think sometimes they don't forgive us for being foreign,' Gianluca says, politely but firmly, as the press draw closer. 'But that's wrong, because we aren't stealing anything. We're just working to make English football even better, and our loyalty to the club is absolute.' Even the FA Cup final had been pulled apart – not for tactics, not for the football, but for the birthplaces of those on the team sheet. The contrast was stark. Aston Villa started with eight English players. Chelsea had one: Dennis Wise, their captain. By now, the headlines had written themselves.

Some called Chelsea 'Vialli's Foreign Legion'. Others labelled their transfer strategy 'foreign affairs'.

The bare truth is, by this point, that Gianluca Vialli is simply ahead of his time. He has always been his own man, always willing to take a different path if he believed it led to success. But perhaps – just perhaps – this time he hasn't realised that English football isn't quite ready for the future he has already embraced. That same future he came to represent when, four years earlier, he arrived not just at Chelsea, but in a league that welcomed him with open arms – full of excitement, full of promise, eager to see what he could bring.

Looking back, the English press now put it plainly: 'In the year 2000, most Premier League players were still British, and English fans still remembered a time when a Scottish player was considered exotic. After spending his entire life in Italy, [suddenly Gianluca Vialli] found himself dealing with a foreign culture and a radically different league.' With the best of intentions, he may simply have moved too fast. 'Nowadays, we accept that teams can be fully multicultural,' the experts say. 'But in the mid-90s, that wasn't the case in England.'

Then there's the other charge – that he spent heavily on international signings, only to walk away with nothing but the FA Cup. Vialli, always the pragmatist, tries to set the record straight. 'We spent £24 million and brought in £15 million from sales. The net spend is just £9 million,' he says, holding up the numbers like a mirror. Nine million isn't excessive – not for a club trying to grow, trying to compete in Europe, trying to build something meaningful, one brick at a time. But chairman Ken Bates isn't convinced. And his patience is beginning to fray.

Ken Bates is a hard man to read. A Londoner by birth, a boyhood QPR fan who once dreamed of making it as a footballer, he built his fortune in logistics but never lost his love for the game. In 1982, he bought a near-bankrupt Chelsea for the symbolic sum of one pound. Like many businessmen who enter football, he doesn't always separate club from company. He struggles with the idea that not every investment yields instant returns. And when it comes to timing, his track record speaks volumes. Just two and a half years earlier, he had sacked Ruud Gullit without warning.

In May, when Chelsea lifted the FA Cup at Wembley, Gianluca handed the trophy to Ken Bates in the stands. The chairman gave him a fatherly pat on the head, then raised Gianluca's arm in triumph. It was a moment of celebration. But was it sincere? Or, more to the point, how much of that Wembley euphoria still lingers in the mind of a chairman who had hoped for the league title – and ended up with a cup? If the press are to be believed, not much.

Vialli's contract runs until 30 June, 2001, but with just a year remaining, there's no talk of renewal. And in football, silence tends to speak louder than words – especially when the man in question has brought more silverware to the club than any manager before him. Gianluca, ever composed, flips the narrative, insisting that a year is long enough to prove he is the right man to continue the job. But even in that phrasing, the fragility of the moment comes through. This is a man who has won four trophies in two seasons – half of all the major honours Chelsea had ever claimed before his arrival – and yet here he is, being asked to prove himself all over again.

Beyond Bates' shifting moods, though, another problem is brewing. One more dangerous than contract negotiations or media noise. A chill has settled between Vialli and parts of his squad. And in football, everyone knows the rule: it's always easier – and cheaper – to change the manager than to move on half the dressing room.

Ironically, the tension is coming from the very players he fought to bring in. Seasoned internationals. Champions. Professionals who didn't come to sit on the bench. Expectations haven't been met. Playing time has been inconsistent. And now the frustration is spilling into the open. The two Frenchmen are making noise. Frank Leboeuf speaks out from France: 'Vialli has problems with everybody, with Albert Ferrer and many others. It's normal for a coach to get along with his lads, but not for him.' Chelsea's chief executive, Colin Hutchinson, tries to soften the blow, suggesting that something may have been lost in translation. But few in London are buying it. The damage is done. The dressing room is restless. And the pressure is mounting.

Meanwhile, Gianluca seems to have lost the trust of two players who might have been expected to stand in his corner. The first is Didier Deschamps. They had shared two seasons together at Juventus, but their reunion at Chelsea proved more difficult than either imagined. 'I felt very frustrated on the pitch and also in my relationship with Vialli,' Deschamps says. 'It was hard, because I had a very different opinion of him as a player from the coach he became.'

The second is Gianfranco Zola. After two sparkling seasons – one under Gullit, the next under Gianluca – he spent much of his third year in London on the bench, caught in a rotation system that his manager sees as vital to fighting on multiple fronts. Dan Petrescu feels similarly hard done by. 'The fans wanted me to play, but Vialli didn't,' says the Romanian full-back. 'And his word is final. Vialli never said anything to me, but the message was very clear.'

Winning the Charity Shield – beating the invincible Manchester United 2–0 at Wembley on 13 August, 2000, thanks to goals from Jimmy Floyd Hasselbaink and Mario Melchiot – briefly lifts the mood. It's the fifth trophy Vialli brings to Chelsea. For a moment, the storm clouds part. The win strengthens his position in the dressing room. It gives the squad belief, the fans pride and his critics pause. The Charity Shield may have been labelled a 'curtain-raiser' by some, but for Vialli, it validates the work he'd done transforming Chelsea into a disciplined, modern and ambitious club.

The truce, however, is short-lived. A run of poor results follows: one defeat and three consecutive draws in the league. Five matches in, Chelsea sit tenth in the Premier League. For a chairman obsessed with the title, a slow start can feel like a fatal blow.

## 4. ITALY, 1995

> 'I believe that I won't play for the national team again.'
>
> GIANLUCA VIALLI

Gianluca Vialli doesn't play at the 1994 World Cup in the United States. Without him, Italy lose the final to Brazil and return home with nothing but the symbolic title of runner-up. 'The national squad is unpopular with people because Sacchi and Matarrese are unpopular,' he says when asked why, despite finishing second at USA '94, the Azzurri fail to ignite real passion. Antonio Matarrese is the all-powerful president of the Italian Football Association.

At the end of March 1995, the national team meet at Coverciano, preparing for back-to-back Euro '96 qualifiers against Estonia and Ukraine. Sacchi's Italy are not in their finest moment. The road is still long, but the home defeat to Croatia in mid-November has made it steeper. 'Why get upset? This week we beat Arezzo and Fiorentina's Youth Team . . .' Gianluca's mocking remarks, naturally enough, don't go unnoticed. Arezzo plays in the semi-professional

Serie D, the fifth tier of Italian football. The wound clearly hasn't healed.

With his goals and leadership steering Juventus towards the Scudetto, the press has begun voicing again, why isn't the national team manager recalling Vialli into the national squad? After all, Sacchi never stated once and for all that Gianluca's days with the Azzurri were over.

Feeling the pressure, Sacchi faces the journalists in a hastily arranged press conference and tries to set the record straight. The room is filled. Arrigo begins with the World Cup exclusion. 'Vialli wasn't called up two years ago,' he says, 'because of his performances with Juventus were unconvincing. He was playing as a holding midfielder, and on top of that, he suffered a serious injury.' A technical choice, not a moral one as the whispers went. As for why Vialli isn't called up now, despite his form with the Bianconeri, Sacchi is blunt. He says he prefers 'to focus on other players who helped Italy finish second at the World Cup – Casiraghi has never been in such good form, and Zola is having an outstanding season.' A debt of loyalty, then.

The problem is, nobody believes Sacchi.

A technical choice? Journalists remind him that Vialli's exclusion was decided 'before Casiraghi exploded in the League.' No moral issue? Then why, only a few weeks prior, did the Football Association president say, 'For Vialli to return, he must apologise'? Though Matarrese never said it, most assume the apology is for his remarks at USA '94, when Gianluca theatrically stated that, after being excluded from the Italian national squad, he was cheering for Brazil. The fact he had publicly admitted he would not support the Italian national team had detonated like a bomb at the time. Italy is a country that magically closes ranks whenever the Azzurri play. To confess you were rooting against them – despite everyone's admiration for

Brazilian football – felt like heresy to most. The Federation did not take it well. And Sacchi never forgot.

Italy beats Estonia 4–1. Then, four days later, the Azzurri win again in Kyiv against Ukraine. Another month and they win also in Lithuania. Qualification for Euro '96 is now locked. But then comes the second friendly match in celebration of the Swiss Federation's one-hundredth anniversary – a bruising 0–2 defeat against Germany, Italy's football nemesis. And this time, even though it's only a friendly, the backlash begins. For the fans, deliberately leaving out a top player who had long been a symbol of the Azzurri and who is in blistering form feels like too much to take.

'GIVE US VIALLI BACK,' scream the headlines the next day. Throughout the match with Germany, the Italian fans made their fury known. Whistles. Chants. A wall of noise against the direction the Italian national squad has taken. One morning paper calls it 'a Dantean Inferno. Matarrese and Sacchi the targets. All because of Vialli – who isn't there, but lives in the people's hearts, especially when the national team is defeated.' The supporters chant his name. They wave banners mocking Sacchi. And when Matarrese leaves the VIP box at the final whistle, they surround him – demanding, shouting, pleading for Vialli's return.

Sacchi refuses to even listen. 'The match has nothing to do with it,' he says flatly. 'They brought him up before we even played,' he scorns. 'There was a clear plan.' Matarrese goes for a softer line. He doesn't contradict his manager – he can't, their fates are tied – but he tries to calm the storm. 'Naturally, I can't act as a mediator, but I hope this matter gets resolved, one way or another,' he says after the commotion in the stands. And before leaving, he makes a promise: 'We'll work to solve an issue that could damage everyone.'

To most it feels like an elegant balancing act – a way to leave Zurich without undermining Sacchi, while hinting at reflection to calm the storm. Few believe him. But then, two months later, the improbable happens.

At the end of August, as the Azzurri prepare to face Slovenia in Udine in another Euro '96 qualifier, Matarrese speaks in public in conciliatory terms about Vialli. In private he goes further. He works behind the scenes, pressing Sacchi to give Gianluca another chance – the Juventus ace fans have not forgotten, the centre-forward they still dream of seeing lead the Azzurri attack.

Matarrese is a skilled diplomat. His career within UEFA leaves no doubt. His persuasion carries weight. When he is at his finest, not even Arrigo can say 'no'. And so, in the final week of August 1995, Sacchi and Vialli finally meet – in total secrecy.

Between Sacchi and Vialli it's an armed truce. The rift runs deep, too deep to be healed in one meeting. But Sacchi agrees to bring him back. No promise of a place in the starting eleven – only the call-up. For Gianluca, at this stage of his career, it's enough. Once you're part of the squad, anything can happen. Football works this way. He knows it well. What matters is being part of the group.

Truth is, Gianluca isn't fully fit. His knee, as he says, 'creaks'. In the opening Serie A League match against Cremonese – the club from his hometown, the one that raised him – he lasts only 56 minutes before surrendering. As he walks off the pitch, he also walks out of the squad list that Sacchi will announce the following Thursday.

With the call-up slipping away, word of the rapprochement between the two is leaked. Lazio striker Beppe Signori – long one of Gianluca's loudest critics in the Azzurri squad and naturally feeling his position under threat with Vialli's return – goes public with his mounting frustration. 'Sacchi said he discussed the matter with the team,' he reveals. 'He didn't speak to me personally . . .'

Signori fumes over not being consulted. Gianluca feels something colder. He learns his recall was put to a vote – his future with the Azzurri decided in a locker-room ballot.

Then Sacchi makes it even worse. A few days later, he acknowledges what everybody suspected yet no one had said aloud – that Vialli was left out of the 1994 World Cup because other players didn't want him along. Not Signori this time, but the whole AC Milan bloc. Sacchi's loyalists. The players that had won everything there was to win in the world with him and who now form the backbone of this mid-1990s Italy squad.

At this point, Sacchi's promise means little. A call-up for the next match – the qualifier against Croatia in Split, on 8 October – if Vialli's knee holds. Arrigo's words fall flat. Now it is Gianluca who has doubts. Heavy ones. Doubts about wanting to be part of an Azzurri team that rejected him 15 months earlier.

What follows is a long, agitated night. No sleep. Only thoughts, circling.

By morning the decision is taken. Brave. Final. Irreversible.

'I spent a restless night because I saw interviews that I didn't really like,' Gianluca says the next day, standing before a wall of microphones at Juventus' training ground. His voice is steady but the weight hangs in the air. He pauses. 'They confused me and left me very bitter. I believe that I won't play for the national team again.' Each word lands hard. Slow. Deliberate. The voice of a man who knows. He's caught inside something larger than football. A game behind the game. And Gianluca Vialli has decided he won't play it any longer.

'Maybe it's an act of weakness – judge for yourselves. But I no longer intend to wear that shirt,' he says. 'I don't accept my call-up being put up to a referendum by my teammates.' His voice stays steady. The voice of a man who knows he's carried an injustice for more than a year. 'I found it unfair. I never imagined player approval would be needed for a national squad call-up. If I came back,' he admits, 'I'd look at my teammates . . . and knowing some of them vetoed me a year ago – I don't like it. I cannot swallow it. And knowing myself, it would make me very unhappy.'

He exhales. Quieter now. 'In order to play, I need to feel happy, calm and at peace. Maybe,' he concedes, 'it's a weakness because there are players who are colder. But me,' he stops for a beat, 'I listen to my heart.'

Gianluca Vialli says 'goodbye' to the Azzurri. 'It was a clash of personalities,' he would remark years later. 'I was used to speaking my mind. With Sacchi, there was no balance between tension and serenity. He excluded me, convinced my doubts would bring negative energy into the group.' Then, with the generosity of hindsight, he said: 'I was wrong to refuse when, twice, he called me back – before and after the 1994 World Cup. I was too touchy. You should never refuse the Azzurri shirt.'

## 5. CHELSEA, 2000

> 'He was a wonderful ambassador for this club. With Luca, you felt Chelsea was in safe hands.'
>
> RICK GLANVILL

Bates acts on instinct.

And just like that, Vialli is gone. The official reasons are debated, but the real accusation, whispered behind boardroom doors, is that Vialli had lost his nerve. That he no longer took the risks required to win. Once a fearless striker, they were now seeing a manager too cautious, too concerned with not losing to go out and win. And in the era of three points for a victory, draws – too many of them last season, too many in the first month of this one – began to look a lot like defeats.

In the end, Gianluca pays for his inexperience – something he could never fix overnight. It's the price often paid by those who go straight from the pitch to the touchline. The instincts are there, the mind sharp, the authority genuine, but not yet weathered. Not yet tested by years in the dugout. It's an English pattern, one that wouldn't last much longer. 'He was given an offer he simply couldn't refuse,' the pundits commented. 'But in the end, he paid the price for the experience he didn't have.' Just like Ruud Gullit before him.

The much-publicised tensions with certain players – amplified by the press and echoed whispers – can also be read as something else: a sign of Vialli's struggle to manage difficult moments. 'He didn't have enough knowledge in his managerial bag. He lacked the experience to navigate tough situations.' And when the results began to dry up, 'he started internalising everything. He worried too much when he couldn't find the answers. Towards the end, he often seemed to lose confidence in his own decisions,' they recall now, gently, at Stamford Bridge. And so, the decision.

Chelsea had just brought in Christian Panucci on loan from Inter Milan. Then, on the morning of 11 September, the rumour mill stirs – Gianluca wants Paolo Di Canio, looking to prise him from West Ham. Another Italian. Another international. And that, it seems, is the tipping point.

Vialli is summoned to the club offices for five o'clock that afternoon. Of course, he's seen the signs. Any manager who survives in football learns to read the game off the pitch as well as on it. But still, he doesn't see this one coming – not like this. Not from Ken Bates. 'I drove from the training ground to visit the board,' Vialli would later recall. 'When I arrived, they asked me to sit down.' Gianluca thinks it's about his contract, finally. And why not? He's still the most successful manager in Chelsea's history. Fresh off winning the Charity Shield. A victory over Sir Alex Ferguson's invincible Manchester United, no less. Surely, this is the conversation about his future? His value?

Instead, it's the footballing equivalent of a two-footed tackle. 'I was thinking of how much to ask,' he'd admit years later. 'One or two million pounds. Instead, Colin Hutchinson said: "You once told me that after three years, you either have to change the manager or all the players. We decided to change the manager."' Just like that.

The decision takes the dressing room by surprise. Just as it had when Ruud was dismissed, out of the blue, back in February '98. And yet, for all the noise around Vialli's foreign signings, for all the criticism aimed at him for bringing too many internationals into the squad, in the end, the only voices raised in his defence come from the English players. Graeme Le Saux doesn't hold back. 'All the players are shocked, and no one had any idea this was happening.' Dennis Wise, the captain, echoes the mood. 'Everyone was disappointed. Luca is a good friend of mine.'

The rest of the dressing room stays silent. It's the press who speak loudest. They don't pull punches. 'Chelsea's decision to sack Vialli was largely precipitated by his distant and insensitive treatment of players, especially Gianfranco Zola, which came straight from the Gullit manual of man-management. Such behaviour played a major part in the Dutchman's downfall. Now it has done for Vialli.'

Football, after all, is a ruthless business. One moment you're lifting trophies, the next you're out the door. Zola – who in the heat of the moment some even tipped as Vialli's potential successor – is pointed to as the real flashpoint between the manager and the board. 'Suddenly Vialli started to blank Zola and drop him without explanation,' the papers claim. 'It may have been an attempt to avoid charges of favouritism, to draw a line between manager and ex-teammate. But it was insensitive – and unsuccessful.'

Beyond what's written, the Chelsea community is stunned. Not just because the club has parted ways with the most successful manager in its modern history, but because of who Vialli was. What he represented. It isn't just a sacking. It feels like a rupture. It's the warmth that people remember. The openness. The way he treated people.

'At the old Harlington training ground,' Jon Harley would recall – one of the many young English players Vialli brought into the first team – 'every first-team player would have to walk down the corridor past the youth-team changing room, and he was one of the few who would always stick his head in and say: "Good morning, chaps." He knew everyone's name. Whoever had the job of his boot-boy was lucky, because Luca gave them time. He asked questions. He wanted to know what was going on in their lives. But the truth was, there was no one he wasn't interested in. He was, simply, a true gentleman.'

And despite the press – always eager to stir the pot – grumbling about the wave of international players he brought to Chelsea, those who lived inside that dressing room, English passport in hand, tell a different story. A truer one. One of Gianluca's greatest strengths, they insist, was his ability to unite players from all corners of the footballing world under one badge. 'Luca created an environment,' they recall. 'We had a diverse group at Chelsea, and he was the first manager of a topflight English club to pick an entirely foreign starting eleven. Yet within that multicultural squad, there was real camaraderie – and that was thanks to Luca.' They add, with a smile, 'He could be passionate and serious, no doubt about that. But then he'd flip the mood – go into jokey mode. You never knew when, but it always worked.'

Chelsea release the standard statement to the press and the world. Respectful, polished, distant. They express 'great admiration for the results Gianluca Vialli has achieved in his two and a half years in charge' before adding, with corporate finality, 'in a broader context, we believe it is in our best interests to seek a change of direction.' That change of direction takes shape a week later with the arrival of another Italian – Claudio Ranieri, who, 16 years later, will write a fairytale of his own – guiding Leicester City to an historic Premier League title.

But behind the official line, the club knows the truth. This was a decision open to interpretation – and ripe for criticism. They have sacked, without warning, the manager who, in just over two years, delivered as many trophies as Chelsea had in the previous 93. And so, they do what football sometimes still allows, they afford him the honours of war.

'We parted on good terms,' says chief executive Colin Hutchinson. 'There were no arguments, and given the circumstances, the meeting was handled with dignity.' He makes a point of fairness. 'Every player we signed under Luca was a quality player.' And one more truth, rarely stated aloud: 'None of the players knew until the announcement. It was a shock. When I arrived at the training ground to break the news, the atmosphere said it all. You could feel how much the squad cared for Luca.'

In the wake of Gianluca's sacking, the club's community rallies around him with heartfelt support. Fans, many of whom had embraced Vialli not just as a manager but as a symbol of Chelsea's continental flair and growing ambition, express sorrow and gratitude. Banners reading GRAZIE

LUCA would soon appear at Stamford Bridge, and radio call-ins and forums will fill with tributes to the man who had delivered silverware and style. His reign had brought the club the League Cup, FA Cup and European glory – and, more than that, a new sense of identity.

While the tabloids scream with headlines like 'Sensational Sacking', Gianluca Vialli stays silent. No outbursts, no blame, no desperate attempt to control the narrative – just silence. Dignified, composed, as always. It's only years later that he reflects on it, and even then, his words carry the same measured grace that defined his playing days and his time on the touchline. 'That was unexpected,' he admits. 'It's never a pleasure when they sack you. In a way, it makes you become a better manager, because you need to go through that sort of experience to toughen up. Getting sacked is part of the job, basically. You've got to accept it.'

But despite the wisdom that comes with the passing of time and perspective, being sacked by Chelsea was, for Gianluca Vialli, one of the most painful moments of his career. 'That afternoon,' he would recall, 'more than football breaking my heart, I was heartbroken by Ken Bates and Colin Hutchinson.' It wasn't just the end of a role, it felt like a personal rupture, a sudden dismissal from a club he had helped transform, where he had built relationships, delivered trophies and laid the groundwork for a new era.

The emotional weight of that moment, the sense of unfinished business, was matched with one other in his footballing life, the night in 1992 when Sampdoria lost the European Cup Final to Barcelona at Wembley. That too had broken his heart, because it was his last match for a club he loved, because he had missed key chances, and because he held himself responsible for the outcome. Both moments left scars. Both marked the end of something precious. And in both the pain ran deeper than sport. For Vialli, these were the two instances when football stopped being joy and became sorrow – the only times, he would say, when football truly broke his heart.

The adventure ended sooner than expected. But once the dust had settled, once the noise of another managerial change had faded away, something remained. To Chelsea – both club and supporters – Gianluca Vialli would never be just another player, or just another manager. 'He was a catalyst,' they say. 'He symbolised everything the Blues were trying to become: an inspiring mix of ability and allure. The reason people still love him,' says Chelsea's official historian Rick Glanvill, 'the reason his name is still sung at Stamford Bridge, is his personality. Luca was charming, mischievous in just the right way, interesting, sophisticated. He was a wonderful ambassador for this club. With Luca, you felt Chelsea was in safe hands. His portrait is the first on the Shed Wall,' the Chelsea Hall of Fame carved into the wall of the old stadium, where people patiently wait in line to take selfies or family portraits with him – 'Gianluca is there not just for what he won with us, but above all for his personality. He won us all over.'

What made Gianluca Vialli's time at Chelsea so striking wasn't just that he was a former Champions League winner, or that he became the first Italian to manage in the Premier League. It was the fact that the son of a well-to-do father – some even mistakenly called him a billionaire – raised in a 60-room villa near Cremona, could so naturally, so humbly, embed himself in the dugout of a club built on working-class roots, grit and graft.

Gianluca had always known there were those who judged him a certain way because of his background. And it always hurt. In Italy especially, some stereotypes are hard to kill. But what truly defined Gianluca Vialli was never family wealth, it was the education he received in an ordinary household. And having an ordinary family, last time anyone checked, was never a crime. 'I don't believe someone has to be poor to find the motivation to succeed,' he would say years later. 'I believe you're either naturally driven or you're not. My drive came from wanting to play football – and to do it as well as I possibly could. It was never about money. It was about the challenge, the joy of playing, the desire to win, and the dream of turning a passion into a profession.'

'Middle class – that's what we are,' said Gianluca's mother in one of her rare public remarks. 'We're doing well. We don't complain. My husband works, and he has five grown children – how could he possibly be rich? Gianluca's elegance doesn't come from money. It comes from the tradition of a family that includes engineers, professionals, even a university rector.'

There was no trace of entitlement in Vialli's approach – not in Italy, and not in London. Despite his privileged background, he never looked down on the culture of English football. He understood it, respected it and, remarkably, earned its respect in return. He didn't try to remake Chelsea in his image – he worked to blend in, then quietly elevate it. He brought in tactical sophistication and continental professionalism, yes – but never at the expense of the club's identity. He celebrated the team's fighters as much as its artists. Dennis Wise got just as much credit as Gianfranco Zola.

What stood out most was how unbothered he was by class boundaries. He loved the banter, the tea-room humour, the wet Tuesday night in Grimsby, if that's what the job demanded. The players saw it. The fans felt it. He made Belgravia and The Shed End feel part of the same story. Vialli didn't just manage Chelsea – he belonged to

Chelsea. In doing so, he proved that class isn't about where you come from, it's how you carry yourself. And though he arrived with silk shirts and continental charm, what mattered most to supporters was that he rolled up his sleeves, led with dignity, and made them believe they were good enough to compete with the best.

GRANA PADANO

# PART EIGHT

# BELONGING

## 1. WATFORD, 2001

> 'A very successful manager I admire told me to stay calm, that a manager only takes the real step up after his first sacking. Now I'll find out if that's true . . .'
>
> GIANLUCA VIALLI

At this stage in his life, even after the shock of being shown the door, Gianluca Vialli believes his future still lies in management. Italy is calling. Plenty of clubs back home would welcome him with open arms. And just a few weeks before the unexpected sacking, when asked by the Italian press, he had said: 'When I came to London, I said I needed time to learn before managing in Italy, because our league is the toughest of all. Now, I believe I'm ready.'

But the truth is, Vialli doesn't feel any great pull to return. His life, both on and off the pitch, is in England now. More precisely, in London. English football, once a distant fascination, has become something much deeper. It's in his system now. 'In England,' he said, 'supporters identify with their club so deeply that booing your own team is almost like booing yourself. It's about identity.' For

Gianluca, that sense of belonging matters. 'When you walk on the pitch, the atmosphere brings the best out of you.'

And then there's another reason to stay. For just over a year, he's been in a steady relationship with Cathryn White-Cooper, a South African-born Englishwoman and a respected interior designer. His long relationship with Giovanna Moro, his childhood sweetheart from Cremona, had quietly ended not long after he took over at Chelsea in the spring of '98. Life had changed. So had he. Now, he says, he feels more settled. More grown-up. For the first time, he talks about being ready to become a father. And with a new partner and a city he's come to love, it's in London that he wants to build a family.

That's not to say everything about England makes perfect sense to Gianluca. He finds certain social circles difficult to read – particularly the stiffness of the British upper class. And he still can't quite understand why people walk around with holes in the soles of their shoes, though he suspects it's a quiet way of saying that there are more important things in life than appearances. At the same time, he finds himself drawn to the capital's architecture – not just the grand palaces that leave tourists in awe, but the quieter character of the city: the rows of red-brick terraces built for working families, full of life and history, and the white colonnades that circle Regent's Park like a composed salute to a more formal age. London, he realises, wears its layers openly – beauty in brick as much as in stone.

'His success with the English can be summed up like this: he's a foreigner who came to England and never moaned about the weather or the food,' says journalist Beppe Severgnini, who spent his own years in London. 'Vialli fits in here because he's a mix of cunning and intelligence, charm and grit. He knows that in England, they weigh you up and judge you. Then, if you haven't scandalised them, they let you in.'

From the sofa in his living room, in the house he shares with Cathryn in SW3, Vialli keeps an eye on Serie A. He watches the matches on TV, keeps up with the rhythm of Italian football. He stays in touch with Marcello Lippi – still close, always will be. And in the quieter moments, he finds himself drawn to *Friends* – the TV series that's just starting to catch on in England. He's a fan already, long before the show ever takes off back home.

His interests, though, stretch well beyond football and sitcoms. British politics absorbs his attention. Economics magazines land on his coffee table and don't just sit there – he reads them with the same focus he once gave to match reports. He is, as far as anyone can remember, the only football manager ever invited to lunch by the publisher of *The Economist*. Gianluca accepts without hesitation. The conversation is in English, and the topics are a world away from the touchline. He holds his own with ease until the meeting ends, and the entire editorial staff suddenly crowd in for autographs. It's only at that point that football finds its way back into the room.

London was never just a city for Gianluca Vialli. It was a turning point. A stage, a sanctuary and, eventually, a home. He arrived with a suitcase full of hopes and a reputation that gleamed with Serie A silverware. What he found was something rarer – a city that allowed him to evolve, to reinvent, to belong.

At first, it seemed an odd match – an Italian superstar joining a club still clawing at ambition, a London side that hadn't yet tasted the modern glories of Arsenal or Manchester United. But Vialli saw more than just a new contract. He saw a city in flux and a club on the cusp. He saw a place where reinvention was not only possible but welcomed. He came as a player, then became a manager, and over time something even more permanent: a Londoner.

There was freedom in London. In its culture, its humour, its contradictions. He once said that in England, people 'loved football, not just footballers.' That distinction mattered. In Turin or Genoa, he had been both idolised and dissected. In London, he could just be. Whether sipping espresso in Belgravia, riding his bike through Hyde Park, or plotting tactical tweaks at Cobham, he found a rhythm that suited him. Not just the pace of the game, but of life.

'Most of us,' the English press would later write, 'expected Vialli to return to Italy. What was left for him here?' It was a fair question. Chelsea had moved on. Claudio Ranieri had arrived. And yet, from the stands at Stamford Bridge, the chants of VIALLI, VIALLI could still be heard, week after week.

At any rate, Gianluca stayed. And he used the time well. He began working towards his UEFA coaching badges. He picked up golf.

Then, on 2 May, 2001 – less than eight months after Chelsea had shown him the door – a phone call came from north London.

---

Watford FC is not Chelsea.

Not even the Chelsea Vialli walked into as a player back in the summer of '96. For most of its century-long history, Watford had been a club of the lower leagues, bouncing between the second and third tiers of English football. Their golden spell came in the mid-1970s, when pop star Elton John – lifelong fan, majority shareholder and eventually chairman – stepped in and gave the place a jolt of colour and ambition. His arrival brought excitement, headlines and, from time to time, a brief run in the topflight.

Now, in 2001, Watford are back in the First Division – the equivalent of Serie B in Italy. A solid club, with loyal support and honest roots, but far from the glamour or resources Vialli had known at Stamford Bridge. So when the news breaks, few can make sense of it. Why would an international name, the most successful manager in Chelsea's history, take charge of a second-tier side? 'Did he love London so much that he'd do anything just to stay?' the papers asked.

The answer, in part, is yes. Gianluca does love London. But it's not just the city. It's the life he and Cathryn are building in it. That matters, too. Still, beyond wanting to remain in the capital – even if the drive from central London to Watford, with the traffic and the crawl up the M1, feels like a journey of its own – this is, above all, a professional decision. A step. A test.

At this point in his life, Vialli still sees his future in the dugout. And he wants to earn his way there properly. 'I wanted to test myself in a different environment, without the advantages I had at Chelsea – a top club, and one on the rise at that,' he would later explain. 'I thought the challenges awaiting me at Watford would make me a better manager, better prepared for the next job.'

In other words, he knows he started from the top – on the bench at a high-profile, ambitious club – and now he wants to earn his stripes in the hard yards. 'After my sacking, I had a lot of time to think,' he says. 'Once the shock wore off, I realised that if you're in this business, things like that are part of the game. A very successful manager I admire' – almost certainly Marcello Lippi – 'told me to stay calm, that a manager only takes the real step up after his first sacking. Now I'll find out if that's true . . .'

Watford itself is a town of just over 100,000. A northern suburb of London, about 18 miles from Buckingham Palace – and not far off the same from Gianluca and Cathryn's home in Knightsbridge. But Vialli is meticulous, and he doesn't want to waste hours in traffic. So, he sells the Knightsbridge home and buys in Hampstead, in the city's north. It's closer to Vicarage Road, closer still to the club's new training ground in St Albans. It doesn't cut out the motorway entirely, but it brings him nearer to the new routine. Back at Chelsea, he used to dodge the traffic on a Vespa – just like the old days with his childhood friend Fabrizio Frittoli, zipping across Cremona on a moped. One steering, the other gripping the football bags and trying not to fall off. But Watford is too far for that. So, he moves house. Moves north. Cuts down the commute. Focuses on the work ahead.

'Graham Taylor, who had been with us for the previous five years, told us he was leaving, and we wanted to replace him with another big name,' recalls Tim Shaw, Watford's CEO at the time of Vialli's appointment. The first contact comes through Brian Anderson, one of the club's co-directors and a personal acquaintance of Gianluca's. With the board's blessing, he reaches out. For a club aiming to grow – on and off the pitch – Vialli feels like the right call. 'Because he had been an international player and had won a lot with Chelsea as a manager, Luca was the right man for a club looking to grow, especially after launching an ambitious development programme,' says Shaw.

There's momentum building at Watford. ITV Digital has just signed a lucrative broadcast deal with the Football League, bringing a sudden influx of money into the First Division. For the first time in the club's long history, Watford becomes the outright owner of Vicarage Road, its home since 1922. In this atmosphere of progress and optimism, the appointment of a high-profile, high-cost manager like Vialli feels like a natural step forward.

There is one early concern. Would someone who has been a star at Juventus, lifted trophies with Chelsea and earned global status truly understand what it means to manage in the second tier of English football? Would he grasp the difference in scale – and expectation? Those doubts don't last long. 'Once Luca showed that he understood the reality of the situation,' Tim Shaw recalls, 'we all realised his arrival was an opportunity too good to pass up.'

Vialli's arrival is met with enthusiasm. It feels like a new chapter. 'A breath of fresh air,' fans say. Even Graham Taylor, a legend at Watford, gives his full support. He had just completed a second spell at the helm, five years this time, but his name had long been etched into the club's identity. His first stint – from 1977 to 1987 – saw him take Watford from the Fourth Division to second place in the old First Division. He is, by any measure, part of the club's soul. Therefore, when Taylor turns up to the press conference to introduce his successor, it says something. 'For the first time in the club's history, the outgoing manager attended the press conference to introduce his successor,' people at Watford still recall today. Taylor stays close in those early weeks, offering his support and helping Vialli get to know the rhythms and values of the club.

The contrast with Stamford Bridge is striking. 'We are like a family club,' Vialli says, 'but we want to have a professional set-up, which is how I like it.' There's something in the closeness of the place that speaks to him. The connection between club and supporters is immediate and sincere. Watford regularly holds open forums with fans, where no topic is too small – or too big, 'from sandwich stands inside the stadium to tactical discussions about the team, or even kick-off times,' Gianluca recalls. 'We pushed midweek games back from 7 p.m. to 7:45 p.m. so that people had time to get to Vicarage Road after work.'

It's all part of what makes Watford different. 'I found a fantastic atmosphere here,' Gianluca would say. 'A club on a human scale – like US Cremonese, where I grew up as a footballer.'

## 2. US CREMONESE, 1981

'A wonderful environment, with managers who taught not just football, but life.'

GIANLUCA VIALLI

Gianluca Vialli's first brush with his hometown team came when he was still in elementary school. For days, *La Provincia*, Cremona's local newspaper, ran the same message: on a certain day, at a certain time, any boy who wanted to could show up and play in front of the US Cremonese scouts.

Gianluca and his close friend Fabrizio Frittoli were buzzing. They decided to go. Their excitement was contagious – it even convinced the eldest Paloschi brother, one of the courtyard's brightest talents, to join them. 'It wasn't a real trial,' Frittoli remembers. 'It was one of those open sessions where they let everyone play. Luca Paloschi and I didn't even get on the pitch. But Gianluca did – right away. And he scored a goal.' Despite the goal, nothing came of it. No call. No offer. But no one had promised anything, and by the end of the afternoon, none of them were disappointed. The result didn't matter. The door was now ajar.

The years that followed were spent where they'd always played – on the parish pitch. Gianluca would have gladly joined US Corona, the team from the Cristo Re oratory. But they didn't have a squad for boys his age. 'I was too young,' he'd later recall. 'Back then, they only had an Allievi team, and I wasn't old enough to play yet.' But Cristo Re wasn't the only oratory in Gianluca's life. Every summer, the Vialli family spent their holidays in Grumello, a small town just outside Cremona. And there, the oratory did have a team for his age group.

'My first official registration,' Gianluca would recall, 'was with Unione Sportiva San Bartolomeo di Grumello.' The club made an effort. Someone would drive from Grumello to Cremona, pick him up for training, and take him home again afterwards. It was 1975. He was 11. He was the youngest. The smallest. He stayed for one season. Then everything changed.

The following spring, during one of the football tournaments at Cristo Re, a visitor appeared at the edge of the pitch. Franco Cistriani, an Italian literature teacher by trade, in his spare time coached the football team at US Pizzighettone – a small club in a town 20 kilometres east, just beyond Grumello, on the Adda River, which then was the border between the provinces of Cremona and Milan. Professor Cistriani had come to see his son play, but someone else caught his eye. 'He came to see his son,' Gianluca would later remember. 'But instead, he left thinking about me.' It was 1976. The young Vialli was in his first year of middle school. Not even 12. And soon after, he signed for Pizzighettone. A new team. A real coach. And his first step onto the path that would shape the rest of his life.

'Gianluca went to Pizzighettone,' Frittoli recalls. 'Then he told Cistriani that his brother Maffo and I were good players, too, so they took us as well. I hardly ever played. He got a few games, but then they found out he was too young. Even though he'd scored a mountain of goals, he wasn't allowed to play in the first team anymore.'

It was a bureaucratic problem. Gianluca's birth year was correct – 1964 – but he wouldn't turn 12 until 9 July, and the cutoff came nine days too soon. He was underage by less than a fortnight. When Cistriani realised it, he had no choice: Gianluca had to be withdrawn from the squad. There was no younger team to drop him into. Pizzighettone ran just the one youth side. That was the end of it. 'I begged and pleaded, but the local football federation wouldn't budge,' Gianluca would later recall. He kept training, of course. But matches were off-limits. For a boy who had already made an impression, it felt like a door closing just as things were getting started.

Gianluca, his brother Maffo and Frittoli stayed at Pizzighettone for a year. Then, their paths split. Frittoli and Maffo moved on to Pontevico, another small-town club not far from Cremona. For Gianluca, something unexpected happened: the doors of US Cremonese opened.

He had played just five matches in the white-and-blue shirt of Pizzighettone, but in those five matches he had shown more than enough. Enough to convince Cremonese that they were looking at a boy with not just talent, but presence.

The transfer fee was 50,000 lire (around £30). A modest figure, even for the time. The move had to be completed by 30 September, 1977, 'subject to a favourable medical examination to be conducted by US Cremonese,' read the official document – still preserved to this day. It was signed by Vice President Giuseppe Miglioli for Cremonese, and President Pierluigi Piacenza for Pizzighettone. Next to Gianluca's name, just 13 years old, was the signature of his father, Gianfranco – 'the parent exercising paternal authority.'

'Luca went to Cremonese first,' Frittoli remembers. 'But since we were close friends, I often gave him a ride on my scooter to the Campo Federale, where they trained. One afternoon, I dropped him off and rode away. The next day, he rang my doorbell to tell me that after I left, he'd gone looking for me. He'd spoken to Babo Nolli, the youth coach at Cremonese. And Nolli wanted to meet me.'

Now, how many kids, when the gates of paradise crack open, think to bring their friends along? How many boys, when joining a new club, or beginning to emerge as natural leaders, stop to say, there's someone else you should see? Someone (almost) as good as me.

*That* was Gianluca Vialli.

Everything else – everything he would go on to do in life, as a footballer, a manager, a pundit, a businessman, a philanthropist, a husband, a father – was simply the natural consequence of the way he thought and the way he carried himself. He was a good man. A decent man. A man who knew he had been blessed – with rare talent and with a mind that could see the game, and the world, with clarity. He balanced heart and head. He welcomed competition. He didn't just accept it, he sought it out. He wanted others to rise, to reach the heights he aimed for, or at least to be given the chance. Only then, he believed, would he truly know how far he could go.

At US Cremonese, Gianluca found what he needed. 'A wonderful environment,' he would later say, 'with managers who taught not just football, but life.' Mario Montorfano, a loyal defender who spent his entire career with the Grigiorossi, remembers Gianluca's first days well. 'He was a complete mess. Later, he became precise, punctual, meticulous. But back then, if he was in a hotel room, you knew – it was chaos. One time, we argued about it. For a two- or three-day camp, you let it slide. But in Berceto, at the pre-season camp, we stayed for three weeks . . . shoes here, socks there . . . total disorder. He was a real mess.'

The football, though, told a different story, and he quickly climbed through the ranks. Gianluca's professional debut for Cremonese came on Sunday, 10 May, 1981. He was 16. The match was a third-tier Serie C fixture against AC Parma. It's worth noting that when manager Guido Vincenzi called him up to the first team, he didn't do it gradually. He didn't ease him in. He skipped the Primavera squad altogether. 'Whenever the regulations allowed it, Vialli always played in at least a category above his age group,' recalls sports journalist Giorgio Barbieri, who began his reporting career around that time. 'He was always with the older players because, even back then, he was so good.'

The match ended 0–0 – another solid step towards promotion to Serie B for the Grigiorossi. Gianluca came on in the 80th minute, replacing right-winger Bresciani. 'There were ten minutes left,' he would later recall, 'and manager Guidone Vincenzi said: "Kid, it's your moment! Get out there!"'

But that debut, full of promise, would always carry a certain aftertaste. 'I get on the pitch, first ball I touch, I skip past two, get into the box, and they absolutely clatter me – a stone-wall penalty. The ref doesn't give it. Five minutes later, I get another ball, beat another man, take a shot, and it misses by this much . . . And then a Parma player comes over and says, "Hey, kid, if you don't knock it off, I'll put my boot through your face."'

'I didn't understand at first,' Gianluca would acknowledge. 'Then a teammate came over and said, "Look, Luca, there's three or four minutes left, we're all dead on our feet, and we've all decided we're happy to let this one finish as it is . . ."' It was a shock. The welcome to the senior game he hadn't quite expected. 'That was the day I lost my footballing virginity,' he said. 'The joy of making my debut, but also the shock of discovering something I'd never expected.' Still, the next day's papers were full of praise for the young Vialli. And it was only the beginning.

Vialli climbs fast. In the official US Cremonese team photo for 1981–82, his face is missing. Despite his spring debut, manager Guido Vincenzi doesn't think he's ready yet. To his credit, Vincenzi will quickly change his mind. By mid-September he throws the Grigiorossi new golden boy into the game. Gianluca comes on in the 63rd minute, replacing veteran Giancarlo Finardi. He runs hard. Hungry to leave a mark. It changes nothing. Cremonese are swept aside 0–3 by Sambenedettese. That day, however, Gianluca is the only Cremonese player the press praises. A dim light in a dark afternoon.

The first autumn fogs settle. Cremonese are having a tough time. No wins. No rhythm. Vincenzi takes his chances. On 4 October, with first-choice striker Sauro Frutti sidelined, the seasoned manager turns to 17-year-old Gianluca Vialli for his first professional start. The stage is the Bentegodi in Verona. The match ends 1–1. Promising. Vialli shines. After the whistle, the opposing centre-half hunts him down, still out of breath. 'How old is this kid? Seventeen? Well . . . he's going places!' Journalist Giorgio Barbieri remembers it vividly: 'Gianluca had something above all others. Despite his young age, he was already sly, clever. Vialli was cunning, even though he was a boy.'

The following Sunday, the first-choice strike is back. Fit. Ready. But Vincenzi keeps faith in Vialli. Gianluca starts, No. 7 on his back – the No. 9 will come later, though in his heart he's always been a centre-forward. Ten seconds into the second half, it happens. His first professional goal. A poacher's goal. A predator's finish. One quick touch after a scramble in the box from a free-kick. History made in an instant. After the match, Gianluca shrugs it off: 'No emotion on my goal. In those moments, you don't have the time.'

Despite the goal, it takes another whole month before he starts again. Vincenzi rates him, but he's cautious – 17 is young. Playing for your hometown team carries weight. Too much pressure can break you. But Gianluca is restless. At 17 he already knows his worth. Knows the role he can play in this team. Polite but firm, he makes his case for a place in the eleven. By now he's been orbiting the first team for months. He knows his teammates. Admires them. Respects their talents. But he's also realised something else: aside from experience, he's no less than any of them. And when the new year comes – and the table looks bleak – Gianluca returns to the starting eleven. That moment marks the beginning of a climb that will carry him to the very top of the football world.

When the manager turns to him to rescue a season sliding towards relegation, Gianluca takes the weight of the team on his shoulders. He does it with his football, his drive and his goals. But there's more. He doesn't lead only from the pitch. For someone so young, and despite the nickname the press gave him – they call him *Viallino* (small, little, young Vialli), the boy has presence. And courage. In the dressing room, teammates listen when he speaks. So, when the senior players decide to take matters into their own hands – to force the club to replace the manager – it's to Gianluca they turn.

One afternoon in mid-April, captain Stefano Di Chiara and Gianluca Vialli walk into the downtown newsroom of *Mondo Padano*, the city's weekly paper. Its sports pages carry real weight in Cremona. They ask for Giorgio Barbieri, the leading football writer.

'First of all, I didn't expect such a strong stance from the team. Sure, I knew there were tensions over Vincenzi's management, but I didn't know the dressing room had turned against him,' Barbieri recalls today. But the surprises didn't stop there. 'When they sat down at my desk, I was sure Di Chiara would speak – he was older, the captain. I thought Vialli was only there because he was from Cremona. But after the introductions, it was Vialli who spoke. And he spoke with conviction, with clarity. He didn't even have a driver's license yet, he was that young, but he spoke with the strength and the authority of a veteran. I listened and thought to myself: this boy will become a great player, because he has a sharp mind.'

It works. One week later, Vincenzi is out; Emiliano Mondonico is in – the youngest professional manager in the history of Italian football. For Gianluca, Mondonico's arrival is another push forward. The new coach had trained him in the youth ranks, helped shape him as a player. From the day they met, the young manager and the younger striker had been in perfect sync. 'Mondonico immediately saw him as the symbol of the team,' recalls sportswriter Giovanni Ratti.

With Mondonico on the bench and Vialli on the pitch, Cremonese achieve what most deemed impossible: they survive. A year later they climb higher still, pushing for promotion to Serie A before falling short in a three-way play-off with Como and Catania. Vialli is 19 now, and his talent impossible to ignore. The big clubs are circling. Juventus lead the chase. But in the end, it's Sampdoria that closes the deal. Cremonese president Domenico Luzzara sells him in secret. No announcements. No leaks. For an entire year, Vialli plays on with Cremonese, not knowing that he is already a Sampdoria player.

Exactly one year later, on 4 June, 1984, in a wild 3–3 draw against Palermo at the Stadio Zini, Cremonese secured an historic first ever promotion to Serie A. And at the heart of it all was Gianluca. His goals have made the difference, yes, but it's more than that. He has become the team's heartbeat. The youngest player in the squad, yet its natural leader. 'We are the main architects of this promotion, and today we rightly feel like giants,' he said that day, drenched in rain, sweat and champagne.

He was the hero. The face of the climb. The symbol of a club that had grown up alongside him. His story over the previous three years was the story of Cremonese itself. From a debut in Serie C, through the heartbreak of a play-off loss, to the glory of promotion. He had gone from promising talent to leading man. 'At 16, they threw me into the fire in Serie C, then three years in Serie B,' he would say later, speaking at the height of his international success.

'It was an incredible launchpad, and I feel a huge debt of gratitude to everyone here.'

After 105 appearances and 23 goals, his time in Grigiorosso came to an end. Even with the leap to Serie A, Gianluca Vialli had outgrown his hometown club. What he left behind was something more than numbers, 'the image of those curls, with something buzzing underneath – like an exposed live wire, a contagious joy for playing football. A joy for winning, yes, but above all, for playing. A love for the game that spread to everyone around him.'

WATFORD

# PART NINE

# LESSONS IN YELLOW

## 1. WATFORD, 2001

> 'It was massive for a club like ours. A global star, a man with his kind of gravitas . . . I had to pinch myself to make sure I was not dreaming.'
>
> TOMMY SMITH

'I have missed you!' Gianluca smiles at the journalists packed into the small press room at Vicarage Road, Watford's home ground, on the day of his official unveiling.

There's warmth in the room. Familiarity. And Gianluca gets ahead of the questions, making one thing clear from the start: 'I had a great time at Chelsea and obviously things happen in life and things go wrong.' But, he adds, 'I am not resentful of Chelsea. I am just here to do a good job and take this club to the next level and improve my skills as a manager. I had to think carefully about this proposal,' he admits, 'but it took me a couple of weeks to realise that this is the club where I wanted to start again, where I want to give my best. I want to take Watford to the next level.'

At Watford, Gianluca feels something he never fully felt at Chelsea – complete trust. 'At Chelsea, even though I achieved a lot, they did not have great confidence in me. I did not feel 100 per cent supported,' he will say, with quiet honesty. Here, it's different. 'The club and I share the same philosophy. We know we're not going to win the Premier League, but we've got an ambitious plan. We want promotion, we want to build something that lasts. And most of all,' he adds, with a smile that shows he means it, 'we want to enjoy ourselves.'

Enjoyment. That word matters to Gianluca. It always has. 'My pleasure,' he says, returning to a theme that's followed him his whole career, 'comes from doing my job in the best possible way. Whether it is at Chelsea or Juventus or Watford, it doesn't really matter.'

He's not bothered that Watford can't afford five-star hotels for away matches. He doesn't mind that he's inherited the club car that his predecessor left behind – not that he's driving it himself. He still doesn't quite trust himself behind the wheel on the wrong side of the road. For now, he has a chauffeur.

'He is still lean, despite not having played regularly since May 1999,' notes the English press, impressed as ever. No surprise there. Gianluca has always looked after himself. A firm believer in the old Latin saying – *mens sana in corpore sano*. At Chelsea, he trained alongside his players. Even during his break from football, he never skipped the gym. Now, at Watford's new training ground in St Albans, he's right back in the mix. He joins the five-a-sides, gets stuck in. And when he loses, he fumes – same as ever.

The only break in his disciplined routine are cigarettes. He knows he should quit. 'Smoking's bad for you. No question about that. One day, I'll stop. But right now,' he confesses, settling into his new role, feeling the weight of the dugout again, 'it'd be too hard.'

Off the pitch, he's become something of a style icon. Always was, really – now it's just second nature. 'Blue shirt, beige jumper, grey overcoat, grey trousers, brown suede shoes,' notes one reporter, taking it all in. And always, the briefcase. Neatly packed. Inside: his notes, and a book by Sven-Göran Eriksson – the man who nearly coached him at Sampdoria, the summer Gianluca moved on to Juventus. Even back then, he'd been drawn to the intellectual side of the game. To the theory, the systems, the thinking behind the play.

Watford fans can hardly believe their eyes. Having Gianluca Vialli as their manager feels like a luxury – like a promise of something greater. Club chairman Elton John, never one to hide his heart, makes his feelings plain: 'I am incredibly excited that we have appointed Luca. When the board said they were thinking of getting Vialli, I said that as a player he was one of my favourites. As a manager, he did an incredible job at Chelsea. It is one of the most stunning coups we have pulled off.'

Gianluca gets to work straight away. He knows what he wants. He has a clear idea of how a football club should operate – and he isn't here to play catch-up. His Watford will be a modern club. European. Better yet, Italian. Even more than his Chelsea ever was. In his view, that's the foundation of a winning side: a club that trains and functions like a team with serious intent. A club that keeps up with the times.

Gianluca believes English football can keep its spirit but add sophistication. He respects the traditions, the terraces, the winter fixtures and the unfiltered noise of matchdays. But he also challenges the old ways. His respect is never blind. He wants English football to grow, and he plays his part in its modernisation. For all the trophies he lifted throughout his career, perhaps his greatest legacy is helping English football believe in better.

Thanks to Gianluca's vision, for the first time in its history Watford has a dedicated goalkeeping coach, a club doctor, two physios, two fitness scientists. Preparation becomes a priority. Double sessions. Tailored fitness plans. Training built around performance, not tradition. Matchday routines are reshaped, too. No more players arriving in separate cars. From now on, the squad, the manager and the entire staff travel together – on the team bus. A small detail, maybe. But meaningful.

The players notice. They respond. 'To me, Luca was a legend. I grew up watching his goals on TV. I could hardly believe he was my manager,' says Tommy Smith, a young forward who will go on to finish the season as the club's top scorer. Eleven goals. A breakout year. But it's more than that. 'The whole place was buzzing,' he says. 'It was massive for a club like ours. A global star, a man with his kind of gravitas. And for me, as a striker like him, those first few weeks – I had to pinch myself to make sure I was not dreaming.'

Nowhere is the shift more obvious than on Watford's pre-season tour of Italy that July. Two stops: Lecco, where they play AC Milan, and Genoa, where they face Gianluca's beloved Sampdoria. 'The whole world seemed to have come to Lecco just to see Gianluca,' one footballer recalls. 'Of course, we knew he was famous, but watching players like Ronaldo waiting their turn in the stadium corridors just to shake his hand – that's when we truly understood his greatness.'

Vialli's presence changes everything. Graham Taylor has just stepped down after five strong seasons – the last ending with a solid ninth-place finish. But now, the club's ambition shifts. The message from above is clear: promotion must be immediate. Gianluca signed a three-year deal, but no one's talking about three years. The clock is already ticking. The new season hasn't even kicked off and the pressure is sky-high. The football world is watching. Expectations aren't just high, they're non-negotiable.

'A new era is taking shape at Watford under the leadership of Gianluca Vialli, and anything less than a serious push for automatic promotion will be considered failure,' declares the BBC that summer. 'The Italian's reputation comes with weighty expectations, especially after a frenzied transfer window.' And what a window it was. Marcus Gayle. Ramon Vega. Stephen Glass. Stephen Hughes. All personally picked by Vialli. All far beyond what most clubs at this level would dare to chase.

With money spent and names brought in, there would be no excuses now. Not that Watford were being reckless. The board's backing of Gianluca – his transfer list, his vision, even his appointment – was a gamble, yes, but a measured one. A gamble made possible by ITV Digital's golden handshake. The new broadcasting deal promised around £3 million a year to every First Division club. Enough to dream big.

Vialli didn't ask for favours, he asked for commitment. Committed investment. Six key signings. No half-measures. When he agreed to take charge, that was the condition. Watford agreed, signing off on a bold plan that banked the club's ITV revenue for the next three years to fund the new project. It was all or nothing now.

And then came the first match.

'The season opener was a rude awakening,' recalls one of the players who started that day – a day that had arrived with so much promise: 11 August. Manchester. Watford away to City. A heavyweight clash on the opening weekend. The build-up was everything you'd expect. ITV chose it as their first live broadcast of the season. Two clubs with topflight ambitions. Two clubs carrying pressure on their shoulders.

City, for now, were still human. Still a club rebuilding after a drop they hadn't planned for. But they had strength, depth and Kevin Keegan in the dugout – a former

Liverpool hero, former England manager and a man who knew exactly how to take a team up the rankings.

At Watford's training ground in St Albans, there was a sense of purpose ahead of the match. Gianluca had prepared meticulously. He knew what this match could mean. Get something at Maine Road – better still, win – and the season would lift off like a rocket.

For the first 20 minutes, Watford hold their own. They stay compact. Keep the ball moving. They look organised. Confident. Like a team that know they belong in the conversation. But bit by bit, City begin to show their class. Just before the half-hour mark, the pressure hits. Espen Baardsen, Watford's keeper, is called into action. Once. Twice. Three times. Three big saves, back-to-back, each one more important than the last. Thanks to Baardsen's brilliance, they reach the break level: 0–0. Still in it. But the second half would be different. The deadlock wasn't going to hold forever.

At first, luck seems to favour Watford. A free-kick from the edge of the box rattles the crossbar, then the post, before trickling out for a goal-kick. Inches from glory. Inches from warning. On 58 minutes, they finally crack. Now City smell blood. They surge forward. Another cross. Another header. Another thundering shot – off the bar again. But this time, the ball doesn't bounce out. It drops kindly. A City striker pounces. 2–0. Game over.

As Gianluca readies his final roll of the dice, desperate to turn the tide, disaster strikes. Paul Robinson, already on a booking, picks up a second yellow. Sent off. Watford are down to 10 men and hanging on. And City, ruthless now, don't wait long. Before full-time, they add a third. A scoreline as emphatic as it is unforgiving.

The headlines belong to Manchester City. The plaudits, the TV packages, the praise – they go one way. But Gianluca isn't interested in shifting blame. 'We should have done better. It was difficult for us to control the game,' he says, his voice steady, his tone even. 'We managed it for over twenty minutes, then started the second half well – but it wasn't enough. If we want to be the best, we have to play like that for the full ninety.'

3–0. No excuses. No sugarcoating. It hits hard. But Gianluca Vialli doesn't linger on the pain. 'We know we're not at our best yet. We can improve. We know what we need to work on. We must stay positive. It's only the start of the season – so we keep working.' And they do.

A week later, in his first home match at Vicarage Road, Watford give him a win. A 3–2 victory over Rotherham United. The kind of game that should settle nerves, maybe turn a page. But it doesn't. The team stutters. Struggles to find rhythm. Ten games in and the table speaks plainly: three wins, two draws, five defeats. While Manchester City power forward, Watford drift.

They're not lacking talent. That's not the issue. The question is whether this group fully understands what Gianluca is asking of them. At Chelsea he coached top-level players, individuals who sometimes needed little more than a nod and a system. At Watford, it's different. The danger isn't that players will ignore him, it's that some of them simply can't deliver what he's drawing on the board. 'Sometimes you could see Luca getting frustrated,' says Tommy Smith. 'He'd ask us to do things that we just couldn't pull off. Not everyone is born with his ability. Not everyone could do what came naturally to him. And at times, you could see it got to him.'

Gianluca had tried to plan for this. He knew the gap between expectation and execution could be brutal. That's why he pushed so hard for Premier League-calibre signings – players who'd seen the top of the mountain. He hoped their presence might lift the entire group, raise standards across the board. But topflight experience doesn't always translate. Especially not in the Championship. It's a grind. Heavy pitches. Tight turnarounds. No time to settle.

And then there is the target on their back. 'We know that everywhere we go to play, and for all the clubs that play against us, it will be the match of their season,' Gianluca warned in the summer. 'It will be Watford because of Elton John, because of myself, because of Ray Wilkins being in charge, or because of all the Premiership players who are in the team.'

He wasn't wrong. Watford felt it every week. The raised intensity. The jeers from the stands. The hunger from the opposition. Gianluca felt it, too. The sting of misunderstanding. The press, the fans, even some colleagues couldn't quite grasp why a man with his reputation would take a job in the second tier. 'I suspect,' he would later reflect, 'that a lot of people, especially in England, saw it as a step backwards.'

Then there was the hostility. Crude, ill-informed. Not always about him, exactly, but aimed at foreign managers, foreign players, foreign methods. 'There was still a lot of ingrained racism in English football at the time,' some observers say, 'probably made worse by the Bosman ruling and the influx of foreign players.' But Gianluca didn't flinch. He tuned it out. This was part of the job, part of the challenge. And instead of snapping back, he flipped the script – signing autographs for wide-eyed ball boys before they could even ask. 'His manner is as gentle and dignified as ever,' the English press wrote. They may not have fully understood why he was here, but they were still drawn to him. Vialli never bored anyone – not with his choices, not with his presence.

But fascination doesn't win football matches. Watford continued to struggle. And slowly, Gianluca began to realise just how lonesome he was. The change he brought to the club was massive. Too massive, maybe. The vision, the structure, the standards – it was a revolution. And revolutions need time; something that Watford didn't have. 'The change was seismic,' his players would later recall. 'Luca changed our daily routine, our food, our diet. In training, we didn't run as a group, we ran individually. And he knew exactly how long you'd run. He could tell if you weren't putting in enough effort.'

This was, however, still a club shaped in Graham Taylor's image. And everything Gianluca did – how the team trained, how they warmed up, how they sat at dinner – was measured against what Taylor had done. Or what he hadn't. 'Luca was frustrated. Saddened, even,' says one pundit. 'Graham Taylor was everywhere. At some point, he realised he'd never be able to change the club the way he wanted.' Taylor's football was direct. Training was always with the ball. No frills. No science. Gianluca was the opposite – systems, analysis, structure. Outthink, don't just outrun. Each player had their own fitness programme. Gym work. Recovery. Sports scientists. Nothing like it had ever been seen at Watford before.

And then there was the human side. Taylor was close to his players, was one of them. Gianluca couldn't afford to be. He was only 36, and he still looked like he could lace up and play. He kept a careful distance. Respect, not friendship. That's where Ray Wilkins came in. 'Ray' to everyone. The bridge. The translator. The soft edge to Gianluca's sharp lines. Vialli? He was always Gaffer. Never Gianluca. 'You could always talk to him if you needed to,' said one player. 'But you couldn't really build a relationship with him. I suppose that was deliberate. Only now do I realise just how young he was at the time.'

As results worsened, the divide widened. The new signings had Premier League wages. The old guard noticed. They understood the logic – big players brought in to win promotion – but logic doesn't soften resentment. 'If we'd started winning, everything would have sorted itself out,' says Tommy Smith, then just 20. 'But the defeats started to divide us. That's when the first complaints about Gianluca, his training methods, and how distant he was from us, really began.'

But as the season dragged on, a bigger and very personal question surfaced – was Gianluca Vialli really cut out for this? He had succeeded at Chelsea. He wanted to stay in the game. But slowly, reality crept in. Coaching didn't excite him the way playing had. 'When you're a player,' he explained, 'your main concerns are training well, getting plenty of rest and being ready for match day. When you're a manager, you have to organise, take care of people, always be one step ahead. I feel responsible for everything that happens at the club. It's hard to enjoy yourself, to have a laugh. It's hard to relax.'

It wasn't just the results. It was the life. The rhythm of management. The weight of it. The way it never really lifts. Gianluca had always been obsessed with winning, but as a player, he could unplug. He could laugh, play, joke, take the edge off. As a manager, there was no switch. No release. 'Just the other morning, my girlfriend told me I'm aging – she says I look much older than I did seven months ago when I took this job. And you know what? I agree. And honestly, I don't like it.'

In March 2002, speaking with journalist and author Amy Raphael, Gianluca let the mask slip. 'My goal is to do this job as well as I can, but also to enjoy myself and have a life. I mean, I can't exactly complain about my lifestyle – there's no doubt about that. But I need to learn to think about something other than football. If I don't dedicate most of my time to the game,' he admitted, 'I feel as though I'm neglecting it. I find it difficult to switch off.'

There were still glimpses of his passion for the sport. At the training ground, jogging alongside Ray Wilkins, you might catch a laugh, a shared joke, a flash of the old Vialli – the one who played with joy. But those moments were rare now. The truth was simple, and heavy: coaching was draining the pleasure from the game. 'Being obsessed is a price you have to pay in order to be successful,' Gianluca said in the late winter of 2002. By then, Watford were stuck in mid-table. Promotion was gone, the season's ambitions long since written off.

Manchester City dominated the campaign. It was their final stint in the second tier, and they made sure of it. Watford never really entered the race. There was a flicker of hope – an 11-match run with just one defeat: six wins, four draws. But the momentum didn't last. Inconsistency returned. The Hornets finished fourteenth. Nineteen defeats, 15 wins, 59 points – 40 short of City's title-winning tally.

Still, not everything was lost. 'We got through four rounds in the League Cup and only went out in the quarter-finals,' CEO Tim Shaw recalls. 'That's to say, there were positives as well.' There was a sense – even amid the frustration – that the groundwork had been laid. Veterans like Filippo Galli had brought calm and experience. With time, the three-year plan might have worked. And Gianluca certainly intended to see it through.

The season had been draining, yes, full of doubt and frustration. But he had a contract. He was prepared to honour it.

## 2. JUVENTUS, 1996

> 'I need to understand if I truly deserve to stay. Playing well is hard work, and I don't like the feeling of being merely tolerated.'
>
> GIANLUCA VIALLI

With the Scudetto stitched to his chest and Juventus marching towards the Champions League final, the spring of 1996 should have been a sweet time for Gianluca Vialli. Captain. Leader. The man at the heart of it all.

But it isn't. There's a restlessness in him. A shadow over his season.

It's the contract. The deal runs out in June. Roberto Bettega – the Juve legend turned club president – says the door at Juventus is always open. But there are strings. They want Gianluca to stay . . . only on their terms. Shorter deal. Lower wage. In July, Gianluca will turn 32. At Juventus, that number screams the end of the line.

The papers smell it. 'A restless Vialli,' they print. 'While the rest of the squad celebrate the present, he's wrestling with his future. Will he stay in Turin? Will he walk away? Will he even remain in Italy? England seems to be whispering to him. London, especially. Arsenal's name is floated.' But it's smoke – never fire. When Chelsea make their move, quiet at first, then sudden, the story will gather pace, fast and unstoppable – one clear direction, one new life.

But before the Blues, there's Glasgow Rangers. Real interest, not just rumours. Executives fly to Turin to meet with him. They sit across from Gianluca in a quiet room, Claudio Pasqualin at his side – for the first time in his career, Gianluca isn't carrying the weight all by himself. Until now, every move, every contract, every decision had been his and his alone. At most, he'd seek his father Gianfranco's advice. And *papà* Vialli, never an agent, never a meddler, would give his view without an agenda. But now it's different. Bigger. More complicated by the day.

Pasqualin gets to work straight away. Juventus sends signals. For Gianluca, the money matters, yes, but not as much as time. He wants two years. Juve offers one. Even Gianni Agnelli steps in. He has always been an admirer – of the player as well as the man. 'If he wants to stay, he stays,' Agnelli tells the press. 'It depends on him. 90 per cent.' Gianluca is pleased but doesn't commit: 'They asked me to renew the contract,' he discloses. 'I'm grateful for their trust, but since I don't like misleading anyone, I need to understand if I truly deserve to stay. Playing well is hard work, and I don't like the feeling of being merely tolerated.' Classic Vialli. Polite but pointed. A line that lands clean, sharp, and leaves the room just a little unsettled.

The situation is tangled. Gianluca isn't stalling. He isn't playing games. This isn't about squeezing Juventus for leverage. Before deciding whether to stay – before even talking numbers – he wants to know, needs to know, what kind of player he'll be a year from now. Gianluca has never chased money for its own sake. It isn't who he is. 'The financial side definitely won't be decisive,' he states. 'I don't have to make more money through Juventus. It'll come down to interests that must align.' In other words, it isn't about the zeros on the contract. It's about purpose. And knowing exactly where he stands.

What has always driven Gianluca Vialli is his place in football history. One can trace his entire club career through that lens. He didn't walk away from Cremonese at the first spark of glory. He stayed at Sampdoria until the dream was complete, until the biggest prize was theirs. Then he chose Juventus at the height of his powers – a club built to win, a place where trophies were always within reach. 'The desire is there. The passion, too,' he says when asked about staying in Turin. In the meantime, the fans have made their verdict clear. They chant his name. They wave their banners. They beg him not to go.

In the first leg of the Champions League semi-final in Turin, Gianluca Vialli finally scores his first European goal of the season. The Delle Alpi explodes. Thirty thousand voices lose themselves in joy. 'Stay with us,' they chant, again and again, the pleas running down the terraces like thunder. Gianluca can't block it out. More than once during the match, he raises his arms, wide and grateful, to the black-and-white ends of the stadium. 'I felt the supporters closer than ever tonight,' he says afterwards, his voice catching, just slightly. 'These things touch you. The respect and affection of the fans – it helps.' The respect is universal. Even the Turin press – owned, like Juventus, by Fiat – drops its usual caution and takes a side: 'The more time passes, the less sense there is in letting go of a leader like Gianluca.'

But by now, it's too late. Gianluca Vialli has made his choice. He's leaving. He's had enough – of Juventus, of the endless negotiations, of Italian football's suffocating politics. He sees the game changing. He understands the meaning – and the opportunity – of the Bosman ruling faster than most.

By mid-April, his position is clear. 'If we ever reach the point of separation, I just hope the Juventus executives behave, as they always have with me, with fairness and consistency,' he says. No drama. No bitterness. But no going back either. 'I don't want strange situations created,' he adds, 'the fans swayed one way or my cause used for other agendas. I only ask for sincerity and respect between gentlemen – the way it was at Sampdoria. Nothing more.' And with that, Gianluca Vialli's story with Juventus is, in essence, over.

All that's left now is one last fight. One last appearance. One last night. The 1996 Champions League final against Ajax. Juventus struck first. Ravanelli pounced and the Bianconeri were ahead. Ajax answered before the interval through Jari Litmanen, cool and precise. After that, the night tightened into a tactical arm-wrestle. Space vanished, every pass was hunted. Chances came in flashes, dangerous but fleeting. Neither side found the blow that could end it – not in the second half, not in extra time. Inevitably, it drifted towards penalties.

Gianluca knew that walk. In this same stadium he had missed against the United States in the 1990 World Cup. Two years later, he had even broken his foot taking a penalty against Roma. When the list of takers was discussed, he asked Lippi not to put him among the first five. If it came to a sixth, then he would go. Lippi agreed. In the end, it was not necessary.

On the pitch of the Stadio Olimpico in Rome, it is Gianluca who lifts the trophy. Captain. Champion. For a moment, it feels like the perfect ending. But when he steps into the dressing room, the air changes. The celebration stays outside. Inside, it's all different. Suddenly, it dawns on him. This was his last match with Juventus. Yet it's a world apart from four years ago at Wembley, after his last night with Sampdoria. Back then it was pure heartbreak. The end of a love story. Tonight, despite his hands on the Champions League trophy, it's another kind of ache. Colder. Sharper. He's given everything he had – and won. Yet, he no longer belongs.

'They say Vialli collapsed onto the bench in the dressing room,' the papers write the next morning. 'His eyes – empty, glassy – fixed on a white wall. He wouldn't speak or move. Not until midnight. It's his way to empty himself completely. To pour everything – heart, body, soul – into every gesture. Every victory. Even every defeat.'

## 3. WATFORD, 2002

> 'Luca was devastated . . . He came to Watford because he believed in the project. And a year later, we simply couldn't keep the promises we had made.'
>
> TIM SHAW

Suddenly, it was over.

At the end of the season, Watford parted ways with Gianluca – one year into a three-year deal. It wasn't strictly about football, it was also about finances. His chapter at Watford ended not with a bang, but with the flourish of an accountant's pen.

In the spring of 2002, ITV Digital collapsed. The broadcast revenue that had underwritten Vialli's vision disappeared overnight. Clubs across the First Division were plunged into crisis. Watford, like many, acted quickly. Ray Wilkins was the first to go. Then Gianluca. Their contracts were simply unsustainable. Vialli would end up in court to claim the two years' wages still owed to him. He wasn't alone. Across the league, high-profile managers – many on Premier League salaries – were quietly shown the door.

By now, Elton John had stepped aside as chairman. His successor, Graham Simpson, was blunt. 'We probably made an error in appointing Vialli,' he said. 'But not a footballing error – a financial one.' Watford had backed his plan – higher wages, top players, a modern staff, upgraded facilities. It was all part of a long-term strategy. But without the money, there was no strategy left. No forward motion. Just survival.

'If we could have afforded to keep Luca,' Simpson reflected, 'who knows what he might have achieved in another two years? He never got the chance to prove it, because we simply couldn't afford to keep him.' There was no bitterness. No scapegoating. 'Maybe, if we'd been wiser, we'd have done things differently,' he added. 'But everything we did, we did for the good of Watford. It was a gamble – and it didn't pay off.'

Tim Shaw, CEO at the time, still echoes that view today. 'If ITV Digital hadn't collapsed, I believe Luca would have stayed. At least until the end of his second season.' Beyond that, as always, results would have spoken. 'But I can say this categorically,' Shaw insists. 'The vast majority of the board wanted to keep him – if only we could have afforded to.' A year later, Shaw himself would be gone, too – another cost-cutting casualty. His role would never be replaced.

The players backed Gianluca to the end. 'Everyone's gutted to see him go,' said midfielder Gavin Mahon. 'It's really sad news. I haven't got a single bad word to say about him.' And then, a parting truth: 'Clubs don't give their managers enough time to build something. Maybe right now, they simply can't afford to.'

Regardless of the context, the support, the circumstances – Gianluca Vialli was hurt. 'I'm very disappointed by the decision of the club, especially as my work at Watford was still in the early stages,' he said. He couldn't shake the thought – Lippi had won the league with Juventus in his second season. Boškov had done it with Samp in his fifth. But he would never get to see his own project through.

For Tim Shaw, it wasn't just the sacking that stung. 'Luca was devastated – not just because he was let go. What really hurt him, and I'm sure of this, was that we, through no fault of our own, had gone back on our word. He came to Watford because he believed in the project. And a year later, we simply couldn't keep the promises we had made.'

Gianluca Vialli's experience at Watford was brief, challenging and ultimately unfulfilling, but not without significance. Reality proved quite complicated. The squad never quite clicked. His attempts to implement a more sophisticated, possession-based style clashed with the gritty, hard-working ethos the club had long embodied. Results faltered. Watford finished fourteenth in the First Division – well below expectations. Gianluca would later acknowledge the experience as humbling. Vialli always maintained that in life, as in football, you either win or you learn something. From his time at Watford, he walked away with lessons.

Though the results were disappointing, the episode revealed another side of Gianluca Vialli – a manager willing to step outside the elite bubble, to take risks and to learn from failure. He would carry those lessons into his later work with Italy's national team, into punditry and leadership roles off the pitch. Watford was not a triumph, but it was part of the journey. And for Vialli, even setbacks had value, if met with honesty and grace.

Two sackings in two years left Gianluca questioning everything. The truth had probably caught up with him. Gianluca was finished with management. Watford would be the last team he ever led. 'Maybe management was just too brutal a profession for someone like him,' said one who knew him then. 'Too much pressure. Too few moments of peace.' And so, at 37, he stepped away from managing.

Gianluca Vialli's greatest contribution to English football was possibly helping it grow – without losing its soul. He had arrived in 1996 at a time when the Premier League was still shaking off its rough edges. There was passion in abundance, but professionalism was patchy, and continental ideas were often met with suspicion. Vialli brought credibility, sophistication and a fresh perspective. As a player, he added class and experience. As a manager, he introduced discipline, tactical intelligence and modern preparation methods – nutrition plans, double training sessions, performance psychology. He helped turn Chelsea from a cup team into a club that believed it could belong at the top, and he tried to do the same at Watford.

But his impact went deeper than trophies. Vialli helped change the way English football viewed foreign influence. He wasn't just a 'foreign manager', he was one who adapted, who respected tradition and who earned the trust of players and fans. He showed that ambition and artistry could sit comfortably inside a club with working-class roots. That you could modernise without cleansing. He also humanised the role of the manager. He led with elegance, humility and humour – qualities that softened rivalries and set new standards. In many ways, Vialli helped English football embrace the future without forgetting who it was.

# PART TEN

# GRACE UNDER PRESSURE

## 1. LONDON, 2017

> 'I'm afraid of dying. I don't know what will happen when the lights go out. I don't know what's on the other side. But in a strange way, I'm excited to find out.'
>
> GIANLUCA VIALLI

It starts with a pain in his leg. Sharp. Constant. The kind you can't quite shake. The doctors call it sciatica – an inflamed nerve pressing against his spine. Nothing serious. Something manageable. But the pain won't go. Not after six days. Not after six weeks. Sleep becomes a struggle. Gianluca's weight begins to drop.

A second opinion reveals a hernia. Surgery follows. The procedure is a success, but the pain stays. So, Gianluca calls Italy's former star goalkeeper and long-time friend, Gianluigi (Gigi) Buffon. Gigi had missed part of the 2010 World Cup with a back injury. He knows people. Knows who to trust. He recommends a specialist. Gianluca books in for another operation. Again, the surgery goes well. Again, the pain lingers.

This time, he knows that something isn't right. There is something deeper going on, something no one has spotted yet. For the first time in his life, he feels truly helpless. Emotion wells up for no reason. Steps become hard work. He feels emptied. Hollowed out. 'It's so damn hard,' he says later. 'So hard that you feel finished.'

Then come the stomach cramps. The vomiting. The nausea. He can't eat. Liquorice becomes his last defence – just to keep something down. His eyes turn yellow. The sickness is total. He cancels his work with Sky Sports and flies to Italy for more tests. This time, the diagnosis is clear. And devastating. Pancreatic cancer. The same disease that took Luciano Pavarotti. Steve Jobs. One of the deadliest there is. 'I found out that pancreatic cancer is one of the worst cancers,' he would recall. 'So I was shocked, confused, helpless, hopeless.'

The doctor tries to offer hope. 'There are good chances,' he says. 'Good chances of what?' Gianluca thinks. And when the answer sinks in, he feels lost. Surgery is scheduled. Urgently. But Gianluca needs space. He retreats to Grumello Cremonese, to the family home, to a quiet apartment he'd kept for moments like this – moments where he needs to think. 'I manage to bring some order to my emotions,' he will later say. 'If there's one thing I've learned in life, it's how to prepare for the hard things.' And he does.

At first, he elects not to tell his parents. 'You feel that you are letting someone down,' he would explain. 'You don't want your parents to see you in a lot of pain. There is also all this shame. I've always been perceived as a tough guy. A strong guy with a lot of determination. To not be in that position made me uneasy.' When he does tell his parents, as always, his family closes in around him.

The five Vialli siblings remain close. His parents, now in their eighties, still anchor the family. Grandchildren, great-grandchildren – it's a full house. Gianluca makes a quiet promise to his father: 'I won't leave this world before you and Mum.' He tells himself: the Viallis are built to last. But still, he writes his will. 'And in doing so,' he reflects, 'I see everything in my life for what it really is – just things. But me, my wife, our daughters, my brothers and sister, my mother and father, my friends – we are so much more.'

The surgery goes well. Better than expected. Fourteen days in hospital become six. While Cathryn flies back to London to be with their daughters, Gianluca returns to Grumello. Mila, his sister, looks after him. 'She spoils me like we're still kids,' he says. 'And on some mornings, with the pale winter sun streaming through the curtains, it feels like time has never passed. Like I haven't lived a life yet.'

He returns to London before Christmas. The whole Vialli clan gathers in England. They surround him, Cathryn and the girls. There is warmth. Love. Light in the darkest time. Then, on Boxing Day, he and Cathryn decide it's time to tell the children. 'And as I speak to them, and they cry, and I cry,' he will say, 'I realise something. Cancer isn't this great enemy to be defeated. It's not a battle where I have to kill it. It's a challenge – to change myself.'

London is home now. It's where he and Cathryn have built their life. After Watford, he never returned to management. 'I realised there are things that are more fun and far less stressful than managing,' he once said. 'Let's just say I stopped for a combination of reasons. And there's also the fact that I got married – whereas before, I was married to football.'

His football brain had in time found a new outlet – television. As a pundit for Sky Italia, he's become a trusted voice. Honest. Clear. No-nonsense. He never forgot what it meant to be a player. For a while, he worked alongside Paolo Rossi – 1982 World Champion, boyhood idol. At first, it must have felt surreal. But managing? That door never reopened.

His name was mentioned often – Juventus, QPR, Sampdoria, even Cremonese. Always with hope. Always with affection. He was at one point linked with a bid to buy QPR, alongside Formula 1 boss Bernie Ecclestone and former businessman and Team Benetton sports manager Flavio Briatore. Nothing came of it. Same with Samp. And in Cremona, many hoped one day he'd return to rescue the club where it all began. But he didn't.

He stayed in London. In a red-brick house in Chelsea, with Cathryn, Olivia and Sofia. Stamford Bridge just down the road. On the Shed Wall, his image is the first one to greet visitors – etched into the bricks of a club he helped transform. Chelsea suits him. The tree-lined streets. The slow traffic. The river just beyond the rooftops. Coincidence or not, it feels familiar. The rhythm of the place, the quiet elegance, it echoes Quartiere Po. The neighbourhood of his childhood.

In London, Gianluca reinvented himself – this time as an entrepreneur. One of his proudest ventures is Tifosy. The name nods to the Italian *tifosi* – the fans – but the concept is forward-looking, quietly revolutionary. A company built to pioneer crowdfunding in professional sport. Once again, Gianluca Vialli is ahead of the curve. 'Our business is about giving football clubs the necessary finance to build something that is not just eleven players on the pitch but everything that goes with it,' he explains. In other words, 'our business is about making clubs more sustainable.' That was always his way. Not just the game, but the structures around it. Not just the team, but the vision.

Always one of the most respected footballers of his time, Gianluca was inevitably at the top of every official betting agency's list when sports betting became legal in Italy. Six-figure offers poured in. He turned them all down. Knowing how alien betting was to the Italian mindset, and how easily the process could become flawed and damaging, he chose to stay completely out of it.

When he realised, once and for all, that he would never return to the dugout, he did something else. He wrote a book. Not a memoir, not a retelling of medals and matches. That was never his style. He chose something harder – something he genuinely cared about. A subject that had fascinated him for years: the difference between English and Italian football. *The Italian Job*, he called it. A nod to his love for the now-iconic 1969 film and his appreciation of Michael Caine – style, wit and swagger, all things Gianluca admired.

Co-written with journalist Gabriele Marcotti, the book was sharp, funny and disarmingly honest. Less autobiography than cultural detective work, it explored how English football was a game of heart, pace and directness, built on passion and muddy pitches. Italian football, by contrast, was chess with boots on: tactical, cautious, obsessed with control. Gianluca didn't judge, he compared. He listened. He questioned why one nation feared losing while the other dreamed of winning. He spoke to players, managers, referees, fans. It was a conversation – one he hoped would outlast him. Maybe he was thinking back to that book by Sven-Göran Eriksson – the one he carried in his briefcase during his time at Watford. The one that shaped the way he saw the game. Now it was his turn. This wasn't about nostalgia. It was about analysis. Ideas. Culture. He wasn't managing anymore, but he was still thinking. Still studying. Still moving.

In January, treatment begins – two rounds of chemotherapy, punctuated by radiotherapy, at a hospital just around the corner from home. The diagnosis remains private. Very few know. Even his closest friends are told only part of the story. He says it's a hernia. Minor. Nothing to worry about. It's classic Gianluca. He doesn't want people's concern. Doesn't want to be seen differently. Doesn't want pity.

'I need to protect both myself and them,' he explains. More than anything, he wants to protect the image. Not the public one – the personal one. He wants to protect the way people look at him. Not as a patient, but as the man they've always known. Honest as ever, he adds: 'It's also a burden. People will call to show they're thinking about you. I thought that, instead of spending time on the phone, I needed time for myself.'

Even Roberto Mancini doesn't know the full story. Not at first. 'He never told me about his illness,' Mancini would later say. 'One day, he just said he had this problem, that he was getting treatment.' But there was no sadness in Gianluca's voice. 'He was thinking positively – because Luca was always a fighter. He was optimistic, and he told me, "I never told you because I didn't want you to suffer."' He hadn't told many people. For exactly that reason.

Surrounded by his family's love, Gianluca resists. 'I think a lot. I read. And the paradox is that I almost feel grateful for what's happened to me,' he says. 'It's a condition I would have gladly avoided, of course. But it gives me the opportunity to reflect, to reorganise my life – spiritually.' He knows the fear. Not just worry or discomfort. Real fear. The kind that closes around your chest and doesn't let go. 'The kind,' he says, 'that locks you in the bathroom, crying. The fear of not being able to say the words that need to be said.'

But Gianluca believes – fiercely – that the mind matters. That a positive mindset can shape outcomes. His doctor at the Royal Marsden Hospital in Chelsea, Professor Cunningham, agrees. That same neighbourhood, that same quiet stretch of west London where he and Cathryn have built their life, is now the frontline in the fight. This, like everything else in Gianluca's life, will be met with courage. With discipline. And with hope.

He begins to collect words – short thoughts, sharp truths, lines to hold on to. 'A goal without a plan is just a wish.' 'Dream as if you'll live forever, live as if you'll die today.' 'Falling down is an accident. Staying down is a choice.' He writes them down. Stores them. Lives by them. One day, they will become a book – not just about cancer, but about how to live when life stops going to plan. He pictures himself older. Still here. Still walking beside Cathryn. Olivia and Sofia, grown into young women. Daughters ready for the world. And the treatment begins to work.

'We portrayed ourselves as tough guys that could deal with anything without showing any weakness. But I now realise the power of vulnerability and that, actually, it can be a powerful tool to get inside people's hearts. It creates empathy – and empathy is everything,' he will confess. 'I'm not ashamed of saying we all cry – sometimes because we are scared. In my case I was crying because I was scared of the unknown. I did not know whether I was going to be fine or not. It's different than if you cry because you've lost a match,' he would reveal.

'I know now that you need to let out the pain,' he says. 'I wasn't particularly good at showing my emotions and I kept things inside. It's not good. Now I realise that whenever I want to cry, I cry. There's no shame. And if you want to laugh, you laugh. I try not to cry in front of people that might get very emotional. I try to cry by myself. When I'm in a comfortable place, I don't hold anything inside. I just let it out, and I feel better afterwards.'

When he feels strong enough, he returns to public life. At first, he covers up the weight loss – a jumper tucked under a shirt and blazer buys him time. But the face tells its own story. Gaunt. Drawn. Changed. The whispers start. The questions. What's happening to Vialli? Finally, he decides it's time. No more hiding. No more silence. And when Gianluca finally speaks, when he tells the world what he's facing, something shifts. Something bigger than sympathy. People see him – really see him. Maybe for the first time.

As a player, he had divided opinion. At Sampdoria, he was the rival. At Juventus, he was a target. Even with the national team, he never quite unified the nation the way others had. But now there are no sides. No rivalries. No colours. No debate. Now, there is only admiration. Not just for what he did, but for who he is. Gianluca Vialli. The man. The fighter. The example.

He refuses the language of war. 'If I saw this as a battle against cancer,' he says, 'it would probably destroy me.' Instead, he gives the disease a different role. 'I see it as a travelling companion – one I hope will eventually get tired and say: "Alright, I've toughened you up, I've taken you on a journey, now I'll leave you in peace."'

And something remarkable happens. The tribalism of football disappears. The club lines vanish. Cremonese, Sampdoria, Juventus, Chelsea, Watford – yes, those fans still feel something special. He is, after all, theirs. But now he belongs to everyone. In Italy, he becomes something else entirely – a national treasure. Abroad, across the footballing world, he is embraced as something greater than an icon. He is living proof of grace under pressure.

'Like everyone else, it hit me suddenly,' he says. 'And I faced it the way I used to face things as a footballer – by setting long-term goals.' The first? Not to die before his parents. To live long enough to walk his daughters down the aisle. Words that don't need decoration. Then came the short-term goals. 'The surgery. The recovery. The chemo. The radiotherapy. And then?' He smiles. 'A holiday in Sardinia – with a body worth showing off again.' Even here, even now, Gianluca Vialli finds a way to smile.

He never pretends to be fearless. 'I worked on it. I put myself in the right psychological condition to face it,' he says. People talk about his strength, about how brave he's been. But in an interview with Italian TV show host Fabio Fazio, he lays it bare: 'I have to tell you, I was scared to death. More than once. There were tough moments – but that's how it was.' Still, something grows from the pain. A deeper clarity. A shift. 'It's hard to say,' he admits, 'but I think this experience – one I would have gladly avoided – has made me a better person.' And with his usual grace, he adds: 'In all this bad luck, I think I've been lucky.' Cancer changes you, he says. It sharpens the way you see the world. 'You value things more – your family, your time. You reflect. You learn to take care of yourself.' And most of all: 'If it happens, you have to use it – to become a better person.'

There's wisdom in his voice. Not platitude. Not performance. Just lived truth. 'Illness isn't just suffering,' he says. 'There are beautiful moments, too.' It becomes a recurring theme whenever he speaks about this chapter. And still, it catches people off guard. 'Life – this isn't my quote, but I fully believe it – is 20 per cent what happens to you and 80 per cent how you react to it. And illness can teach you a lot about who you really are.' He pauses. Then finishes the thought. 'It can even be an opportunity.'

As always, Gianluca Vialli doesn't hide. He presents himself exactly as he is – open, unguarded, unafraid to speak plainly. No filters. No illusions. He shows his fears, his doubts, his weaknesses – because to him, strength has nothing to do with pretending to be invincible. 'I've been a strong player and a strong man, but I've also been fragile. And now, I stand before you with my flaws, my fears and my desire to do something meaningful.'

That honesty lands with real force. People admire his courage – not just for facing cancer, but for admitting he's afraid. There are no big speeches, no defiant soundbites. No false bravado. He doesn't know how this will end – and he doesn't pretend to. But bitterness never touches him. Nor does self-pity. He refuses to see cancer as an enemy. Instead, he treats it as a companion. A presence he didn't ask for, didn't want – but one that, now here, must be lived with. Understood. Endured. Even learned from.

What comes through is clarity. Dignity. And a depth of character the whole world now sees – not just in the footballer, but in the man. 'I now know that I have a duty – to behave a certain way towards people, towards my wife, towards my daughters.' Gianluca has come to understand something most only face much later in life: children don't just listen to their parents, they watch them. 'I'm convinced that our children follow our example more than our words.' And so, he accepts this new reality with care. 'I know I probably won't die of old age. That means I have less time to set an example. I hope to live as long as possible,' he says, 'but I feel much more fragile than before.'

That fragility sharpens his focus. 'Every action now makes me stop and think: "Is this the right example I'm showing my daughters?"' For Gianluca Vialli, being a role model isn't about dramatic gestures. It's about consistency. Perspective. The quiet lessons. 'I try to show them that happiness depends on how you look at life. I try to teach them that you shouldn't put on airs, that you should listen more and talk less, that you should improve yourself every day, that you should laugh often and help others.' And then, with the calm of someone who has come through the fire, he adds: 'In my view, that's the secret to happiness.'

He goes further. 'I believe the purpose of life is to find a purpose in life.' It's not something you stumble into, it's something you build. You choose it. You commit to it. 'When you find a reason worth solving problems for, worth getting angry or joyful about, it becomes much easier to feel that pull towards happiness.' But happiness, he knows, is not a constant state. It's not about smiling through everything. It's about depth. And contrast. 'I try to show my daughters that it's okay to be vulnerable, to cry, to be sad. You have to accept those emotions, absorb them – knowing that they will pass.' And then comes the truth that only experience can offer: 'After all, if you're never sad, how can you truly understand how beautiful happiness is?'

His mindset remains clear. Forward-facing. Defiant in the best sense. 'If you give up once, it becomes a habit.' Still, he doesn't deny what creeps in. The thoughts. The fear. 'I'm afraid of dying,' he says, simply. 'I don't know what will happen when the lights go out. I don't know what's on the other side. But in a strange way, I'm excited to find out.' And then, he reaches a realisation. Quiet. Profound. 'The concept of death exists to help us understand and appreciate life.' The urgency to live fully. The desire to finish what he's started. To make the most of every moment. These aren't burdens. They're gifts. 'In that sense,' he says, 'I feel very lucky.'

The call from the Italian national team comes at the perfect time. Gianluca Vialli, still fighting his illness in private, is invited to join the Azzurri as head of delegation. It means standing shoulder to shoulder with Roberto Mancini – his lifelong friend, now manager of the national team. 'It's an honour to be called up,' he says publicly. But behind closed doors, he's even more candid. 'I'm not well. But this has given me an unbelievable energy boost. I'm happy because I get to experience football again – the way I love it.' That love had never left him. And now, it lights up his days again.

At a reunion dinner with his old US Cremonese teammates, Gianluca appears as a surprise guest. Journalist Giorgio Barbieri is there. 'He looked physically unwell,' he recalls. 'But in that moment, I saw a happy Vialli.' Gianluca pulls him aside. 'The joy of representing the national team will help me in my fight against this illness,' he says.

His friends rally, as they always have. But time moves differently now. Even Mancini admits it: 'So much changed from that day – the hope that he would make it, the way time moved.' And sometimes, the emotions get the better of them. When that happens – when the tears come in public – the fear grows. Because with pancreatic cancer, everyone knows that survival isn't just about strength. It's about time. And luck.

The first battle ends well. The cancer retreats. The body responds. Victory would only come with time. But the first fight is won. Gianluca now undergoes full check-ups every three months. Finally, there's cautious optimism in London as in Cremona. Cold showers are, however, always just around the corner. By March 2019, the cancer has returned. 'We thought everything was going ok. And then, all of a sudden, you get a temperature. You go for a blood test, and they say: "Let's make sure there's nothing sinister. I found out then. It was back."'

'To be honest,' Gianluca says, 'I asked myself: "Did you really think you were going to get away with cancer that easily?"' 'The second time,' he confesses, 'was definitely tougher because it's the cumulative effect. I wasn't so strong and there was some despair. You're thinking: "Oh, my God, this guy is back."'

At the end of the year, after two separate nine-month spells of chemotherapy, he's given hope. Finally, he's declared cancer-free. 'They call it NED,' he explains. 'No evidence of disease. I'm perfectly aware it will take a while before I'm given the all-clear. Unfortunately, these things have a tendency to come back. But at the moment I am in a good place. I hope to stay in a good place until I die of old age.'

When the Covid-19 pandemic hits, Gianluca's in London. He spends the lockdown in his Chelsea home with Cathryn and the girls. His parents are in Cremona, a town hit particularly hard by Covid. Typically, his mind is with those who suffer. 'In London I only know two people that tested positive. Thank God I have not lost anyone I know in this country. But it's different in Cremona, where there are only 80,000 people. London has six million people. You feel it more in a smaller place. In a way I feel I should be there with my people. I felt so bad reading that people were dying in hospital without their loved ones. It's a tragedy.'

After the pandemic, Gianluca is better. The reality is a rollercoaster. Despite everything – resilience, treatment, optimism, love – pancreatic cancer is a cruel opponent. A relentless shadow. But there are moments. Small victories. Like one Sunday morning, when Gianluca takes a quiet walk through the fields of Grumello and visits La Beata Vergine della Speranza, the 18th-century chapel behind his family home. On Instagram, he posts a photo and a simple caption: 'The time of gratitude.' And then there are harder days. Months later, he admits: 'The unwanted guest is still with me. Sometimes more present, sometimes less.'

Whenever possible, he returns to Grumello. One wing is now his retreat – a peaceful apartment filled with light, books and quiet. He wants to breathe the air of home. He wants to be near his parents, his siblings, the grandchildren running through the hallways. He wants Olivia and Sofia to know this place – to understand where he came from, what made him, what matters most. And he wants time with friends. With some – especially the ones who've known him since those earliest days – he speaks openly. About the illness. The future. His hopes. His fears.

But he never gives up. He fights for himself, yes. But also, for those who see in him something greater – something enduring. 'I know I matter to others,' he says. 'They think, "If he can do it, so can I."' And so, he stays present. If you call and he doesn't answer, he calls back. If he misses you, he leaves a message. Always cheerful. Always full of light. One day, he sends a voice note to Marco Nicoletti – his old strike partner from the promotion-winning season at Cremonese. 'Ciao, Marco. Thanks for the message,' Gianluca says, warm as ever. 'Sending you a big hug . . . and also a bit of gratitude for all the goals you set up for me . . . even though I set up more for you!' Then comes the laugh. That unmistakable laugh – wide, alive, full of mischief. The kind that stays with you.

Then, in the spring of 2022, almost without warning, Gianluca sounds the alarm again. From the Italy camp in Palermo, where the European champions are about to face a crucial World Cup qualifier, he delivers a quiet but sobering message: 'I don't know how long I have left. There's no time to waste.' The words land hard. They're not shouted. They don't need to be. Everyone understands.

Weeks earlier, during a filmed interview with TV host Alessandro Cattelan on a golf course, Gianluca had already left what now reads like a spiritual testament: 'I try not to waste time. I tell my parents that I love them.' And then, with the calm of a man who's stopped pretending life is endless: 'I've realised there's no point in wasting time on bullshit. Do the things you love. Do what you're passionate about. The rest? There's no time for it.'

These words and the spring announcement catch everyone off guard. After Euro 2021, after standing side by side with Mancini and the Azzurri every step of the way, the feeling – carefully guarded but deeply felt – was that Gianluca had beaten this, too. That he'd done it again.

But the fight isn't over.

In September, Cremona welcomes back one of its own. US Cremonese, newly promoted to Serie A after 26 years, play their first home match. And there, in the stands at the Zini Stadium, is Gianluca. He wears red with grey trim – the club colours. The crest stitched to his chest. The cap pulled low, the same grey as his trousers. His face is thinner now, more lined. But the smile is there. The sun has kissed his skin. The old glint still lingers in his eyes.

Around him, familiar faces. Just a few seats away, Professor Mondoni, the man who taught him to dribble – though back then it was with a basketball. Heads turn. People nod, smile, wave. They remember. They always will. The young man who ran down this very pitch, who later became their pride, their champion. They still love him.

Then December delivers the blow. Midway through the month, a statement arrives. From London. Quiet, direct. Gianluca announces he's stepping down. 'After a long and difficult "negotiation" with my wonderful team of oncologists, I've decided to pause – hopefully just temporarily – my professional commitments, both present and future. My goal is to channel all my physical and mental strength into helping my body get through this stage of the illness, so that I can return soon, ready for new adventures to share with you all.'

A negotiation with the doctors – that's pure Vialli. Turning pain into something wry, something a little easier to carry. Always the joke to soften the blow. But anyone who'd seen him just weeks earlier – appearing in a special about the Sampdoria title-winning side of '91, or heard his voice crack on a Zoom call with the Juventus Champions League team and Marcello Lippi – knew the truth. The illness was back. Stronger. Closer. Those who loved him worried. Messages came in. The football world rallied. But this time, Gianluca – back in hospital – didn't answer.

Antonio Cabrini, family friend and former Italy teammate, found another way. He wrote him a letter, published it in *La Provincia* of Cremona. He remembered Mexico '86. 'That adventure wasn't too fortunate for the national squad,' he wrote. 'But it brought us back together, after those childhood years in Cremona. Our parents were friends. Among us kids, you were the youngest – the pup of the pack.'

In closing, Antonio delivered a note of hope. 'We Cremonesi are stubborn. Hard-headed. We don't give up. Back when I played,' he wrote, 'they called me "the one who keeps running even after the pitch runs out." Same goes for you, Luca. Keep running. Keep pushing. Because the pitch never ends.'

# PART ELEVEN

# HOUSE OF REDEMPTION

## 1. ITALY, 1988

> 'This group – these days – will stay with Vialli forever.'
>
> AZEGLIO VICINI

The announcement comes from Gabriele Gravina, president of the Italian Football Association. Gianluca Vialli is the new head of delegation for the Italian national teams. It's 11 November, 2019.

It didn't come easy. Gravina had to push, insist, coax. It took all his persuasion to bring Gianluca on board. Vialli hesitated at first – the weight of the role, the expectations, the timing, what it might demand of him, not just professionally but personally, the return to a stage he had once left behind. But in the end, Gravina gets his man. He knows that Vialli can bring not just stature but steel. And in tournament football, that can make all the difference.

Gianluca's new job, his first active role in football after leaving Watford in the summer of 2002 is to stand beside manager Roberto Mancini, to help guide the Azzurri. The old Sampdoria partnership is back. Two friends. Two leaders. Together again – this time, for Italy. Gianluca takes it in quietly, with gratitude. The national team has always felt like unfinished business – a chapter in a brilliant career that never quite closed. But this isn't the hour for regret. 'I am happy and proud to take on this role,' he says at Coverciano, the Azzurri's training ground, on his first official day. 'I also feel humble, because I know who has preceded me in this job – Gigi Riva.'

Riva, the legendary *Rombo di Tuono* (Roar of Thunder), speaks that day with calm authority. 'The right man for a delicate job,' he says of Gianluca's choice. 'He has been a champion, he has managed, he has worked as a top-level executive. Players, you see, can be fragile. It takes next to nothing to throw them off course. A leader who knows what to say – and more importantly, knows when to listen – is essential.'

Gianluca is moved. Those words, coming from Gigi Riva, carry weight. They come from a man he once idolised – from a voice that still echoes with the power of another era. Perhaps Riva doesn't remember now, but Vialli does: in his first season at Cremonese, it was Riva who first tipped him for greatness. A quiet word, a line in print, a belief placed early. To be welcomed now – not as a promise, but as a peer – feels like something closing. Not an ending, but a circle drawn clean.

---

Gianluca Vialli's personal story with the Italian national team was never an easy one – part pride, part pain, a journey lit by moments of joy but shadowed by the feeling that something had always been just out of reach. The ending – fractured, bitter, full of silences and sidelong glances with Arrigo Sacchi – is well known.

Yet the beginning had been electric.

Gianluca was just past 20 when he got the call for Mexico '86. The squad was stacked with the champions of 1982 – battle-hardened, world-class, untouchable. And yet there he was, the only fresh face among them. Not there as a favour. Not there just to learn. There to play. And when the Mexico World Cup ended in disappointment and the Italian Football Association cleared the decks, Vialli became the face of the rebuild. The goals started coming. The leadership followed, natural, as ever. In those first years after the reset, Gianluca didn't just lead the line, he led the team.

His golden spell came between 1987 and 1988. That was when he became the heartbeat of a side designed for one purpose: to win the 1990 World Cup that would be hosted by Italy. On home soil. Under pressure. In front of everyone. Some of Vialli's goals in that two-year period became the stuff of which legends are made – so too the courage it took to even try them.

In June 1987, in Zurich, Gianluca strikes twice in a 3–1 win over reigning world champion Diego Armando Maradona's Argentina. Officially, the first one is logged as an own goal – an Argentinian defender knocking it over his own line – but anyone who recalls the move, or watches the footage today, knows whose goal it really was. With today's rule, it would be assigned to Vialli without any discussion.

Gianluca takes the ball on the left, drives to the edge of the box, feints inside, then cuts suddenly wide. The defender is lost and can only chase. Gianluca now goes for the byline, skips past a second man trying to close him down, and drills a low diagonal shot across goal. The keeper is beaten, and another defender, scrambling back, only helps it in.

The second is just as decisive.

Two minutes from time, playmaker Giuseppe Giannini slips him a ball on the edge of offside. Gianluca charges again down the left of the box, defenders in pursuit, the goalie rushing out. With the outside of his foot, Gianluca pushes the ball forward, looking to round Nery Pumpido. The goalkeeper gets a hand to it, but the ball stays alive at Vialli's feet. He drives on and, with an enviable calm, slides it home past three desperate defenders – Italy's third seal on the match.

Both are goals in pure Vialli style. Goals of power and intelligence, where the brains work with the same speed, and finesse, as the feet. Two goals. One left foot, one right. Gianluca Vialli is honing his talent to its peak. He's becoming a leader. They still call it Vicini's Italy, from the name of the manager. Soon it will be Vialli's Italy.

Yet the goals that truly mark his early career with the Azzurri are those he scores between the autumn of 1987 and the spring of 1988. Some in matches decisive for qualifications to Euro '88. Others against one of the future finalists. Goals that leave opponents and spectators – and teammates – open-mouthed. Goals where Gianluca's talents match his instincts, his composure, his obvious belief in himself – the kind of belief that dares where others would never even try, for fear of failure.

His first brace comes against Sweden in Naples. It is the penultimate qualifier on the road to the 1988 European Championships in West Germany, and it is the night Italy secures their place at the event – at the Swedes' expense.

Gianluca wears the No. 11 shirt. He looks loose, confident, electric. The ease of execution leaves the crowd stunned. A ball is played long down the left. He cushions it with the outside of his right foot, keeps it moving, and drives into the box, shadowed closely by a defender. The angle's tight. Four yellow shirts are waiting. So is the keeper. Everyone expects a cross. He shoots. Not with his right – the foot that's brought him most of his goals – but with his left. And he barely seems to hit it. Just a smooth stroke, almost casual. The ball curls and climbs and smashes into the top corner at the near post. The net bulges. The crowd rises. Vialli keeps running, arms to the sky, socks rolled low at the ankle like a South American player – just the way he likes it.

Ten minutes later, Sweden equalise. Just like that, the momentum shifts. But Vialli isn't done. Not even close. He's only halfway through the job. Before the break, he seals qualification with another goal – this one even more outrageous. The assist comes again from midfielder Luigi De Agostini, who floats a high, looping ball that drifts over the entire Swedish back line. It looks like it's going nowhere. But before it drops, Vialli reads it. Times it. And meets it with his right foot, on the volley. He doesn't catch it clean. Not really. He hits it full-on, with the top of the boot. But it's a messy strike. The ball skips off the turf, rises again, and crashes against the underside of the bar before folding itself into the net. A goal that's part instinct, part violence, part luck.

Gianluca, true to form, plays it down. Modesty intact, he credits fortune – the blindfolded goddess, he says – for guiding his boots. If others see magic, he shrugs. If the crowd begins to dream, he cautions them gently. But the press isn't having it. The travelling writers, the veterans from Italy's great dailies – they've seen enough to know better. And they all write what Gianluca won't say himself.

'VIVA VIALLI' headlines the revered journalist Gianni Mura from the press box at San Paolo Stadium. 'Sweden remain a tough, awkward opponent, never to be taken lightly. But Italy now have something more – a kind of joyful recklessness that leads young Vialli to attempt two shots no sane man would try . . . and to score them both. Vialli is becoming, without quite meaning to, the leader of this team. He's a rare type: refined technique, powerful frame, and a hunger to play that sometimes carries him too far. In a country used to champions who hoard their gifts, we may need to get used to this new prototype – a player defined by uncontainable generosity.'

Gianluca Vialli doesn't fall for the trap of easy praise. He's too smart for that. Too grounded. He moves quickly to defuse the talk of leadership. 'It'll take three or four years at this level before I can be called that,' is as far as he'll go. Measured. Modest. Just enough to satisfy the press without giving the story any more oxygen.

He also waves off the comparisons to Gigi Riva, inevitable for any Italian striker. The symmetry is striking. But Gianluca isn't interested in symmetry. Not yet. And still, the signs are impossible to miss. He might not wear the armband, but he's already leading – in presence, in poise, in moments that matter. 'When people speak of the spirit of this team,' one Italian paper prints that week, 'these two goals will be remembered. You need real courage to even attempt them. And Vialli has it.'

After scoring in the final, now-meaningless qualifier against Portugal, Gianluca Vialli adds another brace to his growing collection – this time in Bari, in a friendly against the Soviet Union. It's 20 February, 1988. Three and a half months out from the European Championship. And while it's labelled a friendly, this one carries weight. The Soviet Union are no soft touch. Managed by the legendary Colonel Valeriy Lobanovskyi, they've just breezed through their qualifying group unbeaten. This is a proper test. And Vialli passes it – twice.

Italy take the lead in the 7th minute. Franco Baresi converts from the spot after Vialli, breaking through the Soviet defence, is taken down by the keeper. It's a clear penalty, no arguments. A strong start – but it doesn't last. Just before the 20-minute mark, the Soviets equalise with a free-kick. And then the match changes shape. Then comes the storm – Vialli's storm.

On the half-hour, Italy win the ball back near the Soviet third. Giannini is sharp, slides it forward to Vialli. Gianluca lets the ball run, shifts his weight, and with a stride into the box unleashes a right-footed rocket into the top corner at the near post. Power and precision. The Soviet keeper can only watch – just as his Swedish counterpart had done three months earlier – as the ball rips into the top of the net.

Five minutes later, he's at it again. This time, it starts with Fernando De Napoli – winning a duel at midfield and launching Vialli in behind. The No. 11 bursts between two defenders in white, stretching forward into a sliding finish. He stabs the ball past the onrushing keeper with the toe of his boot – cool, instinctive, unstoppable. It rolls in just inside the near post. The match is over. 'The good people of Bari rise to applaud – moved and grateful,' writes legendary sports reporter and author Gianni Brera that evening. 'At this rate, Luca from Cremona is charging into the Walhalla of Italy's great goalscorers – the last of whom, in time, was Luis Riva, the thunderclap.' The headline the next morning says it all: 'EVEN THE USSR SURRENDERS TO VIALLI.'

After his recent performances with the Azzurri – the braces against Sweden and the Soviet Union – Gianluca Vialli's star shines brighter than ever. 'His light is so intense now,' one journalist writes, 'that the blue shirts of his teammates risk fading beside it.' But this is Vialli. And that's not how things work around him. He scores, yes, but he always shares the glory. The squad knows it. Feels it. Loves him for it. They stay tight around him, not in awe, but in step. 'He's the best striker in the world,' says Roberto Mancini. 'He's a phenomenon. We're the supporting cast,' the rest of the squad chime in – proud, and hopeful for what lies ahead.

The rendezvous with destiny would come at Italia '90. But first, in the summer of '88, Vialli's Italy headed north to West Germany for the European Championships. The air feels charged – the sort of summer when everything hums with possibility. The favourites are elsewhere: the hosts, West Germany; the Netherlands of Gullit and Van Basten; the relentless Soviet Union. But this is a young Italy, vibrant and hungry. The whispers back home are cautious, superstition as ever keeping dreams on a short leash. Still, beneath it, there's quiet defiance. The Azzurri aren't flying to Germany as a sacrificial lamb. Not this time. Not with Vialli and Mancini – the *gemelli del gol* (the Goal Twins) – carrying the hope of a nation still young enough to believe.

The moment feels charmed.

Just months earlier, thanks to Vialli's goals, the Italian military team had been crowned world champion in their category. Confidence is flowing. The new generations look ready to take charge. Giuseppe Giannini, the elegant Rome playmaker who teed up Gianluca's first goal against the Soviets in Bari, doesn't hold back: 'Vialli is an extraordinary player – full of power, able to give the team that extra gear. We play to his strengths, and he scores. Franco Baresi, now the unquestioned general at the back, offers his verdict with the calm authority of a man who rarely gets it wrong: 'He'll be the star of Euro '88.' The stage is set. And Gianluca Vialli, about to turn 24, is ready to take Europe by storm.

Compared to today, the 1988 European Championships feel almost intimate – a tight, compact tournament. Just eight teams. Two stage groups. No second chances. No safety nets. The top two from each group reach the semi-finals, crossing over to face the best from the other side. Win that, and you're in the final. Five matches to conquer Europe. Italy landed in Group One, alongside the hosts West Germany, Spain and Denmark. Across the divide, Group Two looks almost brutal: the Netherlands, the Soviet Union, England and Jack Charlton's Ireland.

Italy opens their campaign against the Germans in the tournament's inaugural match. Never just another game, when it's played in Germany the weight of the match doubles. There are the usual rivalries, pride and old scars, but when it's played in Germany there's something else – thousands of Italian migrants in the stands waving flags, chanting louder, wearing their origin with pride. Men and women who came to Germany to build better lives for themselves, hopelessly longing for the place they left behind. For them, nights like this aren't just about football, they're about redemption. About proving something.

On the eve of the match, the tension is thick enough to touch. 'The urge to joke around is slowly disappearing,' Vialli states. 'This one against the Germans is decisive: if we win or draw, the path ahead gets easier. If we lose, it's uphill all the way.' Some journalists note how pale he looks, how his face seems drawn. Gianluca brushes it off. 'It's true,' he admits, 'I'm tense, I'm focused. None of us believe we will beat West Germany – yet, deep down, we believe.'

The *Daily Mail* states that Vialli is destined to become 'the Italian Bobby Charlton'. Coming from the English, it's the highest praise Gianluca could ask for. Back home, the expectations are no lighter. For well over a year, he's been hailed as the natural heir to Gigi Riva. And now – partly for the number on the back of his shirt at this European Championships – the latest comparison is with Paolo Rossi, who wore 20 in Spain six years ago. Never mind that their playing style couldn't be further apart.

Against West Germany the game finishes 1–1. The scoreline flatters the hosts. But taking a point off them, in their own stadium, is no failure. Mancini gets the goal – his first with the national squad. Gianluca battles for every ball. Tightly marked. Kicked, pulled, hacked at. Smothered for the whole 90 minutes. 'You can't always be the protagonist,' he says afterwards, calm, measured. 'In a lot of situations, fouls were committed on me and on some of my teammates, and the referee didn't call them.' He lets it hang, then shrugs it off, turning to the bigger picture. 'This isn't about individuals – it's about the collective. And tonight, Italy gave the answers everyone was waiting for.'

The goal that didn't come against the Germans arrives against Spain – and it's worth the wait. A strike straight from the Riva playbook, 'a moment of brilliance on an Ancelotti pass, with Altobelli's clever dummy opening the space.' Gianluca reads it early. He lets the ball glide across his body to the left. One touch. One opening. One superb finish. The goal doesn't just win the match, it all but books Italy's place in the semi-finals.

Young Italy impress with their spirit, their courage, the way they chase victory without fear. Gianluca has three clear chances. 'If I'd put them all away, I'd be a phenomenon,' he jokes afterwards, flashing a grin. But he's the match-winner regardless. The goal against Spain lifts a weight off his shoulders. 'I felt the responsibility so much,' he reveals the next day, surrounded by reporters. 'I couldn't sleep. My heart was pounding. I was afraid of letting people down. This goal – important, decisive – took that weight away. It freed me.' Before leaving the reporters to their stories, one request: 'Don't talk about Vialli's European Championship anymore. I don't accept being singled out ahead of the team.'

Even if they wanted to, the reporters covering the Azzurri this June in Germany couldn't stop talking about Vialli. Italy next beat Denmark 2–0 in their final group match and fly to the semi-finals. Despite three clean chances, Gianluca doesn't score. But he creates the opener – slipping Alessandro Altobelli what he himself calls a 'golden ball'. With three minutes left, De Agostini seals the win, finishing off another move born from Vialli's feet. And the next morning, inevitably, the headlines scream: 'IT'S ALL BECAUSE OF VIALLI.'

In the semi-final, the Azzurri face the Soviets – the same team they defeated in Bari that winter. The match takes place in Stuttgart, the city where Italy's 1974 World Cup campaign collapsed. Superstition still carries weight in Italy. But many believe this Italy – Vialli's Italy – is strong enough to defy even that. 'On the pitch where, 14 years ago, Gigi Riva – the king of Azzurri strikers – played his final match for the Italian national team, Gianluca Vialli, heir to "Thunderclap Riva", sits his Russian exam while dreaming of Munich,' the seat of the final, write the Italian dailies on the day of the match. Gianluca stays put, answering in his own fashion: 'Riva, with the chances I had in these first three games, would have scored more than one goal.'

In the semi-final, the USSR edge past Italy, but the 0–2 scoreline flatters them. At 0–0, Gianluca had two big chances, both missed by inches. Italy fall. But there's no shame. No collapse. This young side has announced itself on the European stage – and Gianluca Vialli is at its heart.

'Vialli,' says Italy's manager Azeglio Vicini at the end of the campaign, 'scored less than he deserved. But we leave Germany with proof of our quality, with international praise ring in our ears, and with the certainty that offensive football is the right way forward. This group – these days – will stay with Vialli forever.'

'It was a team made up of players who knew each other really well,' Gianluca would later recall. 'We'd played plenty of matches together at Under-21 level, and we were joined by more experienced players like Baresi, Ancelotti and Altobelli. There was joy, real happiness in being together. There was harmony. We were true friends, and what brought us together wasn't just the pride of wearing the blue shirt – which we wore with great humility. It was more than that.'

Gianluca is named by UEFA in the Team of the Tournament at Euro '88 – a nod to the impact he's made, even without the goals to match the headlines. By year's end, he places seventh in the Ballon d'Or voting. At 24 years old, already among Europe's elite. And everyone senses he's only getting started.

## 2. ITALY, 2021

> 'Roberto says that meeting up again with the national team makes us realise how much time has passed. I say this experience will make us feel young again.'
>
> GIANLUCA VIALLI

'The national team means being together again,' Roberto Mancini says after Gianluca is appointed head of delegation. 'And after so many years, that's a truly wonderful thing.' His old goal twin replies with a smile: 'Roberto says that meeting up again with the national team makes us realise how much time has passed. I say this experience will make us feel young again.' If only Boškov could see them now. He'd be proud of his boys – though he always said that, between the two, it was Vialli who had the numbers to be a great manager.

Gianluca stands with his head completely shaved. The battle with the unwelcome guest is still ongoing, and it shows. But this is a new day. A clean slate. And he means to live it fully. 'It is a prestigious role,' he says, 'one that lets me do what I've always wanted – stay in touch with young players and offer my experience as a player, coach and executive to them, to Roberto, and to the Federation. I have played around 80 matches for Italy, including with the Under-21s. I know what it means. It puts pressure on you, but it also gives you the chance to leave a mark – as men, even before as football players.' Then comes the glint in his voice, that old mix of hope and steel: 'I have won two bronze medals with Italy – at Euro '88 and at Italia '90. Let's hope we can do better.'

He slips on the navy-blue tracksuit and throws himself into it. A guitar appears, along with a guitarist. Gianluca pulls out his phone, reads the lyrics through his glasses, and starts singing Lucio Battisti's '*La Canzone del Sole*'. He's off-key, as always, but it doesn't matter. This is a ritual. And he's all in.

He always loved to sing. Being off-key never bothered him. Back in Cremona, as a student, he'd formed a band with his mates. Even as a star with Samp and the national team, he'd return to Grumello each summer, grab the drums, and throw a party in the park outside the family villa. In December 1990, when his world had caved in after Italy's World Cup debacle, RAI TV invited him on a popular variety show that stopped in Cremona for a week of live broadcast. He was invited on the Monday – his day off – and he needed no convincing. Mondays were always spent in Cremona in those days: a cocktail at Novecento, a sandwich at Ugo's, a chat with friends, maybe a stop at the Baldesio rowing club. At noon, on live TV from the Teatro Ponchielli opera house, he gave a wildly off-key but utterly heartfelt rendition of Claudio Baglioni's '*Questo Piccolo Grande Amore*'. Nobody cared. Least of all Gianluca.

Now, back at Coverciano, word gets around the dining hall that Vialli is singing. Players, kit men, physios, staff, waiters – everyone comes in. A chorus forms. They clap, they laugh, they all sing. Attilio Lombardo, now on Mancini's staff, records the moment on his cell phone.

Gianluca's role will be vital in this national squad. He's not the manager. He's not even the assistant. That job belongs to Roberto, assisted by the old Samp crew – Lombardo, Fausto Salsano, Giulio Nuciari, Alberico Evani.

Gianluca is the bridge between players and staff, between heart and head. He joins every training session, laces up his boots, runs beside the lads. It keeps him fit, yes, but more than that, it sends a message: I'm with you. I'm one of you. The walls come down fast. 'In this national team,' one journalist writes, 'Vialli is the charismatic leader, the head coach of minds, the motivator, the advisor, the confidant.'

His gestures are small but meaningful. Gianluca is building the kind of culture he once longed for when wearing that Azzurri blue shirt himself. The managers he admired most were the ones who could blend discipline with humanity. In this squad, Mancini is the authority. Vialli brings the touch. Gianluca even invents a tradition: the Gagliardetto ritual. Every new call-up receives a personalised pennant with their squad number. It's a borrowed idea – from England, the country that gave him so much. The handover is ceremonial. The entire squad attends. The senior players line up at the front. Gianluca speaks, softly but firmly, about what the shirt means. Then he hands it over. A keepsake. A reminder. A beginning.

Mancini's Italy soars. They qualify with ease for the European Championship. Then the world shuts down. Gianluca locks down in London with Cathryn and their daughters. Euro 2020 is postponed to 2021. And when the Azzurri meet again, Gianluca is still there in his new role. He is thinner, but his spirit is unchanged. The warrior has not surrendered. And he is more determined than ever to ensure this Italy doesn't either.

The tournament opens in Rome. Italy sweep past Turkey in the first match at the Stadio Olimpico. It's a strange edition of the Euros – games scattered across the continent, the final set for Wembley. But for Gianluca, the real story begins on the afternoon of 16 June. Italy are due to face Switzerland. The team bus is already rolling out of the hotel forecourt – doors shut, engine running. But where is

Vialli? The ever-punctual Gianluca has somehow been left behind. He waves, sprints, flags it down. The driver stops. The doors swing open. Gianluca climbs aboard. That night, Italy win 3–0.

It should have been a one-off. A minor mishap, a funny story for the team dinner. But football is a game of superstitions. Four days later, it happens again – only this time, deliberately. The bus rolls forward. Gianluca chases. Doors open. He steps in. Italy beat Wales. Three matches. Three wins. A new tradition is born.

By now, the choreography is set. Mancini boards first, then the players – Francesco Acerbi at the front, Gianluigi Donnarumma at the back. And just before departure, Gianluca, running to catch the bus, as if late. The routine is invariably the same. The mood on board is relaxed, focused, unified. The man who once led Sampdoria's frontline now leads in a different way. Quietly. From behind the scenes. As the Azzurri move from Italy to England, then Germany, and back to London for the final stages, the ritual continues. The bus pulls forward. Vialli arrives. The doors open. Only then does the journey towards the stadium begin.

Inside the squad, the bond is real. On the pitch and off it. Gianluca never steps on Mancini's toes. The tactics are not his job. He sings the anthem with the staff. He celebrates every goal. He turns his back, like the rest of the bench, during the penalties against Spain. He shares a glance with Roberto before every kick-off and after every final whistle. But his influence goes beyond the touchline. He is the presence that calms, the figure that inspires. His role isn't tactical – it's human. Emotional. Almost spiritual. He builds a space where the players feel safe. Grounded. Together. A squad, yes – but more than that, a team.

There's one final step to take now, the final match against the home team.

## 3. SAMPDORIA, 1992

> 'Even at 22, he was a leader. In his blood. In his brain.'
>
> VUJADIN BOŠKOV

The year after the Scudetto, Sampdoria crossed the Alps chasing the greatest prize of all – the European Champions' Cup. And waiting for them, like a shadow that refused to lift, was Johan Cruyff's Barcelona. A team blessed with brilliance – led by one of Gianluca Vialli's boyhood idols, now his latest obstacle. And, in many ways, his personal nemesis.

It wasn't their first dance.

Two years earlier, in the Cup Winners' Cup final, Barcelona had beaten them. The following year, Samp had exorcised that ghost – beating Anderlecht, with Gianluca himself scoring twice. But football, like fate, has a long memory. And it never forgets unfinished business. Vujadin Boškov's men would've picked anyone else. Anyone but Barça. Still, they came to Wembley unafraid. This was no fairytale team. This was a side built on steel and silk – Gianluca Pagliuca's hands, Pietro Vierchowod's muscle, Toninho Cerezo's brain, Mancini's genius, Vialli's fire. And character – above all, character. They had proved that in Sofia a few weeks earlier.

The group decider against Red Star Belgrade – played in 'neutral' Sofia – had become a battle far beyond the touchline. War had reached the Balkans. The match was moved to Bulgaria. The streets were tense. Samp's supporters were ambushed by Red Star's highly politicised ultras. A punch bloodied the team's masseur. Pagliuca barely dodged one himself. The air was thick with fear – sharp, metallic and close. Inside the dressing room, it threatened to boil over. Paolo Borea, Samp's sporting director and the architect of that splendid team, felt it in his bones. 'We feared another Heysel,' he said, still haunted by the deadliest night Italian football had ever known. 'Our wives were in the stands.'

Then Vialli stood up. Not to score. Not to shout. But to sing. He called them into a circle, clenched fists, locked eyes, and began belting out the Sampdoria anthem – loud, shaky, defiant. The others joined in. And suddenly the fear lifted. When they ran out onto the pitch, they played with heart, with hunger – with nothing held back. A 3–1 victory. A place in the final. Boškov never forgot. 'Even at 22,' he said years later of Gianluca, 'he was a leader. In his blood. In his brain.'

Now came the endgame. Wembley. Barcelona. Again.

This time, it had to be different. This was a once-in-a-lifetime chance – because back then, only league champions qualified for Europe's top competition. If you didn't win your domestic title, you stayed home. There was no second act, no safety net. And Samp knew it.

So did Barça.

They'd never won the European Cup, not once. That night at Wembley, both clubs played with history breathing down their necks. For all their flair, for all their talent, what weighed on them was not just the dream, but the fear of waking up. Barcelona looked at Sampdoria and saw an opponent they could handle. But the Blucerchiati? They knew better. They knew this was their moment, their reckoning. One last shot at something eternal. One chance. No repeats. No rematches. No regrets.

That night in May '92, beneath the old Twin Towers of the imperial stadium of Wembley, the air was thick with history and tension. This was no ordinary final. It was a clash between dreamers and giants – between a club that had dared to believe and one that had been bred for glory. And in that clash, Gianluca Vialli had his moments.

Twice, the match tilted in his direction. Twice, the ball dropped onto his right foot – the foot that had decided titles, lifted cups and broken defences across Europe. He needed no invitation, no extra touch. Just the instinct of a striker at the height of his powers. The first effort – a low, vicious drive – sliced past the post by a whisker. The second – a thunderous shot on the turn – shaved the bar with a sound only footballers recognise. The sound of what might have been. A game of inches. A night of heartbreak.

There were two matches that haunted Gianluca Vialli more than any others throughout his career. The first was in June 1983, still a teenager, playing for Cremonese on the final day of Serie B. Promotion to Serie A was within reach. Vialli broke free, one-on-one with the goalkeeper. He could have scored. Should have. But he chose to pass. The shot missed. The dream dissolved. He was young – maybe too young to shoulder the weight. He made amends a year later. More selfish now, more clinical. He carried Cremonese to the promised land.

But at Wembley in May 1992, there would be no sequel. That night marked the end of something rare and beautiful. The golden age of Sampdoria – the era of Vialli, Mancini and Boškov – reached its final chapter under the lights of Wembley. It was a tale of joy, of courage, of a club that dared to dance with the gods. But like all great stories, it had to end.

The European Cup slipped through their fingers. The Twin Towers of the legendary London stadium, once imagined as a gateway to immortality, stood instead as monuments to loss. Wembley – so long a dream – became for Gianluca a place of unfinished business. A sacred ground stained by missed chances. A wound that never truly closed. Not until Euro 2021. Not until he returned, older, frailer, but still standing.

And this time, Wembley gave something back.

## 4. ITALY, 2021

> 'The credit belongs to the man who is actually in the arena, whose face is marred by dust and sweat and blood . . .'
>
> GIANLUCA VIALLI

For Gianluca Vialli, the Euro 2021 final is more than a match, it's something personal, poetic and cruelly exact. A fixture drawn by fate with a sly, knowing grin. For 25 years, London has been his town. His refuge. His home. The place where he built a life, raised two daughters, and came to love a people who once stood on the other side of the touchline.

In earlier interviews, whenever Italy met England, Vialli never masked the conflict. He spoke with the same honesty that marked his game: 'Italy – but not as strongly as when Italy play another side, because I'm living in England, I've got friends here, and I love the people.' But now, in the final at Wembley; the pull of memory, the weight of history, the twin loyalties of heart and soil. For Vialli, this night is no ordinary contest, it's past and present colliding. Italy, his first home. England, the one he chose. And somewhere between the two, the man he has become.

This time it's different. Now he stands in the heart of the Azzurri setup, beside Roberto Mancini – his lifelong friend, his partner in triumph and trauma. And the final is played at Wembley, of all places. The very ground where, together, they had endured their greatest heartbreak of their careers. The wounds had never quite healed. The score had never truly been settled. Now it could be.

Two days before the final – Friday, 9 July – Gianluca turns 57. After lunch, he stands to speak. No fanfare. Just him, a small blue notebook embossed with the crest of the national team in his hands. A man about to say something more than motivational.

He begins to read. 'It is not the critic who counts,' he says, voice low, deliberate. 'Not the man who points out how the strong man stumbles, or where the doer of deeds could have done them better.' The room is still. Dozens of eyes are fixed on him. 'The credit belongs to the man who is actually in the arena, whose face is marred by dust and sweat and blood . . .'

The words sweat and blood are caught in his throat.

He stops.

A flicker of silence. He tries again. His voice cracks.

He isn't just speaking to the players anymore, he's speaking to himself. To the battles he'd fought. To the pain he'd carried. To the boy from Cremona. To the man who never backs down. His tears stay unshed – but only just. In that moment, Gianluca Vialli gives the Italian squad more than a speech. He gives them his heart.

The room is thick with emotion – too much to hold in. Someone calls out, a voice from the heart, offering Gianluca strength. It breaks the silence like a match struck in the dark. These players – grizzled veterans, rising stars, men trained to steel themselves in battle – are undone. They love him. Not in the abstract, not out of duty. They love this man who has led them without grand gestures, who has shown them that strength and fragility are not opposites, but companions. That true courage can walk hand in hand with tears.

Gianluca steadies himself. He breathes. Finds his voice. And reads on.

'The man who strives valiantly; who errs, who comes short again and again, because there is no effort without error and shortcoming; but who does actually strive to do the deeds; who knows great enthusiasms, the great devotions; who spends himself in a worthy cause; who at the best knows in the end the triumph of high achievement, and who at the worst, if he fails, at least fails while daring greatly. So that . . .' His voice falters again, but he keeps going, shoulders squared, '. . . his place shall never be with those cold and timid souls who neither know victory nor defeat.'

The words are not his, but they might as well be. They belong to Theodore Roosevelt – the first President Roosevelt, the Rough Rider, the fighter. He didn't write them from the heights of power, but from the trenches of reflection. They came after the presidency, after the cheers faded. After the triumphs and amid the scars. They came as he prepared for one last doomed charge – his attempt to return to the White House in 1912. A battle he knew he would likely lose but charged into anyway. Because that's what warriors do. And Gianluca Vialli – today, in this room, with this team – is nothing less than that.

After a moment like this, the Azzurri cannot fail. And they don't.

The final goes to penalties. Again. Vialli turns his back. He cannot bear to watch. Not out of fear, but out of love. Superstition. Hope. And then – it's done. Italy wins. And Gianluca turns. Into the arms of Roberto Mancini. That embrace – God, that embrace. It says everything without a single word spoken. About their friendship. About the years. About Wembley, then and now. About what was lost. And what, finally, was found. It is real. It is raw. It is theirs. Even with millions watching. Even with the world leaning in. Some things remain sacred and utterly personal.

## PART TWELVE

# HERE COMES THE SUN

> 'A gentleman in life, a warrior on the pitch.'
>
> CISO PEZZOTTI

'I was lucky,' Gianluca Vialli always maintained. 'Some people say that to be successful, you need to find out early and clearly what you want to do in life. Well, when I was three years old, someone kicked a ball to me. I kicked it back – and I knew. I knew that's what I wanted to do for the rest of my life. I was lucky because I got to do what I loved. I earned good money, had success, met incredible people. I lived in Cremona, in Turin, in Genoa, and then in London. I couldn't have asked for more.'

Wherever he went, he left a trail of affection. In Cremona, Genoa, Turin and London, the reasons were etched in silverware – titles, cups, the weight of history. But that's only part of the story. Even where his time was perhaps cut short, the memory of him lingered, warm and intact. 'With Chelsea fans, I had a fantastic relationship. We fell in love with each other,' he was proud of saying. 'They never stopped encouraging me and when I became the manager, the love and the passion went on. I remember once we went to Old Trafford and we beat them 2–1. I happened to score very close to where our fans were sitting, so I ran towards them, and they became even louder. It was a wonderful feeling. You are basically an extension of the fans on the pitch. You are one of them wearing the shirt of the team you are playing for.'

'The first Italian to manage in the Premier League had won everything in the club game by the time he moved to London in 1996. He became a star of the English game, too, winning fans with his pugnacious style of play, later with his urbane personality. His time at Chelsea was an era of new influences and excitement and Vialli embodied it. He was adored for his demeanour: a class and style that was engrossing and novel, his gregariousness and the endearing attempt at using English idioms,' reported the *Guardian*; that would never be forgotten.

'He got a lot from his career,' says one reporter who'd followed him from the boy with promise to the man who reached the stars. 'And everything he got, he earned. No one handed him anything. He took his chances when they came. I don't think he finished his career with any real regrets. Yes, maybe in the national team, he didn't have much luck – Schillaci got in his way at the wrong time. But that's football.'

That – if anything – was the only wound left open. The Azzurri shirt never seemed to fit quite right. It tugged at him. A regret perhaps soothed by Italy's triumph over England at Wembley. The same Wembley where, in 1992, shoulder to shoulder with Mancini, he had fallen short with that brilliant Sampdoria side shaped in their image. Half of them were there again, now in Azzurri suits and tracksuits, standing behind a new generation. But still – a regret. 'I wish I'd played in a World Cup and been a success,' he once admitted. 'I was happy with what I did at Mexico '86 because I was only 20 and I played all the matches, even though it was always as a substitute. But then,' – he paused, sighed, 'in 1990 everyone blamed me for Italy not winning the World Cup because expectations were so high.'

Ciso Pezzotti, who knew Gianluca as well as anyone ever did, summed him up in a sentence: 'If I had to describe Luca Vialli in just a few words, I'd say – a gentleman in life, a warrior on the pitch.' Italy had fallen for him early. And yet, in a very peculiar way, his home country never fully understood him – not the way Genoa did, anyway. It was England that perhaps saw him most clearly. 'Luca Vialli was one of those players who transcend the clubs they played for,' says an English writer today. 'A very rare phenomenon. One of those characters football produces once in a generation – sometimes even skipping one.'

By the time the trophy was packed and the squad had boarded the plane for Rome, Gianluca lingered behind. He had pushed his body further than most knew over the course of the tournament. The Euros was won. But for him, this was only one of two battles. As London stirred awake, he sat in the back of a car, watching red buses roll out across the city. The platforms at Paddington were crowded again. The newsstands screamed of Italy's glory. But in the quiet, he felt the tug of something more personal.

Off the pitch, London gave him a life that extended far beyond football. It was here he had built his family. His daughters were born in London. He built friendships, launched businesses and, later, even tried television. He had a house, a bike and a corner café. In the mornings he first read *The Times*, then *La Gazzetta dello Sport*. He felt safe here, at ease. 'I'm Italian,' he once said, 'but London is home.'

Even after his time at Chelsea ended, Vialli stayed. He could have gone back to Italy, taken up another club, accepted the revolving door of Serie A. But he didn't. He remained in London, choosing the life he had built, even as the spotlight faded. When the headlines stopped calling, he didn't leave. Because it wasn't about attention – it was about belonging.

Later, when illness came, London became something else: a fortress. It was the city where he faced cancer. In interviews, he described how grateful he was for the privacy and dignity that London afforded him. 'Here,' he said, 'I can be vulnerable without being defined by it.' He underwent treatment at the Royal Marsden Hospital in Chelsea. He walked the streets when he could. He lived as best he could, with courage and grace. The city that had welcomed him in strength now embraced him in struggle. His last professional chapter brought him back to the Azzurri bench, but it was from London that he flew to Coverciano. From London that he packed the suits and notes. From London that he carried the resolve.

Gianluca Vialli would die a Londoner. Not because he stopped being Italian – he never did – but because he let the city into his heart. It was the place that let him breathe, laugh, love. The place that gave him space to be complex, flawed, real. The place that let him live fully. It wasn't the glamour. It wasn't even the football. It was the freedom to be the best version of himself – without noise, without pressure, without masks. In return, he gave the city his honesty, his elegance, his soul.

This morning, on the day after Italy's triumph at Wembley, Gianluca feels the urge to walk. He longs for some solitude. He asks the driver to stop around the corner. He wants to breathe. To absorb what's just happened. To let it settle, quietly, within him. Italy had only won the European Championship once before, in 1968. He was four then, just beginning to chase a ball around the courtyard, still young enough to believe in magic. Professor Maurizio Mondoni, who coached him at mini basketball during his primary school years, still believes today that Gianluca Vialli would have made it in any sport he'd chosen. Gianluca always saw it differently. 'If I hadn't become a professional footballer,' he once said, 'I would have been an architect and worked with my father.'

Now, as he turns onto his home street, something stirs – not the roar of stadiums, but the hush of childhood. The sycamores cast their long, familiar shadows. And in them, he glimpses another street. Another set of trees. Quartiere Po, in Cremona. The Belsit café across from Monteverdi Elementary. A boy with a KitKat in one hand, football stickers in the other. Dreaming – though utterly convinced it would never be real. 'Sometimes, when I look at old photos, old footage, even old football stickers, I think about when I was a kid, dreaming of becoming like Boninsegna, my idol,' he once said. 'And I remember how sure I was that I'd never make it. I thought it was almost impossible to become a professional footballer.'

And yet, he had. He had done it all.

The boy who lifted Cremonese, the young man who delivered the Scudetto miracle at Samp, the leader who conquered Europe with Juventus, the architect of Chelsea's first golden era quickly reaches his door. Inside, Cathryn, Olivia and Sofia are still sleeping. The hush of early morning wraps itself around the house like a soft blanket, part silence, part grace. He is spent – body aching, spirit worn thin. Not only from the long nights and the weight of the tournament, but from the deeper battle he carries within. The one no matchday crowd could see.

But for now, his duty is done. He has turned down the parade in Rome. Skipped the reception at the Quirinale with the President of Italy. He has chosen this instead: this quiet street, this front step, this stillness. The place where love lives. The three girls who give him reasons, even when strength runs low. On this cool midsummer London morning, life can still be beautiful.

# AFTERWORD

When this book reaches its final page, what remains is, hopefully, not a list of trophies nor a sequence of matches replayed by memory. What remains is a presence. Gianluca Vialli's legacy does not reside only in what he won – though he won a lot – but in how he moved through football, and life, leaving things subtly altered behind him.

Vialli arrived in England at a moment when English football itself was changing. The game was rediscovering Europe, opening its door to new ideas, new habits, new ways of thinking. He did not arrive as a conqueror, nor as a foreign star asking to be indulged. He arrived with curiosity, humility and an uncommon intelligence for the world he was entering. He listened, learned and then, quietly, began to lead.

His influence was never purely tactical, though he understood the game deeply. It was cultural. He brought with him an Italian sense of preparation, of detail, of collective responsibility, but he never imposed it. Instead, he translated it. He adapted it to English football's rhythms, traditions, dressing rooms. In doing so, he helped build a bridge between two footballing worlds that had long looked at each other with suspicion, sometimes even with prejudice.

As a player, he embodied generosity. As a manager, he embodied trust. He believed in people often before they fully believed in themselves. He demanded standards, but never theatrics. Authority for him did not need to be raised, it was simply exercised. Those who played with him or for him often speak not of fear but of respect, not of orders but of conviction.

Beyond football, Vialli really represented something rarer still: a way of being. He showed that ambition and kindness are not opposites. That competitiveness does not require cruelty. That leadership can be firm without being loud. In an era increasingly dominated by image, he remained stubbornly authentic. He did not perform himself; he *was* himself.

This book has followed him across borders – geographical, sporting, cultural. But in truth, the most important journey he made was always inward. Gianluca Vialli never stopped questioning himself, refining himself, learning. That restlessness, that refusal to settle into a finished version of who he was, may be his most enduring lesson.

For English football, he was not simply a successful foreign import. He was part of a broader evolution: proof that openness enriches rather than dilutes, that exchange strengthens identity rather than erasing it. For Italian football, he was a reminder that tradition is not something to defend by closing ranks, but something to carry with confidence into the world.

And for those of us who knew him, or simply watched him closely, he leaves behind a quieter inheritance: the sense that decency still matters, that intelligence still counts, and that grace – on and off the pitch – is never out of fashion.

# CAPTIONS

**AUTHOR NOTE**
Gianluca Vialli during the September 1996 Premier League match between Chelsea and Nottingham Forest at Stamford Bridge, London. Photo by David Gadd/Sportsphoto/Allstar via Getty Images

**LONDON**
Ruud Gullit and Gianluca Vialli present the Chelsea #9 shirt, 1996 – The beginning of a partnership that would soon prove as transformative as it was, at times, turbulent. Photo by Alessandro Sabattini/Getty Images

**GREAT EXPECTATIONS**
Gianluca Vialli controls the ball at Old Trafford, 2 November, 1996 – A moment of balance, imagination and technical daring that reflected both his football prowess and the expectations that followed him to England. Clive Brunskill/Allsport

**FAULT LINES**
Gianluca Vialli on the ground – An image that came to reflect a difficult spell, as fault lines began to emerge in his relationship with Ruud Gullit. Photo by Mark Leech/Offside via Getty Images

**IN CHARGE**
Gianluca Vialli lifts the Champion's Cup in Rome, 22 May, 1996 – A defining triumph that would soon shape the authority he carried into a new adventure and, later, a new role. Photo by Alessandro Sabattini/Getty Images

**FORTUNE FAVOURS THE BRAVE**
Gianluca Vialli with the Football League Cup (Coca-Cola Cup), March 1998 – A reward for bold decisions and a reminder that, at Chelsea, courage had begun to find its own fortune. Photo by Mark Leech/Getty Images

**COOL HAND LUCA**
Gianluca Vialli celebrates with Roberto Mancini, Genoa 1990 – Composure, instinct and quiet authority already visible in the player he once was, and in the manager he would become. Photo by Image Photo Agency/Getty Images

**ALONE**

Gianluca Vialli leaves the pitch at Valley Parade, August 2000 – He became increasingly isolated, as tensions with the Chelsea hierarchy began to close in around him. Gary M Prior/Allsport

**BELONGING**

Gianluca Vialli with Cremonese in 1983 – A return to where it had all begun at a time when questions of belonging came back into sharp focus. Photo by Image Photo Agency/Getty Images

**LESSONS IN YELLOW**

Gianluca Vialli at Watford – A brief chapter that carried both promise and disappointment, where lessons of the past returned with a sharper edge. Phil Cole/ALLSPORT

**GRACE UNDER PRESSURE**

Gianluca Vialli – A quiet strength in the face of adversity, where grace, more than ever, became a way of being. Photo by Chris Brunskill/Fantasista/Getty Images

**HOUSE OF REDEMPTION**

Roberto Mancini and Gianluca Vialli celebrate at Wembley, July 2021 – A moment of redemption, where a place once marked by defeat became, at last, the setting of fulfilment. Photo by Alex Morton – UEFA/UEFA via Getty Images

**HERE COMES THE SUN**

Gianluca Vialli celebrates for Chelsea, January 1999 – A moment of unguarded joy that captured both the player and the man, and the light he carried with him. Graham Chadwick /Allsport

**AFTERWORD**

Gianluca Vialli in motion for Chelsea, September 1996 – A career defined by intelligence, intensity and grace, carried from Cremona to London and beyond. Photo by Richard Sellers/Sportsphoto/Allstar via Getty Images

# FURTHER READING

Beppe Severgnini, *An Italian in Britain* (BUR Biblioteca Universale Rizzoli, 2003)

Fabio De Masi, *La Bella Stagione* (2025)

Gianluca Vialli, *Goals: Inspirational Stories to Help Tackle Life's Challenges* (Headline, 2020)

Gianluca Vialli and Gabriele Marcotti, *The Italian Job: A Journey to the Heart of Two Great Footballing Cultures* (Bantam Press, 2006)

Sven-Göran Eriksson, Willi Railo and Hakan Matson, *Sven-Göran Eriksson on Football* (Carlton Books, 2001)

Sven-Göran Eriksson, Willi Railo and Hakan Matson, *Sven-Göran Eriksson on Management: The Inner Game – Improving Performance* (Carlton Books, 2002)

# A NOTE ON SOURCES

The sections devoted to Gianluca Vialli's years in England draw on contemporary reporting and later analysis published primarily by the *Guardian*, *The Independent*, *The Times*, *The Observer*, *The Daily Telegraph* and the BBC, including match reports, features, interviews and televised material. Further sources include a few websites dedicated to football history and culture.

For the years preceding his move to London, this book relies on articles, match coverage, interviews and commentary from *La Gazzetta dello Sport*, *La Stampa*, *Il Corriere della Sera*, *La Repubblica*, *Il Corriere dello Sport*, *Guerin Sportivo*, as well as archival material and broadcasts from RAI, Mediaset and Sky.

For the earliest phase of Gianluca Vialli's career in Cremona, particular reference was made to local reporting by *La Provincia* and *Mondo Padano*, whose articles and chronicles provide invaluable insight into his formative years. This section is also informed by first-hand material, including one of Gianluca Vialli's earliest interviews – published in *Avvenire* in the spring of 1982.

In addition to published sources, this book is also based on original interviews conducted by the author with former players, teammates, managers, club officials, journalists, friends and family members. The names of most interviewees appear in the text itself and are listed in the Acknowledgements on pages 262–3. Some of Gianluca Vialli's quotes are taken from his two books, *The Italian Job*, and *Goals*. For the Scudetto season with Sampdoria, a great source of information was the book *La Bella Stagione* by Gianluca Vialli and Roberto Mancini.

# BIBLIOGRAPHY


## Part One

### 1. CHELSEA, 1996

**English football has always been my obsession**
*La Repubblica*, 18 June, 1996

**an emigrant with a Vuitton suitcase**
Ibid.

**His arrival was the start of something thrilling for English football**
Author's conversation with Amy Raphael, 6 March, 2024

**Luca had just won the Champions League and was a charismatic player, a leader of men**
Author's conversation with Rick Glanvill, Chelsea FC official historian, 7 March, 2024

**cost relatively little but brought immense value in terms of skill, leadership, quality and personality**
Author's conversation with Rick Glanvill, Chelsea FC official historian, 7 March, 2024

**Gentlemen, we talk Chelsea. No Juve, no Italian national team, not a word**
*La Stampa*, 18 June, 1996

**Since he arrived … it has become oppressive, obsessive**
Ibid.

**We can win, but in the way they like it here … by getting the very best out of ourselves.**
*La Repubblica*, 18 June, 1996

**He was a beautiful soul, an Italian man with great charm … he was curious about the world around him**
Author's conversation with Amy Raphael, 6 March, 2024

**When I got here, Hoddle told me I was needed to shake things up … I just hope he helps the team grow**
*La Stampa*, 18 June, 1996

**I can finally have a normal life. In London, no one bothers you on the street**
*La Stampa*, 12 June, 1996

**He was happy to be just another person, not recognised, not stopped in the street. Except by Italian fans, of course!**
Author's conversation with Amy Raphael, 6 March, 2024

### 2. CREMONA, 1964–1980

**I grew up in the Quartiere Po neighbourhood in Cremona. I played football in the courtyard.**
*La Provincia*, 17 December, 2021

**Even after years in London, Vialli carried a deep, almost instinctive bond with his homeland and his people … never forget where they came from.**
*Corriere della Sera*, 7 January, 2023

**I'm proud to be called a provincial ... It helped make me the man I am.**
Gianluca Vialli, interview on the occasion of the fifth anniversary of the Pro-Cremona Association, 2021

**Luca was always three, four steps ahead of everyone else ... You knew he would make it big.**
Author's conversation with Fabrizio Frittoli, 4 August, 2023

**My parents helped me keep my feet on the ground**
BBC, Emotional Tribute to Vialli, 6 January, 2023

**I had worked out a system ... while we played, we did the commentary ourselves**
Contrataque.it, 2 April, 2016

**We were all really good**
*Mondo Padano*, 21 June, 1982

**I was always a forward ... one who liked to roam across the attack**
Gianluca Vialli, *The Italian Job*, page 19 (Italian edition)

**We pounded the wooden garage doors with our shots ... calling out the plays like we were in a World Cup Final.**
*Mondo Padano*, 21 June, 1982

**During the '78 World Cup, whenever Argentina played, we'd rush outside right after the game, fired up from watching them on TV**
Author's conversation with Fabrizio Frittoli, 4 August, 2023

**We could play from four in the afternoon until dinner time ... again from 8.30 to 9.30 in the evening.**
Ibid.

**Sometimes the ball would fly off ... we'd all pitch in and buy a new one**
*Mondo Padano*, 21 June, 1982

**My brother and I spent hours practising bicycle kicks ... it wasn't a coincidence that acrobatics became one of my trademarks.**
Gianluca Vialli, *The Italian Job*, page 19 (Italian edition)

**Sometimes, we'd play against teams from the San Pietro parish ... wasn't afraid to, not even as a kid**
Author's conversation with Fabrizio Frittoli, 4 August, 2023

**Fausto was the first to get me and Luca Vialli into the Cristo Re tournament ... I played at the back wearing a No. 5 jersey. Luca, of course, was up front.**
Ibid.

**The 'kids' were really good ... But those two – those two were the real deal.**
Author's conversation with Fausto Melgari, 26 September, 2023

**The first years of my ministry at Cristo Re were a whirlwind ... but deeply felt by the kids and their families alike.**
A contribution by Don Angelo Scaglioni to the parish book *Santa Chiesa di Dio che cammini nel tempo, 50 Years of the Cristo Re parish*, 2009

**If you brought your own ball ... getting it back at the end of the day wasn't that easy**
Author's conversation with Fabrizio Canesi, 18 October, 2023

**That day, we decided to climb over the back fence ... Both of us sent home until the next day**
Author's conversation with Fabrizio Frittoli, 4 August, 2023

**It was probably the only 'life lesson' that was ever explicitly taught to me on a football pitch**
Gianluca Vialli, *The Italian Job*, page 58 (Italian edition)

**He ran straight at me ... whether it goes your way or not.**
Ibid.

### 3. CHELSEA, 1996

**No regrets about leaving Italy. English football has always been my dream.**
*La Stampa*, 10 July, 1996

## PART TWO

### 1. CHELSEA, 1996

**I'm here to win. Not just matches, but respect**
Ibid.

### 2. SAMPDORIA, 1984

**It was the end of the 1983–84 season … Sampdoria president Paolo Mantovani was there, too**
*Sampdoria News*, 'Vialli e la Sampd'oro', 13 April, 2011

**A lot of scouts had come to see him … Go ahead, give him to Mantovani**
*La Stampa*, 26 August, 1995

**I don't think he was ready for Juve yet … his decision was well thought out and, ultimately, the right one**
Author's conversation with Marco Nicoletti, 20 July, 2023

**Looking back, Gianluca made the right call going to Sampdoria rather than Juve … he wouldn't have had at a big club – attention.**
Author's conversation with Giovanni Ratti, 25 September, 2023.

**We were lucky because we had a president who didn't worry too much about the cost of players … One of those players was Luca**
Author's conversation with Alessandro Scanziani, 19 March, 2024

**Luca was a humble young lad … was a player with real quality, and he was going to go far**
Author's conversation with Ivano Bordon, 20 March, 2024

**He arrived as a young and ambitious forward from Cremonese … making a key contribution**
Author's conversation with Ciso Pezzotti, 10 December, 2023

**When Bersellini arrived as coach … who were strong both physically and technically, it was a matter of waiting for their turn**
Author's conversation with Alessandro Scanziani, 19 March, 2024

**Bersellini wanted to get to know him first … and then, of course, there was his technique**
Author's conversation with Ivano Bordon, 20 March, 2024

**At the start, I was the regular alongside Francis, and Mancini was the backup … I don't intend to get off this rollercoaster**
*La Stampa*, 10 October, 1984

**A likable guy, quick-witted, well-read and mature in his judgment**
*La Stampa*, 26 February, 1985

**He was a great person, even before he was a great player … did it so that the fans wouldn't whistle at me**
Author's conversation with Alessandro Scanziani, 19 March, 2024

**We could be fighting for the Scudetto right now if Bersellini had put Gianluca Vialli in the team at least a month and a half ago**
*La Stampa*, 9 April, 1985

**After the win over Fiorentina, there was great enthusiasm because we had realised – first us, then the fans – that we were a great team, playing to win as much as possible**
Author's conversation with Alessandro Scanziani, 19 March, 2024

**Before the second leg, I can't say that we were sure of victory … he gave them his word that the team would do a lap of honour with the cup**
Ibid.

**In the second leg of the final, Luca Vialli had been the best player on the pitch ... the most beautiful goal of the match**
*La Stampa*, 4 July, 1985

**He has a culture beyond that of his peers**
*La Stampa*, 7 February, 1988

**He's traditional ... whom he met in Cremona when they were both teenagers**
*La Stampa*, 20 June, 1986

**Off the pitch, he is a character ... he has shaken up a sport that doesn't like to change**
*La Stampa*, 7 February, 1988

### 3. CHELSEA, 1998

**I have not come to England to be the big star ... I am careful to ask for it with manners**
*Mail* and *Guardian*, 23 August, 1996

**When he arrived, Gianluca gave himself completely to Chelsea ... the perfect English gentleman**
Author's conversation with Rick Glanvill, 7 March, 2024

**Such modesty comes as a shock ... with piercing blue eyes and a devilish sense of humour**
*Mail* and *Guardian*, 23 August, 1996

**When I play, I score**
*La Stampa*, 28 April, 1997

**His ego was as big as Amsterdam ... didn't want me anywhere near the training ground**
*Sunday Times*, 2 January, 2000

**You see? I put Luca in, and we got beaten. Maybe it's a coincidence, but we always lose with him**
*La Stampa*, 28 April, 1997

**The comment wasn't just undiplomatic, it was cruel and fictitious. Public, casual and devastating**
Ibid.

**Vialli frustrated but not forgotten**
*The Independent*, 20 January, 1997

**I'm not going back to Italy ... of all the Italians who came to the Premier League, I'm the one who's done the worst**
*La Stampa*, 28 April, 1997

**I was thinking of maybe leaving**
Planetfootball.com, 6 January, 2023

**He came with an open heart and filled it with London ... and filled our hearts with him as well**
Author's conversation with Rick Glanvill, 7 March, 2024

**Here, I feel a real sense of freedom ... I wasn't recognised, they wouldn't even let me into a nightclub**
*La Stampa*, 16 November, 1997

## Part 3

### 1. CHELSEA, 1998

**He looked fitter and sharper ... and he's given up smoking**
Planetfootball.com, 6 January, 2023

**Of all the images that define Vialli as a Chelsea player ... could barely stand on their feet**
*The Sun*, 6 January, 2023

**I was playing more, but I was frustrated with the rotation system, which didn't really make sense**
Planetfootball.com, 6 January, 2023

**Last year, we had some misunderstandings. But on a personal level, there was never a problem**
*La Stampa*, 16 November, 1997

### 2. JUVENTUS, 1992

**Never had an ex-player been welcomed back with such warmth and kindness**
*La Stampa*, 11 January, 1993

**I'm starting from zero, but I'll overcome any difficulty quickly**
*La Stampa*, 21 July, 1992

**The critics are ready to stress every mistake I make … I do it willingly**
*La Stampa*, 8 November, 1992

**Gianluca knows his role is important … he always does**
Ibid.

**It was an idea I had been toying with for a while … just needs to adapt to the role**
*La Stampa*, 23 December, 1992

**Gianluca agrees. We have an open dialogue. It's a solution to keep in mind**
*La Repubblica*, 31 December, 1992

**Gianluca Vialli elegantly sidesteps all questions about his potential transformation into a midfielder**
*La Stampa*, 29 December, 1992

**The experiment didn't go perfectly … the experiment should continue**
*La Stampa*, 5 January, 1993

**Never had an ex-player been welcomed back with such warmth and kindness**
*La Stampa*, 11 January, 1993

**Why spend a fortune on a recycled Vialli, a Vialli who is no longer Vialli?**
*La Repubblica*, 31 January, 1993

**I'd love to return to Sampdoria … I'd gladly go back to Sampdoria**
*La Stampa*, 24 May, 1993

**I haven't spoken until now … I wasn't allowed to say**
*La Repubblica*, 25 May, 1993

**If Vialli wants to play up front, he's welcome to … can play together**
*La Stampa*, 8 June, 1993

**These were the same things Boniek and Platini used to say … demanded more from themselves**
*La Stampa*, 7 June, 1993

**I'm sorry if the fans misunderstood me … but that's in the past**
Ibid.

### 3. CHELSEA, 1998

**I found out through the television**
*The Independent*, 13 February, 1998

**It's a joke. It has to be a joke**
*La Stampa*, 13 February, 1998

**Later, I went to Turin and spoke with Lippi and some Juventus executives … had the makings of a manager**
Ibid.

**I'm still a little confused but I'm very happy and I hope I can be the right person for the right job**
*The Independent*, 13 February, 1998

**This is the most unbelievable thing that's happened in my career … you'll understand that's no small thing**
*La Stampa*, 13 February, 1998

**I rang a few friends … I'll need everyone's help, their support**
Ibid.

**It's true, I was an experienced player … I was still just a novice**
Gianluca Vialli, *The Italian Job*, page 117 (Italian edition)

**I have a lot to learn, of course. But I hope I can repay the trust the club has placed in me**
*La Stampa*, 13 February, 1998

## Part Four

### 1. CHELSEA, 1998

**The drama was intense … a pivotal figure in the club's recent history**
Planetfootball.com, 6 January, 1998

**I know that for the players it will be a bit difficult … which is the key to any successful team**
*The Independent*, 13 February, 1998

**After I had got over the shock … I had waited 18 months for Ruud to say that to me**
*The Independent*, 15 February, 1998

**Impeccable in his London look, with his shaved head and neatly trimmed goatee**
*La Stampa*, 18 February, 1998

**Lippi was a great example for me ... meticulous planning in both fitness and tactics, perfection in the details**
Ibid.

**An early sign of what was to come in terms of managerial style**
Planetfootball.com, 6 January, 2023

**He looks ten years younger ... he might just feel a twinge of regret**
*La Stampa*, 19 February, 1998

**Chelsea fans saw a clear display of Vialli's tactical and motivational abilities tonight**
Ibid.

**Now I just hope I can sleep ... felt just like the night before the Champions League final in Rome**
Ibid.

## 2. JUVENTUS, 1996

**if anyone thinks we've already reached the summit ... they're making a big mistake**
*La Stampa*, 26 August, 1995

**He has always had the heart of a leader ... Gianluca always finds the goal when it matters**
*La Stampa*, 5 December, 1995

**The guns are aimed at him ... If we don't, they'll beat me with a stick**
*La Stampa*, 20 March, 1996

**Some thought Gianluca wasn't fit enough ... He led by example**
*La Stampa*, 21 March, 1996

**It had to happen sooner or later ... Just a poacher's goal**
*La Stampa*, 4 April, 1996

**Tonight, more than ever, I felt the fans behind me ... think we've already qualified**
Ibid.

**Suaudeau poured on more fuel ... He called Vialli a 'provocateur, a bully, a cry-baby who runs to the referee for protection.'**
*La Stampa*, 17 April, 1996

**No need for me to be my own lawyer ... Even if it means using someone else as a pawn**
Ibid.

**For me, that match was quite similar to the match I played ... the most complicated game, for me, mentally, to prepare for**
Sky Sports Retro, Gianluca Vialli on winning the Champions League with Juventus

**Physically, we were the best team in Italy ... The absolute leader of a group full of leaders**
Ibid.

**I was nervous when we got to the penalty shoot-out ... I didn't have good feelings about it**
Ibid.

**Luca, do you want to take one ... You might be sixth, if it comes to that**
*La Stampa*, 25 May, 1996

**A goal would have been the cherry on top ... I wanted the whole cake**
Ibid.

**It was amazing ... I nearly fainted on the pitch**
Sky Sports Retro, Gianluca Vialli on winning the Champions League with Juventus

## Part Five

### 1. CHELSEA, 1997

**Vialli's selflessness primes Chelsea's deserved victory … compensation was a trophy**
*The Independent*, 29 March, 1998

**We're still in it thanks to De Goey … we'll need to be perfect**
*The Independent*, 2 April, 1998

**Even after going behind … deserved to go through**
*La Stampa*, 17 April, 1998

### 2. SAMPDORIA, 1990

**there's a heavy air in the dressing room … Afraid of another Bern**
*La Stampa*, 8 May, 1990

**A year ago, I was playing on one leg … only winning will do**
Ibid.

**Ball goes in when God wants**
Eurosport.it, 16 May, 2016

**Not a beautiful goal … It won Sampdoria our first European trophy**
Lords of Football, Ask Vialli interview, 2012

**I'm happy for Mantovani too … you can win and still be a gentleman**
*La Stampa*, 8 May, 1990

### 3. CHELSEA, 1998

**at Chelsea, his teammates adored him … became the enemy**
Author's conversation with Amy Raphael, 6 March, 2024

**I've just lost a friend … as long as he is a manager**
*The Independent*, 29 March, 1998

**It must be possible to be angry sometimes with your friends**
Ibid.

**I'm now playing more in the way that I did in Italy … I accept that**
Ibid.

**There's more discipline now in the way we play … except dropping form in the League a bit**
Ibid.

**I could play … if it's better for me to stay on the bench**
BBC News, 12 May, 1998

**Let's turn a great season into an extraordinary one**
*Irish Independent*, 12 May, 1998

**It was my assistant, Graham Rix … And he was right**
*The Guardian*, 14 May, 1998

**Lucky Luca … A man who wins**
Author's conversation with Rick Glanvill, 7 March, 2024

**Vialli has won more trophies in half a season than most managers do in a lifetime**
BBC News, 13 May, 1998

**We're delighted we won … The next step is the Premier League**
Ibid.

## Part Six

### 1. CHELSEA, 1998

**with Luca, Chelsea are now a real team … they can become the number one team in England**
*The Guardian*, 16 May, 1998

### 2. SAMPDORIA, 1991

**without false modesty, I'd say there's a lot of me in this … on and off the pitch**
*Guerin Sportivo*, 22– 28 May, 1991

**A team for the romantics, a target for the press**
*Il Fatto Quotidiano*, 18 May, 2021

**his Sampdoria were only '*copetera*' … Knockout football suited them**
Author's conversation with Ciso Pezzotti, 12 December, 2023

**The 'Champagne and phantasy' football of the Vicini's band has faded into a pale memory**
*La Stampa*, 1 June, 1990

**We were a carefree, reckless team ... and that isn't entirely a good thing**
Ibid.

**We run a lot but we score little ... Vicini tells me to run, to move, to roam, and I do it**
*La Gazzetta dello Sport*, 16 June, 1990

**When the going gets tough, the tough get going ... it's always my fault**
*La Gazzetta dello Sport*, 29 June, 1990

**I'm bitterly disappointed ... show the full range of what they could do**
*Storie di Calcio*, Italia 90. 'Vialli contro tutti', 17 February, 2017

**I am leaving – don't come looking for me ... and finish as the league's top scorer**
*La Stampa*, 9 July, 1990

**Same age but nothing alike ... they were friends, and they were never rivals**
Author's conversation with Ciso Pezzotti, 10 December, 2023

**He was the good-looking one. I was the funny one. I did the dirty work, and he scored**
*Guerin Sportivo*, 17–23 October, 1990

**We really lived in symbiosis for ten years ... he remained the kind of friend you keep for life**
Roberto Mancini, 'Porta a Porta', RAI TV, 10 January, 2023

**We never actually picked the team ... then he'd do exactly the opposite**
Corriere.it, 6 January, 2023

**Luca is reaching full maturity ... a decisive force in Sampdoria's title charge**
Author's conversation with Ciso Pezzotti, 10 December, 2023

**We had already beaten Juventus, triggering their crisis ... Our world was already special**
*Sampdoria News*, 'Vialli e la Sampd'oro', 13 April, 2011

**A well-earned victory, in every sense**
*La Stampa*, 6 May, 1991

**We were 16 men, a proper team ... he needs to take on board what his players tell him**
Goal.com, 'La Sampdoria Campione d'Italia: Vialli e Mancini e lo storico Scudetto 1990/91', 19 May, 2024

## 3. CHELSEA, 1998–99

**There are various reasons for Vialli's astonishing success ... while maintaining the camaraderie**
*The Guardian*, 30 January, 1999

**The way I saw it ... but I knew I couldn't**
Gianluca Vialli, *The Italian Job*, page 118 (Italian edition)

**Considering his team's meteoric rise to stardom ... He knows what to say and when to say it**
*The Guardian*, 18 April, 1999

**Luca brought style to the Premier League ... even the famously ruthless British press were taken in**
Author's conversation with Amy Raphael, 6 March, 2024

**A testament to his intelligence ... slipping into the local lingo like a natural**
*The Telegraph*, 6 January, 2023

**Well, 'ats off to them**
*The Independent*, 7 January, 2023

**As long as you can, you have to keep your finger in all the pies**
*The Observer*, 3 March, 2002

**his roguish charm**
*Daily Mail*, 6 January, 2023

**Cool Hand Luca**
*The Observer*, 3 March, 2002

**You can hear Vialli's generosity in his answers … but it's the players who must make them work**
*The Guardian*, 30 January, 1999

**Vialli realises that most footballers respond best … so many managers use to convey a sense of authority**
Ibid.

**I'm proud that the fans remember me with such affection … but my future is at Chelsea**
*La Stampa*, 9 January, 1999

**As a manager … I want players who are spontaneous**
*The Guardian*, 30 January, 1999

**he clashed with the ebullient rival manager Carlo Mazzone**
CalcioCasteddu. '*La lite tra Mazzone e Vialli. Sampdoria-Cagliari, stagione 1992–1993.*' YouTube video, uploaded November 6, 2019. youtube.com/watch?v=ETUk1RaXAx8

**Granted, I'm a Catholic in my own way … can lead to damnation**
*La Stampa*, 20 May, 1995

**I hope I am a much better manager now than when I started … for the rest of my career**
*The Guardian*, 30 January, 1999

**Here, I can walk down the street with my girlfriend … I'm finally a free man**
*The Observer*, 3 March, 2002

## Part Seven

### 1. CHELSEA, 1999–2000

**Gianluca Vialli's Chelsea should have won. They dominated physically and tactically**
*La Stampa*, 16 September, 1999

**I don't see the fuss … the internationals played**
*La Stampa*, 27 December, 1999

**This is the most important match in the history of the club … in two years' time only the final will be good enough**
*La Stampa*, 18 April, 1999

**This is when Vialli's managerial inexperience perhaps shone through … saw Barcelona through to the semis**
Thesefootballtimes.com, 4 January, 2018

**'Am I?' he says, almost surprised**
YouTube, 2000 FA Cup Final, Aston Villa v Chelsea, Before Roman Abramovich. Accessible at: youtube.com/watch?v=9sAgVwLsARc&t=868s

**Sir Alex Ferguson once bought himself time at Manchester United … pre-Champions League and pre-Bosman**
*The Guardian*, 21 May, 2000

### 2. ITALY, 1991

**Italy without Vialli? … The risk is real.**
*La Stampa*, 11 November, 1992

**Juventus has nothing to do with this … I'll keep to myself**
Ibid.

**When I was at AC Milan, I wanted him … He needs to fit into my system.**
*La Stampa*, 16 December, 1992

**I have no desire for revenge against the manager … I'll throw plenty of elbows to win back my Azzurri shirt**
Ibid.

**'I didn't expect it,' he said, clipped and curt**
*La Stampa*, 17 January, 1993

**So … unwilling to follow the rigid, clockwork patterns Sacchi demanded**
*La Stampa*, 16 January, 1993

**When it comes to the national team and his relationship with Sacchi … I think it was a matter of character**
Author's interview with Ciso Pezzotti, 12 December, 2024

**At first, he loved me … Someone who needed more than just an order**
Contrataque.it, 4 February, 2016

**I mentioned to one of Sacchi's staff that I had doubts … I was in camp at Villar Perosa**
*La Stampa*, 21 March, 1995.

**Some say the final straw came later … the relationship between Sacchi and Vialli had gone well past breaking point**
Ibid.

**I haven't given up on the national team … he is desperate to be back**
*La Stampa*, 30 October, 1993.

**I don't think it would be fair … three goals today but has played well all year**
TV Interview, 17 April, 1994

**If they call me, I'll go … you can't handle two months of training camp without playing**
*La Stampa*, 21 March, 1994

**It's not easy being Vialli**
*La Stampa*, 31 December, 1995

### 3. CHELSEA, 2000

**I get up every time I mention Alex Ferguson's name … lifting a trophy would be the best way to start the season**
Lords of Football, 'Ask Vialli', 2021

**I think sometimes they don't forgive us for being foreign … and our loyalty to the club is absolute**
*La Stampa*, 27 December, 1999

**Some called Chelsea 'Vialli's Foreign Legion'. Others labelled their transfer strategy 'foreign affairs'**
YouTube, 2000 FA Cup Final, Aston Villa v Chelsea, Before Roman Abramovich

**In the year 2000, most Premier League players were still British … a foreign culture and a radically different league**
*The Observer*, 3 March, 2002

**Nowadays, we accept that teams can be fully multicultural … that wasn't the case in England**
Author's conversation with Amy Raphael, 6 March, 2024

**We spent £24 million and brought in £15 million from sales. The net spend is just £9 million**
*La Stampa*, 12 August, 2000

**Vialli has problems with everybody … but not for him**
*The Guardian*, 16 August, 2000

**I felt very frustrated on the pitch … as a player from the coach he became**
*The Guardian*, 30 August, 2000

**The fans wanted me to play, but Vialli didn't … the message was very clear**
*The Guardian*, 12 September, 2000

### 4. ITALY, 1995

**Why get upset? This week we beat Arezzo and Fiorentina's Youth Team**
*La Stampa*, 18 November, 1994

**Vialli wasn't called up two years ago … Zola is having an outstanding season**
*La Stampa*, 22 March, 1995

**before Casiraghi exploded in the League … For Vialli to return, he must apologise'?**
Ibid.

**GIVE US VIALLI BACK**
*La Stampa*, 22 June, 1995

**a Dantean Inferno. Matarrese and Sacchi the targets … especially when the national team is defeated**
Ibid.

**The match has nothing to do with it … We'll work to solve an issue that could damage everyone**
Ibid.

**He works behind the scenes, pressing Sacchi to give Gianluca another chance**
*La Stampa*, 30 August, 1995

**long one of Gianluca's loudest critics in the Azzurri squad**
*La Stampa*, 3 September, 1995

**Sacchi said he discussed the matter with the team … didn't speak to me personally**
*La Gazzetta dello Sport*, 3 September, 1995

**In order to play, I need to feel happy, calm and at peace … I listen to my heart**
*La Stampa*, 9 September, 1995

**It was a clash of personalities … You should never refuse the Azzurri shirt**
*La Stampa*, 25 November, 2018

### 5. CHELSEA, 2000

**he was given an offer he simply couldn't refuse … seemed to lose confidence in his own decisions**
Author's conversation with Rick Glanvill, 7 March, 2024

**I was thinking of how much to ask … We decided to change the manager**
*The Sun*, 6 January, 2023

**All the players are shocked, and no one had any idea this was happening**
*The Guardian*, 12 September, 2000

**Everyone was disappointed. Luca is a good friend of mine**
Ibid.

**They don't pull punches … Now it has done for Vialli**
Ibid.

**Suddenly Vialli started to blank Zola and drop him without explanation … it was insensitive – and unsuccessful**
Ibid.

**Luca created an environment … You never knew when, but it always worked**
*The Guardian*, 7 January, 2023

**We parted on good terms … You could feel how much the squad cared for Luca**
*The Guardian*, 13 September, 2000

**That was unexpected … You've got to accept it**
*The Observer*, 3 March, 2002

**That afternoon … I was heartbroken by Ken Bates and Colin Hutchinson**
*FourFourTwo* magazine, June 2014

**He symbolised everything the Blues were trying to become … He won us all over**
Author's conversation with Rick Glanvill, 7 March, 2024

**I don't believe someone has to be poor to find the motivation to succeed … the dream of turning a passion into a profession**
Gianluca Vialli, interview on the occasion of the fifth anniversary of the Pro-Cremona Association, 2021

**Middle class – that's what we are … the tradition of a family that includes engineers, professionals, even a university rector**
rivistaundici.com, 6 January, 2023

## Part Eight

### 1. WATFORD, 2001

**when I came to London, I said I needed time to learn … Now, I believe I'm ready**
*La Stampa*, 12 August, 2000

**In England supporters identify with their club so deeply … the atmosphere brings the best out of you**
*The Guardian*, 9 September, 2017

**His success with the English can be summed up … if you haven't scandalised them, they let you in**
Beppe Severgnini, *An Italian in Britain*, Rizzoli, 2003

**Most of us expected Vialli to return to Italy. What was left for him here?**
*The Telegraph*, 6 January, 2023

**Did he love London so much that he'd do anything just to stay?**
*The Observer*, 3 March, 2002

**I wanted to test myself in a different environment … better prepared for the next job**
Gianluca Vialli, *The Italian Job*, page 120 (Italian edition)

**After my sacking, I had a lot of time to think … I'll find out if that's true**
*La Stampa*, 3 May, 2001

**Graham Taylor, who had been with us for the previous five years … an ambitious development programme**
Author's conversation with Tim Shaw, 28 February, 2024

**Once Luca showed that he understood the reality … opportunity too good to pass up**
Ibid.

**A breath of fresh air**
Author's conversation with Tommy Smith, 26 February, 2024

**For the first time in the club's history … introduce his successor**
Author's conversation with Richard Walker, 26 February, 2024 and Tim Shaw, 28 February, 2024

**We are like a family club … people had time to get to Vicarage Road after work**
Gianluca Vialli, *The Italian Job*, page 312 (Italian edition)

**I found a fantastic atmosphere here … where I grew up as a footballer**
Gianluca Vialli, *The Italian Job*, page 120 (Italian edition)

### 2. US CREMONESE, 1981

**it wasn't a real trial … he scored a goal**
Author's conversation with Fabrizio Frittoli, 4 August, 2023

**I was too young … I wasn't old enough to play yet**
Vita.it, 6 January, 2023

**My first official registration was with Unione Sportiva San Bartolomeo di Grumello**
Vita.it, 6 January, 2023

**He came to see his son. But instead, he left thinking about me**
*Mondo Padano*, 2 January, 1984

**Gianluca went to Pizzighettone … he wasn't allowed to play in the first team anymore**
Author's conversation with Fabrizio Frittoli, 4 August, 2023

**I begged and pleaded, but the local football federation wouldn't budge**
Gianluca Vialli, *The Italian Job*, page 60 (Italian edition)

**subject to a favourable medical examination … the parent exercising paternal authority**
Original document, Definitive Transfer Agreement of footballer Vialli 1977/78

**Luca went to Cremonese first … Nolli wanted to meet me**
Author's conversation with Fabrizio Frittoli, 4 August, 2023

**A wonderful environment with managers who taught not just football, but life**
Calcionews24.com, 1996 Gianluca Vialli Interview

**Mario Montorfano, a loyal defender … He was a real mess**
Author's conversation with Mario Montorfano, 4 October, 2023

**Whenever the regulations allowed it, Vialli always played in … even back then, he was so good**
Author's conversation with Giorgio Barbieri, 26 September, 2023

**I didn't understand at first … I'd never expected**
Gianluca Vialli, Interview on the occasion of the fifth anniversary of the Pro-Cremona Association, 2021

**How old is this kid? … even though he was a boy**
Author's conversation with Giorgio Barbieri, 26 September, 2023

**No emotion on my goal. In those moments, you don't have the time**
*La Provincia*, 13 October, 1981

**First of all, I didn't expect such a strong stance from the team … he has a sharp mind**
Author's conversation with Giorgio Barbieri, 26 September, 2023

**Mondonico immediately saw him as the symbol of the team**
Author's conversation with Giovanni Ratti, 25 September, 2023

**We are the main architects of this promotion, and today we rightly feel like giants**
*Mondo Padano*, 4 June, 1984

**At 16, they threw me into the fire in Serie C … I feel a huge debt of gratitude to everyone here**
Calcionews24.com, interview with Gianluca Vialli, 1996

**the image of those curls … love for the game that spread to everyone around him**
Author's conversation with Giovanni Ratti, 25 October, 2023

## Part Nine

### 1. WATFORD, 2001

**I had a great time at Chelsea … I want to take Watford to the next level**
*The Guardian*, 2 May, 2001

**At Chelsea, even though I achieved a lot … we want to enjoy ourselves**
*La Stampa*, 3 May, 2001

**My pleasure … Chelsea or Juventus or Watford, it doesn't really matter**
*The Observer*, 3 March, 2002

**He is still lean, despite not having played regularly since May 1999**
Ibid.

**Smoking's bad for you … it'd be too hard**
Ibid.

**Blue shirt, beige jumper, grey overcoat, grey trousers, brown suede shoes**
Ibid.

**I am incredibly excited that we have appointed Luca … one of the most stunning coups we have pulled off**
*The Guardian*, 2 May, 2001

**To me, Luca was a legend … I had to pinch myself to make sure I was not dreaming**
Author's conversation with Tommy Smith, 26 February, 2024

**The whole world seemed to have come to Lecco just to see Gianluca … that's when we truly understood his greatness**
Author's conversation with Richard Walker, 26 February, 2024

**The season opener was a rude awakening**
Author's conversation with Tommy Smith, 26 February, 2024

**We know we're not at our best yet … so we keep working**
BBC, 11 August, 2001

**We know that everywhere we go to play … all the Premiership players who are in the team**
*The Guardian*, 4 August, 2001

**I suspect that a lot of people, especially in England, saw it as a step backwards**
Gianluca Vialli, *The Italian Job*, page 120 (Italian edition)

**There was still a lot of ingrained racism in English football … the Bosman ruling and the influx of foreign players**
Author's conversation with Amy Raphael, 6 March, 2024

**His manner is as gentle and dignified as ever**
*The Observer*, 3 March, 2002

**The change was seismic … could tell if you weren't putting in enough effort**
Author's conversation with Tommy Smith, 26 February, 2024

**Luca was frustrated. Saddened, even … never be able to change the club the way he wanted**
Author's conversation with Amy Raphael, 6 March, 2024

**You could always talk to him if you needed to … just how young he was at the time**
Author's conversation with Tommy Smith, 26 February, 2024

**We got through four rounds in the League Cup … there were positives as well**
Author's conversation with Tim Shaw, 28 February, 2024

### 2. JUVENTUS, 1996

**a restless Vialli … Arsenal's name is floated**
*La Stampa*, 5 December, 1995

**If he wants to stay, he stays … I don't like the feeling of being merely tolerated**
*La Stampa*, 29 January, 1996

**The financial side definitely won't be decisive … come down to interests that must align**
*La Stampa*, 31 December, 1995

**Stay with us … The respect and affection of the fans – it helps**
*La Stampa*, 4 April, 1996

**The more time passes, the less sense there is in letting go of a leader like Gianluca**
*La Stampa*, 18 April, 1996

**If we ever reach the point of separation … the way it was at Sampdoria. Nothing more**
La Stampa, 19 April, 1996

**They say Vialli collapsed onto the bench in the dressing room … Every victory. Even every defeat**
*La Repubblica*, 24 May, 1996

### 3. WATFORD, 2002

**Their contracts were simply unsustainable. Vialli would end up in court to claim the two years' wages still owed to him**
*The Guardian*. 'News story.' *Football section*, 8 February, 2003. theguardian.com/football/2003/feb/08/newsstory.sport4

**We probably made an error in appointing Vialli … not a footballing error – a financial one**
*The Guardian*, 30 September, 2002

**If we could have afforded to keep Luca … was a gamble – and it didn't pay off**
Ibid.

**If ITV Digital hadn't collapsed, I believe Luca would have stayed … if only we could have afforded to**
Author's conversation with Tim Shaw, 28 February, 2024

**I'm very disappointed by the decision of the club, especially as my work at Watford was still in the early stages**
*The Guardian*, 14 June, 2002

**Luca was devastated … we simply couldn't keep the promises we had made**
Author's conversation with Tim Shaw, 28 February, 2024

**Maybe management was just too brutal a profession … few moments of peace**
Author's conversation with Amy Raphael, 6 March, 2024

## Part Ten

### 1. LONDON, 2017

**it's so damn hard … So hard that you feel finished**
Gianluca Vialli, *Goals*, pp 354–358, 2020

**I found out that pancreatic cancer is one of the worst … I was shocked, confused, helpless, hopeless**
Ibid.

**There are good chances … it's how to prepare for the hard things**
Ibid.

**You feel that you are letting someone down … not be in that position made me uneasy**
Ibid.

**I won't leave this world before you and Mum … we are so much more**
Ibid.

**She spoils me like we're still kids … Like I haven't lived a life yet**
Ibid.

**And as I speak to them, and they cry, and I cry … to change myself**
Ibid.

**I realised there are things that are more fun and far less stressful … I was married to football**
Goal.com, 'Il Vialli allenatore: Una carriera breve ma da vincente', 6 January, 2023

**Our business is about giving football clubs the necessary finance … about making clubs more sustainable**
*The Guardian*, 9 September, 2017

**I need to protect both myself and them … instead of spending time on the phone, I needed time for myself**
Gianluca Vialli, *Goals*, pp 354–358, 2020

**He never told me about his illness … 'I didn't want you to suffer'**
Roberto Mancini Interview, 'Porta a Porta', RAI TV, 10 January, 2023

**I think a lot. I read … the fear of not being able to say the words that need to be said**
Gianluca Vialli, *Goals*, pp 354–358, 2020

**We portrayed ourselves as tough guys … different than if you cry because you've lost a match**
Ibid.

**I know now that you need to let out the pain … I feel better afterwards**
Ibid.

**If I saw this as a battle against cancer … 'now I'll leave you in peace'**
Oggi, 20 March, 2022

**Like everyone else, it hit me suddenly … with a body worth showing off again**
RAI TV, 'Che tempo che fa', 2 December, 2018

**I worked on it. I put myself in the right psychological condition to face it … to become a better person**
Ibid.

**Illness isn't just suffering … can even be an opportunity**
Ibid.

**I've been a strong player and a strong man … desire to do something meaningful**
TG Poste, 6 January, 2023

**I now know that I have a duty … I feel much more fragile than before**
Netflix, *A Simple Question*, Alessandro Cattelan, Episode 3 (featuring an interview with Gianluca Vialli), 18 March, 2022

**I believe the purpose of life is to find a purpose in life … truly understand how beautiful happiness is?**
Ibid.

**If you give up once, it becomes a habit … I feel very lucky**
Ibid.

**It's an honour to be called up … the way I love it**
Author's conversation with Giorgio Barbieri, 26 September, 2023

**So much changed from that day – the hope that he would make it, the way time moved**
RAI TV, 'Porta a Porta', Roberto Mancini, 10 January, 2023

**We thought everything was going OK … 'Oh, my God, this guy is back'**
*The Guardian*, 16 May, 2020

**They call it NED … in a good place until I die of old age**
Ibid.

**In London I only know two people that tested positive … It's a tragedy**
Ibid.

**The time of gratitude … Sometimes more present, sometimes less**
*La Provincia*, 17 December, 2021

**I know I matter to others … 'If he can do it, so can I'**
Netflix, *A Simple Question*, Alessandro Cattelan, Episode 3 (featuring an interview with Gianluca Vialli), 18 March, 2022

**Ciao, Marco. Thanks for the message … even though I set up more for you!**
Author's conversation with Marco Nicoletti, 20 July, 2023

**I don't know how long I have left. There's no time to waste**
Oggi, 24 March, 2022

**I try not to waste time … The rest? There's no time for it**
Netflix, *A Simple Question*, Alessandro Cattelan, Episode 3 (featuring an interview with Gianluca Vialli), 18 March, 2022

**After a long and difficult 'negotiation' with my wonderful team of oncologists … new adventures to share with you all**
Tuttosport, 14 December, 2022

**That adventure wasn't too fortunate for the national squad … Because the pitch never ends**
*La Provincia*, 15 December, 2022

## Part Eleven

### 1. Italy, 1988

**I am happy and proud to take on this role … I know who has preceded me in this job – Gigi Riva**
*La Gazzetta dello Sport*, 11 November, 2019

**The right man for a delicate job … and more importantly, knows when to listen – is essential**
Calciocasteddu.it, 11 April, 2020

**VIVA VIALLI … a player defined by uncontainable generosity**
*La Repubblica*, 15 November, 1987

**It'll take three or four years at this level before I can be called that**
*La Stampa*, 15 November, 1987

**When people speak of the spirit of this team … Vialli has it**
*La Repubblica*, 15 November, 1987

**The good people of Bari rise to applaud … the thunderclap**
*La Repubblica*, 21 February, 1988

**EVEN THE USSR SURRENDERS TO VIALLI**
*La Stampa*, 21 February, 1988

**His light is so intense now … blue shirts of his teammates risk fading beside it**
Ibid.

**Vialli is an extraordinary player … He'll be the star of Euro '88**
Ibid.

**The urge to joke around is slowly disappearing … yet, deep down, we believe**
*La Stampa*, 10 June, 1988

**You can't always be the protagonist … Italy gave the answers everyone was waiting for**
*La Stampa*, 11 June, 1988

**a moment of brilliance on an Ancelotti pass, with Altobelli's clever dummy opening the space**
*La Stampa*, 15 June, 1988

**If I'd put them all away, I'd be a phenomenon … It freed me**
Ibid.

**Don't talk about Vialli's European Championship anymore. I don't accept being singled out ahead of the team**
*La Stampa*, 16 June, 1988

**IT'S ALL BECAUSE OF VIALLI**
*La Stampa*, 18 June, 1988

**On the pitch where, 14 years ago … sits his Russian exam while dreaming of Munich**
*La Stampa*, 22 June, 1988

**Riva, with the chances I had in these first three games, would have scored more than one goal**
Ibid.

**Vialli scored less than he deserved … will stay with Vialli forever**
Ibid.

**It was a team made up of players who knew each other really well … It was more than that**
YouTube, Uno storico Europeo: Gianluca Vialli racconta Germania vs Italia – EURO 1988

### 2. ITALY, 2021

**it is a prestigious role … Let's hope we can do better**
*La Gazzetta dello Sport*, 11 November, 2019

**In this national team, Vialli is the charismatic leader, the head coach of minds, the motivator, the advisor, the confidant**
*Il Messaggero*, 23 June, 2021

### 3. SAMPDORIA, 1992

**we feared another Heysel … Our wives were in the stands**
*La Stampa*, 10 January, 1993

### 4. ITALY, 2021

**Italy – but not as strongly as when Italy play another side, because I'm living in England, I've got friends here, and I love the people**
*The Observer*, 3 March, 2002

## Part Twelve

### Chapter 1

**I was lucky … I couldn't have asked for more**
Sky Sports Retro, Gianluca Vialli looks back on his career, 2015

**With Chelsea fans, I had a fantastic relationship … You are one of them wearing the shirt of the team you are playing for**
*Evening Standard*, 28 March, 2014

**The first Italian to manage in the Premier League … endearing attempt at using English idioms**
*The Guardian*, 9 September, 2017

**He got a lot from his career … Schillaci got in his way at the wrong time. But that's football**

Author's conversation with Giovanni Ratti, 25 September, 2023

**I wish I'd played in a World Cup and been a success … everyone blamed me for Italy not winning the World Cup because expectations were so high**
*The Observer*, 3 March, 2002

**If I had to describe Luca Vialli in just a few words, I'd say – a gentleman in life, a warrior on the pitch**
Author's interview with Ciso Pezzotti, 12 December, 2012

**Luca Vialli was one of those players who transcend the clubs … sometimes even skipping one**
Author's conversation with Amy Raphael, 6 March, 2024

**Here I can be vulnerable without being defined by it**
Netflix, *The Italian Job*, 2022

**If I hadn't become a professional footballer, I would have been an architect and worked with my father**
*The Guardian*, 'Gianluca Vialli: What I know', 16 October, 2011

**Sometimes, when I look at old photos, old footage, even old football stickers … it was almost impossible to become a professional footballer**
Calcio News 24, 1996 interview

# ACKNOWLEDGEMENTS

This is a special book. It tells the story of one of the greatest Italian footballers seen from abroad: how Gianluca Vialli crossed borders and, in doing so, helped shape a league that was not initially his own. It is a story of football, of course, but also of culture, roots, love, shared identity and resilience. For all this – and for the many people who made these pages possible – the following thanks are deeply felt.

My gratitude goes first to Chelsea FC and Watford FC for their generous cooperation, and to Rick Glanvill, the Blues' official historian, and to Richard Walker, head of PR with the Hornets. Thanks also to Tommy Smith, David Noble and Tim Shaw. A personal thank you goes to journalist and author Amy Raphael, to Alex Bell and to Gianluca's Chelsea captain, Dennis Wise.

To understand Gianluca Vialli and the role he played in shaping English football, it was essential to return to his roots. My thanks therefore go to the former boys of Cristo Re, whose voices and memories form the living background of this book, and especially to Fabrizio Frittoli. In Cremona, I would also like to thank Professor Maurizio Mondoni, US Cremonese, Marco Nicoletti, Mario Montorfano, Giovanni Ratti, Giorgio Barbieri, and 1982 FIFA World Cup winner Antonio Cabrini. Beyond Cremona, my heartfelt thanks go to Ciso Pezzotti for his invaluable insight from UC Sampdoria and Juventus FC, to Alessandro Scanziani, Ivano Bordon, Gianluca Pellegrini and Francesca Mantovani.

I am also deeply grateful to my publisher, Matthew Lowing, and my editor, Caroline Hewlett, and to everyone at Bloomsbury for their trust, care and belief in this book. I would also like to thank my agent, Melanie Michael-Greer, for being the first to believe in this project and in me, and for her constant support, advice, and sound judgement.

Thanks to my wife Elisabetta for her guidance and patience through countless drafts, and to my daughter and son, Lodovica and Nicolò, for helping my English find its rhythm and its footballing voice. Finally, my deepest gratitude goes to the Vialli family, in Cremona and in London, and especially to *Mamma* Maria Teresa, brother Nino, Nadia, Edoardo, and Riccardo. Thank you for your trust, your encouragement, your friendship and generosity throughout this journey.

Ben Radford/Allsport